EDUCATIONAL RESEARC~

DAY
LOAN

~r before

This reader is one part of an Open University integrated teaching system and the selection is therefore related to other material available to students. It is designed to evoke the critical understanding of students. Opinions expressed in it are not necessarily those of the course team or of the University.

EDUCATIONAL RESEARCH IN ACTION

Edited by
Roger Gomm and Peter Woods

at The Open University

Published in association with
The Open University

P·C·P

Paul Chapman
Publishing Ltd

Paul Chapman Publishing Ltd
144 Liverpool Road
London
N1 1LA

British Library Cataloguing in Publication Data

Gomm R. and Woods P.
Educational Research in Action
1. Gomm, Roger   II. Woods, Peter
370.7

ISBN 1 85396 242 2

Typeset by Inforum, Rowlands Castle, Hants.
Printed and bound by
Athenaeum Press Ltd., Newcastle-upon-Tyne

ABCDEFGH 9 8 7 6 5 4 3

CONTENTS

ACKNOWLEDGEMENTS

We thank those listed below for permission to reproduce the following copyrighted material:

Ch. 1   P. Atkinson, D. Shone and T. Rees (1981) Labouring to Learn: industrial training for slow learners, in L. Barton and S. Tomlinson (eds.) *Special Education: policy and practices and social issues*, London, Paul Chapman Publishing. Reprinted by permission of the authors.

Ch. 2   C. Wright, Early Education: multiracial primary school classrooms, reprinted with permission from D. Gill, B. Mayor and M. Blair (eds.) *Racism and Education*, London, by permission of Sage Publishing Ltd, and the author.

Ch. 3   P. Woods, The magic of Godspell: the educational significance of a dramatic production, unpublished.

Ch. 4   A. Hargreaves (1992) Time and Teachers' work: an analysis of the intensification thesis, *Teachers College Record*, Vol. 94, no. 1, pp. 87–108. Reprinted by permission of the author.

Ch. 5   J. Gray (1982) Publish and be damned? The problem of publishing examination results in two inner London schools, *Educational Analysis*, Vol. 4, no. 3, pp. 47–56. Reprinted by permission of the author.

Ch. 6   I. Schagen (1991) Beyond League Tables: how modern statistical methods can give a truer picture of the effects of schools, *Educational Research*, Vol. 33, no. 3, pp. 216–28. Reprinted by permission of NFER and Routledge.

Ch. 7   J. Gray, D. Jesson and N. Sime (1990) Estimating differences in the examination performances of secondary schools in six LEAs: a multilevel approach to school effectiveness, *Oxford Review of Education*, Vol. 16, no. 2, pp. 137–58, Carfax Publishing Company. Reprinted by permission of the author.

Ch. 8 R. Alexander, J. Rose, and C. Woodhead, The quality of teaching in primary classrooms, from Department of Education and Science *Curriculum Organisation and Practice in Primary Schools: a discussion document*, London, reproduced by permission of the Controller Her Majesty's Stationery Office.

Ch. 9 M. Donaldson (1978) Failing to Reason or Failing to Understand? from *Children's Minds*, Ch. 4, Fontana, an imprint of HarperCollins Publishers Limited.

Ch. 10 M. Hammersley, An appraisal of 'Labouring to Learn', unpublished.

Ch. 11 J. Scarth and M. Hammersley (1986) Questioning ORACLE's analysis of teachers' questions, *Educational Research*, Vol. 28, no. 3, pp. 174–84, reprinted by permission of NFER Nelson.

Ch. 12 R. Gomm, Figuring out ethnic equity: a response to Troyna, *British Educational Research Journal*, Vol. 19, no. 2, pp. 147–63, Carfax Publishing Company.

Ch. 13 M. Hammersley and J. Scarth (1993) Beware of Wise Men Bearing Gifts: a case study in the misuse of educational research, *British Educational Research Journal*, Vol. 19, no. 5.

INTRODUCTION
R. Gomm and P. Woods

Educational research takes a bewildering array of forms, ranging across a variety of topics and employing diverse types of data and techniques of analysis. This volume provides a sense of this diversity. It covers some very different substantive topics, from examinations as a measure of 'the school effect', through the 'intensification' of teachers' work and the study of multiethnic primary school classrooms, to an investigation of the impact of a production of *Godspell* on the education of those involved. In terms of method, we distinguish between qualitative and quantitative work, placing studies exemplifying these approaches in different sections; though there is no hard and fast line to be drawn between the two, and substantial differences in approach are to be found within each.

All educational research needs to be subjected to careful methodological assessment. Research results should never be taken at face value. In the final part of the book we have collected together some critical evaluations of educational research studies to illustrate the sorts of methodological assessment that often need to be carried out. Two of these articles address studies included in the earlier sections.

The first part of the reader contains examples of recent qualitative research relating to issues of current concern. They illustrate typical processes of data collection, analysis and theory, drawing on different phases and personnel in the educational process. Atkinson, Shone and Rees consider the issue of government intervention in youth unemployment. They study a unit providing industrial training for 'slow learners', a group particularly disadvantaged at times of high unemployment. They use ethnographic techniques to examine the nature of the training provided. General principles of workshop practice are conveyed to students through lectures, with strong emphases on safety procedures and social skills. A common technique is to illustrate undesirable traits by 'showing up' students, and to use this as a basis for moral homilies. Images of the 'good worker' are presented, in terms of appearance, attitude and behaviour. Lectures are given on social relationships, again using examples from ongoing interaction. More formal, routine training is given on a rather haphazard number of topics deemed important for adult life. Students are evaluated by staff observation according to basic categories of intelligence, orientation to work and personal characteristics. These assessments clearly have implications for their training, and feed into judgements about 'work readiness'. The account illustrates the interweaving of formal and informal components, a distinctive work ethos in the unit, and notions of the model worker. The authors could not detect any sense of progression in the students, nor was the appropriateness for the job market of skills and tasks always clear. In sum, the article claims to show how ethnography can uncover some of the hidden assumptions involved in training schemes.

Cecile Wright presents a typical ethnographic study of teacher and pupil interaction in four multiracial, inner-city primary schools. She is particularly concerned to examine classroom processes and their effects. Subtle differences are reported in the way white teachers treated black children. Asian children were sometimes excluded from discussion, or dealt with in a way insensitive to their background culture. On the other hand, Afro-Caribbean children received a disproportionate amount of attention, though mainly for criticism. Teachers appeared to expect bad behaviour and lower educational attainment from Afro-Caribbean children. Wright argues that these children were selected out for criticism, even though white pupils were indulging in similar behaviour. Rastafarian children were particularly subject to prejudice. Teachers tried to take the multicultural nature of classrooms into account, but their lack of knowledge and confidence hampered their efforts and led to embarrassment and awkwardness. Teachers held generalized images of pupils, for example that Afro-Caribbean children are less well motivated towards school and more likely to display 'behaviour problems'. Among the pupils themselves, racial harassment featured prominently in their interaction. Asian pupils in particular were frequently victimized. There was no official school policy addressed to this problem. The article is distinctive for the detailed extracts from classroom interaction.

The next two articles illustrate some of the ways in which ethnographers approach theory. In 'The Magic of *Godspell*', Peter Woods seeks to extend his earlier analysis of 'critical events' from primary to secondary level (Woods, 1993). These are outstanding events in education that bring about radical change in both pupils and teachers. They are marked by distinctive relationships within the participating group, and they have a clearly identifiable structure from initial conceptualization and planning through to an eventual 'celebration'. Favourable conditions for producing a critical event include legitimation within the curriculum structure, a favourable school ethos, a critical agent (usually a co-ordinating teacher) and critical others (other experts recruited for particular purposes). The secondary-school production of the musical *Godspell* that was studied exhibited these features, and was particularly strong in its facilitation of personal, emotional and social development. In considering the learning within this event, Woods seeks to develop David Hargreaves's 'traumatic theory of learning', which Hargreaves advanced to explain adults' appreciation of art (Hargreaves, 1983). Analysis of the *Godspell* experience confirms the traumatic features identified by Hargreaves, with some refinements, but suggests the need to contextualize the trauma within a more general theory. As for structure, *Godspell* turned out to be a multicritical event with three distinct phases, each building on the one previous. Transition from one stage to another was a problem, but here the services of a critical other proved crucial. The *Godspell* production thus gives support to the notion of critical events, and extends the conceptualization.

Andy Hargreaves' article relates a kind of test of the 'intensification thesis', and thus shows how ethnography can interrogate macro-theory. Drawing on Marxist theories of the labour process, the intensification argument claims that teachers are becoming deskilled and deprofessionalized as they have become subject to programmes and curricula devised by others, and deprived of opportunities for reflection as pressures on them have intensified. Yet, because these pressures are couched in technical apparatus, teachers may feel more professional rather than less, thus 'misrecognizing' the process, and unwittingly contributing to it. Hargreaves's research was among Canadian teachers, but its relevance for teachers in the UK, and indeed elsewhere, is clear. Canadian teachers had recently won the right to have two hours 'preparation time' a week. Hargreaves saw the study of how teachers used this time as a critical case for examining the nature and conditions of teachers' work. Was it used to relieve intensification, or to promote it? From interviews with teachers in the Toronto district (thus placing the weight of evidence on teachers' own voices) he concluded that there were plenty of instances that supported the intensification thesis, but there were qualifications that needed to be made to it. Some of these derive from the research, which shows that preparation time can, in fact, relieve intensification. But it can also lead to new problems and struggles not associated with the labour process. Hargreaves concludes that intensification is a real problem for teachers, but that labour process theories do not fully explain teachers' work. Characteristically, this qualitative work illustrates some of the complexities of social life and the contribution that might be made to the testing of all-embracing theories, and to their refinement.

The second part of the reader provides examples of recent quantitative work in the field of education. We have selected most of our examples from the currently topical area of school results. At the time of compilation most of the research in this area has concerned examination results at 16+, and this is reflected in our selection; although increasingly the same kinds of research techniques will be used in connection with SATs scores.

Differences in achievement between the pupils in different schools and LEAs is an increasingly significant area of political debate. John Gray's paper 'Published and be damned?' captures the politics of the moment nicely. However, only recently have educational researchers developed powerful statistical techniques for modelling and measuring the relative contribution to the measurable outputs of schools of the many factors involved. These techniques are generally referred to as 'multilevel modelling'. 'Multilevel' refers to their ability to sort out the relative contribution of factors at various levels: at the pupil level – for example, differences between pupils in terms of prior achievement, measured ability, gender, ethnicity and/or socio-economic status; at the school level – for example, differences between schools which might be attributed to school organization, policy or resourcing; and at the level of LEAs – for instance, differences in population profile and level of resources. The principles of multilevel modelling are described in the paper by Ian Schagen; and the paper by Gray, Jesson and Sime provides a more extensive example of the technique in operation. The technique of multilevel modelling largely supercedes earlier quantitative techniques such as the ones used by Coleman in his well-known American study of the contribution of schools to pupils' academic achievement (Coleman, 1966) and those used by Rutter *et al.* in their influential book, *Fifteen Thousand Hours* (Rutter *et al.*, 1979).

One of the limitations of multilevel modelling is that a separate analysis has to be conducted for each 'output measure'. There is a danger here that concentrating on a single sort of measurable output is taken to imply that maximizing that output is the only important goal of schools. An example is that maximum aggregate examination scores is what the target schools should be aiming for, irrespective of how different groups of pupils contribute to the aggregate, or of other goals that are equally, if not more, important. In reality, of course, schools direct themselves to a wide variety of aims, and try to optimize between outcomes rather than maximize for any one of them. The technique of 'data envelopment' described in the second part of the paper by Schagen is a means of judging school performance on various output measures concurrently. Thus schools can be compared not just in terms of their performance on one measure but in terms of their success in optimizing on several outputs: for example, in hitting a balance between promoting the achievement of their more intelligent pupils and promoting the achievements of their average pupils. The 'right balance' is not, of course, something which can be determined by statistical techniques, but data-envelopment analysis does enable the data to be analysed and displayed in ways that set the school up for judgement on multiple chosen criteria. It has to be said, however, that data-envelopment analysis is a controversial technique among statisticians (Desai 1992). Furthermore, it can only be deployed in relationship to measurable outputs; and not all of the goals that schools pursue are measurable.

The convergence of new developments in statistical modelling with the requirement that schools should be made more accountable in terms of their measured results constitutes an interesting moment in the history of educational research. Whatever one's attitude to them, it is clear that the National Curriculum, standardized achievement testing and the publication of school examination results and truancy rates will transform the British educational system from something which, in quantitative terms, could only be studied expensively and on an *ad hoc* basis into a system that routinely generates large quantities of easily accessible, roughly standardized, or standardizable, data. It seems reasonable to assume that we are standing on the threshold of an era when quantitative techniques of analysis will become more commonly used and more important in policy-making and implementation. Much of their importance, of course, will be given by the political climate within which school data are published, and we will no doubt see a great deal of research designed to demystify the superficial appearances of published 'raw data'. Indeed, research so far suggests that there is a considerable discrepancy between league tables ranking schools in terms of raw results and those ranking them in terms of 'value-added', as judged by the relationship between the achievement of pupils on entry compared to their achievements on exit. Some schools with prestigious reputations and formally excellent results will not look so impressive when judged in value-added terms.

The final reading in this part is an extract from one of the most controversial official reports of recent years, which draws on a large body of educational research, most (but not all) of it quantitative in character. Following the institution of the National Curriculum in 1988, the British government soon turned its attention from content to method, commissioning Robin Alexander, Professor of Primary Education, Leeds University, Jim Rose, Chief Inspector, Her Majesty's Inspectorate, and Chris Woodhead, Chief Executive, National Curriculum Council, to review the evidence and make recommendations about how the National Curriculum could best be implemented in primary schools. They were given seven weeks to accomplish this. Their report was conceived of and produced in a highly charged political atmosphere in which there was something of a moral panic about 'declining standards of education' and the part played in this by so-called 'progressive' methods of teaching. Alexander had just completed some widely publicized research in Leeds (reported in Alexander, 1992), which raised questions about the professional culture of primary education and the prevailing ideology among primary teachers. In the section of the report reproduced here, the authors claim to draw on a range of research. They argue that the task of the primary teacher has changed dramatically since the introduction of the National Curriculum, but that progress is being hampered by teachers' adherence to 'outmoded dogmas' and resistance to subject-based teaching. Much topic work, so popular among primary teachers, has not been sufficiently well planned and focused, they claim. And they put the case for more whole-class teaching, but within a balanced, 'fitness-for-purpose' approach which includes group work and individual teaching. Teachers should expect more of their pupils, they suggest, and that this is an essential condition for higher standards.

As already indicated, the final part of this volume consists of critical assessments of examples of educational research and their use. Donaldson's paper is a critique of well-known experimental work by Piaget. It is a good example of the way in which the findings of an experimental approach can be challenged when the subjectivity of the participants is taken into consideration. This article and the book from which it comes are part of a substantial literature critically reviewing and revising Piaget's influential ideas (Donaldson, 1978).

The next chapter provides a critical assessment of an article by Barry Troyna (1992) based on a case study of a single secondary school in which he claims to show South Asian pupils being disadvantaged in allocations to sets. Troyna's article illustrates the common use of quantitative method on a relatively small scale, to display the differential achievement of pupils of different social classes, genders or ethnic groups, and their differential treatment in terms of streaming, banding, setting or subject choice allocations (see also, for example, Woods, 1976; Troyna, 1978; Ball, 1981; Grafton *et al.*, 1983; Wright, 1986). There are frequently problems in interpreting the results of such work, arising from the fact that it typically focuses on just one school year of pupils, when school year-groups actually vary considerably; and even in the largest schools a single cohort constitutes a very small sample when the interest is in the differential performance or treatment of sub-groups. In his critique of Troyna's work, Roger Gomm argues that the article also illustrates a common tendency in work on educational inequality to move straight from numerical displays of difference in ability-group placements or in examination outcomes, as between different categories of pupil, to claims that this represents inequitable treatment. Quite frequently such claims are made without specifying what equitable treatment would look like. In assessing Troyna's claims Gomm discusses how equity might be modelled for statistical purposes.

In Chapter 10 Hammersley provides a methodological assessment of the study of a training unit for 'slow learners' by Atkinson, Shone and Rees which is included in the first part of the Reader. He examines the central claims made by the authors and the evidence they offer in support of them. He argues that while the study is presented as descriptive in character, it also involves some evaluative claims, though the basis for these is not made clear. He concludes that, while most of the descriptive claims are well supported, not all of them are; and insufficient grounds are provided for generalization from the unit studied to others of a similar type.

The chapter by Scarth and Hammersley is a critique of the use of structured observation by the ORACLE researchers to identify the frequency of different types of teacher question (Galton and Simon, 1980; Galton, Simon and Croll, 1980). Structured observation, using observation schedules to preclassify and then record events, is an alternative to the less structured kinds of observation conducted by ethnographic researchers. The detailed classification of types of behaviour, and the recording of events in these terms, generates quantitative data for analysis in a way that ethnographic observation rarely does. In their paper Hammersley and Scarth do not deny the usefulness of structured observation, but they do draw attention to the difficulties faced by researchers in using observation schedules, and the threats to validity likely to be involved in data produced by them.

The final chapter assesses the Report by Alexander, Rose and Woodhead, a section of which is reproduced in Part 2. This report created a furore in the media and among educationists reminiscent of that which greeted Bennett's (1976) book *Teaching Styles and Pupil Progress*, which was concerned with the same underlying issue – traditional *v.* progressive teaching methods (though many now argue that this crude polarization is out of date). The Alexander report had its critics and its supporters. Among the latter, Brian Simon (1992, p. 91) states

> Here we have a thoroughly intelligent, acute analysis of primary practice, drawing mainly on the considerable amount of research carried through over the last ten or fifteen years, by three people, two of whom (Alexander and Rose) speak with some authority, given their record in this field. The report is readable, down to earth and clearly structured. . . . Generally the report presents a clear standpoint – prescriptive at times, but why not? This both offers a challenge and gives us something to bite on – and discuss.

However, by no means all responses were so supportive. So far, however, there has been little sustained critical assessment of the report focusing on its argument and the evidence it draws on. This is the task Hammersley and Scarth set themselves in their article. They conclude that it constitutes 'a case study in the misuse of educational research'. The evidence, for example that on standards of literacy and numeracy, is very mixed, but this does not prevent the authors claiming that standards have declined. Similarly, as regards the authors' claim about the prevalence of 'highly questionable dogmas' among primary school teachers, there are problems of conceptualization, of generalization across the population of teachers, and of establishing the relationship between cause and effect. Hammersley and Scarth also point out that the report makes an evaluative judgement that children are not achieving what they might in present conditions. But this is a matter of much dispute, as is the way in which the authors rule the crucial issue of resources out of account. Even more significant, Hammersley and Scarth argue, is the manner in which the arguments in the report are presented. This is seen as hierarchical and prescriptive, a mode not best suited to promote discussion among teachers – the report's declared aim.

We would not want readers to think that these critiques are the final word. In fact, some of them have drawn replies. (See, for example, Croll and Galton, 1986; Scarth and Hammersley, 1987; Troyna, 1993; Hammersley, 1993.) In this volume we have tried to show the contribution that educational research can make to our understanding of educational issues. At the same time, we have sought to make clear the problems surrounding the interpretation of the findings of that research, whether qualitative or quantitative. This is particularly important in a context in which debates about educational issues, and research relating to them, occur in an increasingly politicized climate.

REFERENCES

Alexander, R. J. (1992) *Policy and Practice in Primary Education*, Routledge, London.

Alexander, R. J., Rose, J. and Woodhead, C. (1992) *Curriculum Organisation and Classroom Practice in Primary Schools: A Discussion Paper*, Department of Education and Science, HMSO, London.

Ball, S. (1981) *Beachside Comprehensive: A Case Study of Secondary Schooling*, Cambridge University Press.

Bennett, N. (1976) *Teaching Styles and Pupil Progress*, Open Books, London.

Coleman, J. (1966) *Equality of Educational Opportunity*, US Government Printing Office, Washington, DC.

Croll, P. and Galton, M. (1986) A comment on 'Questioning ORACLE', *Educational Research*, Vol. 28, no. 3, pp. 185–9.

Desai, A. (1992) Data envelopment analysis: a clarification, *Evaluation and Research in Education*, Vol. 6, pp. 39–41.

Donaldson, M. (1978) *Children's Minds*, Fontana, Glasgow.

Galton, M. and Simon, B. (1980) *Performance in the Primary Classroom*, Routledge & Kegan Paul, London.

Galton, M., Simon, B. and Croll, P. (1980) *Inside the Primary Classroom*, Routledge & Kegan Paul, London.

Goldstein, H. (1987) *Multilevel Models in Educational and Social Research*, Charles Griffin/Oxford University Press.

Grafton, T., Miller, H., Smith, L., Vegoda, M. and Whitfield, R. (1983) Gender and curriculum choice: a case study, in M. Hammersley and A. Hargreaves (eds.).

Hammersley, M. (1993) On methodological purism: a response to Barry Troyna, *British Educational Research Journal*.

Hammersley, M. and Hargreaves, A. (eds.) *Curriculum Practice: Some Sociological Case Studies*, Falmer Press, Lewes.

Hargreaves, D. H. (1983) The teaching of art and the art of teaching: towards an alternative view of aesthetic learning, in M. Hammersley and A. Hargreaves (eds.) *Curriculum Practice: Some Sociological Case Studies*, Falmer Press, Lewes.

Rutter, M., Maughan, B., Mortimore, P. and Ouston, J. (1979) *Fifteen Thousand Hours: Secondary Schools and their Effect on Children*, Open Books, London.

Scarth, J. and Hammersley, M. (1987) More questioning of ORACLE: a reply to Galton and Croll, *Educational Research*, Vol. 29, no. 1, pp. 37–46.

Simon, B. (1992) Review of *Curriculum Organisation and Classroom Practice in Primary Schools: A Discussion Paper* by Alexander, R., Rose, J. and Woodhead, C., *The Curriculum Journal*, Vol. 3, no. 1, pp. 91–7.

Smith, D. and Tomlinson, S. (1989) *The School Effect: A Study of Multi-Racial Comprehensives*, Policy Studies Institute, London.

Troyna, B. (1978) Race and streaming: a case study, *Educational Review*, Vol. 30, no. 1, pp. 59–65.

Troyna, B. (1992) Underachievers or underrated? The experience of pupils of South Asian origin in a Secondary School, *British Educational Research Journal*, Vol. 17, pp. 361–76.

Troyna, B. (1993) Underachiever or misunderstood? A reply to Roger Gomm, *British Educational Research Journal*, Vol. 19, no. 2, pp. 167–74.

Woods, P. (1976) The myth of subject choice, *British Journal of Sociology*, Vol. 7, no. 2, pp. 130–49.

Woods, P. (1993) *Critical Events in Teaching and Learning*, Falmer Press, Lewes.

Wright, C. (1986) School processes – an ethnographic study, in J. Eggleston, D. Dunn and M. Anjali (eds.) *Education for Some: The Educational and Vocational Experiences of 15–18 Year Old Members of Minority Ethnic Groups*, Trentham Books, Stoke-on-Trent.

PART 1:

Qualitative examples

1

LABOURING TO LEARN?
INDUSTRIAL TRAINING FOR SLOW
LEARNERS

P. Atkinson, D. Shone and T. Rees

INTRODUCTION

The growth in youth unemployment has been matched by an increase in state intervention to manage the 'social problems' thought to be an inevitable and direct consequence. One aspect of this has been intervention in the process of work socialization of young people now no longer necessarily experiencing work itself straight after leaving school. This chapter examines one such intervention measure which has as its client group slow learners. The project is overtly attempting to increase the students' life-chances by preparing them for working life: this involves not only the inculcation of certain industrial skills designed to make them more marketable, but also the instilling of a range of social skills seen to be appropriate in a 'good worker'.

Slow learners, along with the mentally and physically handicapped generally, experience special difficulties in competing effectively in the labour market. Their position has long been recognized as needing some form of positive discrimination policies. However, these policies have been singularly impotent. The Disabled Persons (Employment) Acts of 1944 and 1958, which established a quota system whereby employers of more than 20 persons were to ensure that 3 per cent of their workforce were registered as disabled, have been widely disregarded and are in any case virtually impossible to enforce. As Hudson suggests 'a total of five prosecutions between 1970–75 makes the maximum penalty of £500 an ineffective deterrent' (Hudson, 1977, p. 1703).

If the quota system has been ineffective, it seems unlikely that the initiative from the Manpower Services Commission and the National Advisory Council on Employment of Disabled People in publishing a guide to employing disabled people can have materially effected their competitive edge either. The document, *Positive Policies* (1977), was sent to all employers with 20 or more

staff (about 55,000); it was both supported by the CBI and TUC and wel-
comed by the Warnock Committee on Special Education Needs.

These strategies, focusing as they do on the employers, seem unlikely to
make much of an impact on the job prospects of those young handicapped
capable of working in open employment. During the current high levels of
youth unemployment, when employers can pick the more attractive candidates
from the dole queues for even the most menial of tasks, clearly a different
approach is required if the handicapped school-leaver is to have any chance of
a job at all.

The National Society for Mentally Handicapped Children has for many
years attempted to enhance the life-chances of the mentally handicapped
school-leaver by paying their wages for the first twelve weeks of employment
and recruiting a foster worker to oversee and advise the young person at the
place of work. The Pathway scheme thus introduces employers to handicapped
workers on a no-commitment basis, thereby ensuring even if the employer does
not then take on the young person permanently, he or she has at least had the
benefit of work experience.

The initial response by the government to high levels of youth unemployment was also to provide some form of work experience so that school-
leavers were not hopelessly penalized in the labour market. Of the revamped
schemes operated by the Manpower Services Commission (MSC) since 1978,
it is work experience which accounts for the majority of places under the
Youth Opportunities Programme (YOP). And, according to one source at
least (Gregory, 1980), specialist career officers for the handicapped have
been able to do a 'deal' with employers, persuading them to take a handicapped young person as part of a job lot. Employers have apparently expressed surprise at their employability and kept them on; the capacity of
some mentally handicapped young people to tolerate extremely boring work
has been cited as one reason.

Under YOP there are also a variety of courses aimed at preparing young
people for working life (Working Introduction Course, Short Training
Course), including one specifically aimed at young people with mental or
physical handicaps – the Young Persons Work Preparation Course. In addition, while, nominally at least, a further input has always been an integral
element of YOP, including those on some form of work experience, its emphasis and role has become more significant. The MSC is no longer simply
concerned to provide work experience, it is now concentrating more and more
on aspects of work socialization.

Gregory and Markall (1982) refer to MSC's:

> *transformative* attempt to intervene culturally, ideologically and mater-
> ially in the sphere of education, training, work induction and the identi-
> fication and transmission of 'skills' which not only carry meanings about
> the nature of work and wage labour but which also attempt to structure
> and delimit other understandings and definitions available to and enter-
> tained by the young.

The MSC is now in the business of enhancing life-chances, instilling skills, further education, remedial literacy and numeracy, and, most significant of all perhaps, providing the young unemployed with 'social and life skills'. That includes, as the MSC instructional guides on teaching social and life skills illustrate, how to have the 'right attitude' to work and to employers. Increasingly, then, rather than just offering young people work experience to improve their marketability, MSC is intervening to a far greater extent by moulding young people to the 'needs' of industry.

Industrialists have for many years bemoaned 'declining standards' and illiteracy and innumeracy among young workers. With greater horror complaints have been lodged at the *attitude* of young job-seekers. Indeed in one survey, 43 per cent of employers claimed to have turned down applicants because of their attitude and personality, 29 per cent because of their appearance and manners, compared with 24 per cent because of their 'lack of a basic education' (DE *Gazette*, October 1977; see also MSC, 1980). The concentration of MSC on aspects of work socialization can be seen as a response to the desire by industry for workers with the 'right' attitude.

Clearly the transition from school to work is not simply a linear process with MSC and other agencies acting as 'bridge' between the two worlds by equipping young people with appropriate experience and social skills. The two worlds overlap in multifarious ways – parents and friends are known to play as important a role in shaping the work socialization of handicapped young people as all the official 'gatekeepers' (careers, specialist education services) and voluntary agencies. Nevertheless, increasingly such interventions have shifted in emphasis from allowing the experience itself to be the formative factor in work socialization to more overt instilling of 'right' attitudes.

The rest of this chapter is based on an ethnographic study of one institution designed to ease the transition from school to working life for adolescents who are 'educationally subnormal' or 'slow learners'. (We shall not enter into any discussion at this stage as to the precise definition of the young people involved, since in practice there is no single educational, psychological or social characteristic which delimits the client group.) We shall describe some features of the working of an industrial training unit in industrial South Wales. We shall make no claims as to the 'typicality' of this one institution: indeed, we have reason to believe that in some respects it is rather unusual. On the other hand, we do wish to claim that the issues *raised* by this 'case study' are of more general relevance. In particular, we wish to highlight some aspects of the training and socialization for work that goes on in the training unit, and some of the ways in which the young people there are evaluated and assessed.

THE INDUSTRIAL TRAINING UNIT: AN INTRODUCTION

The unit is part of a college of further education, but is physically distinct and self-contained. It is located on an industrial site, rather than the college campus. The unit consists of a workshop, with woodwork and metalwork machines, an industrial sewing room, a canteen and staff facilities. It can accommodate up to twenty-one students at a time. It is staffed by a manager, whose background is woodwork craft teaching, one other lecturer specializing in woodwork, two lecturers in metalwork (all male), one sewing teacher, one part-time machinist/nurse, and one part-time tutor in literacy and numeracy (all female).

Broadly speaking, three components can be identified in the training provided: specific 'industrial' tasks and skills, 'social and life skills', and remedial numeracy and literacy. We shall not comment on this last aspect in this chapter. In practice the former two aspects are not sharply differentiated. At the time of our observations, the unit's day-to-day work was not organized in accordance with a preset curriculum in the normal sense of the term. Rather, the pace and content of the work was framed by *production* processes. The philosophy' of the unit reflected a belief that students should engage in and be responsible for 'real' work, and most of the tasks they perform are aimed at the completion of contracts placed with the unit by local firms. The range of tasks performed by the students is also determined largely by the sort of machinery available, which in turn constrains the range of contracts that can be attracted by the manager and his staff. The 'curriculum' of the unit, then, is embodied in its physical plant, the contracts which are placed, and the production processes which these imply.

Most of the machine tasks performed by students are simple and repetitive. They require students to conduct a simple set of sequenced activities which form a complete cycle which is then repeated. A typical task of this sort on the metalwork side would include drilling components – placing them in a vice or jig, lowering the drill and raising it again, by simply pulling a lever. While it is more difficult to preset the woodworking machinery, similarly repetitive tasks, such as sawing or planing lengths of timber, are undertaken. The sewing tasks involve the operation of industrial sewing machines, a button machine and a hand-operated press.

The unit takes male and female students. There is a degree of gender differentiation in the allocation of tasks in the unit. Most of the girls are allocated work in the sewing room, except those whose ability is regarded as too low to cope with industrial sewing machines. When the sewing room is not in operation, the girls are usually provided with the more simple tasks in the workshop.

Over and above the routines of productive work, the students also receive more general instruction, through talks and lectures. These arise out of particular incidents that crop up in the course of the day's work.

LECTURES ON WORKSHOP PRACTICE

Certain general principles of workshop practice are communicated to the students as a group, through a lecture. For example, breaches of the safety procedures have been occasions for a lecture on the potential danger of machinery. Such lectures are used to emphasize the necessity of safety procedures and they underline the precept that the students must 'do exactly as you're told', in order to avoid danger.

Other problems which occur, such as continual faulty workmanship, may form the basis of a lecture of this sort. These lectures reinforce the procedures and safety rules of the workshop by demonstrating the potentially dangerous, and sometimes expensive, consequences of failure to obey them. Thus students are enjoined 'always stack materials tidily and correctly'; 'no smoking in the workshop'; 'always switch off machines when leaving them'; 'do as you're told'; 'inform staff if you see something going wrong'.

It is a common ploy of the lectures to include dramatic and vivid demonstrations of matters of danger and safety precautions. For instance, on one occasion the observer noticed the manager hurrying over to where one boy, Dennis, was using a circular saw.

> He switched off the main power and called everybody to 'gather round'. He said something to Dennis which I couldn't hear[1] and then he asked if anyone would put their hand on the bench while he picked up a piece of wood and waved it up and down aggressively.
>
> Someone replied 'No', then the manager said 'Why not?' I was at the rear of the assembled group and as I shuffled forward I saw that it was Tina who was replying to the questions. 'Well this saw blade is travelling at 120 mph and it cuts this wood. What do you think it could do to your fingers?' (Rhetorically). The telephone rang and then the manager asked another lecturer to take over and to 'show them the other display'.
>
> He moved over to the edge planer machine and selected a long length of wood about 6 feet and said something to the effect that 'imagine this was a finger'. He then pushed it against the rotating cylindrical blade of the planer, and in a matter of a few seconds it was reduced to about 18 inches in length. Stuart said, 'You've proved your point' (sarcastically).
>
> The lecturer then said that the saw travels at 120 mph which is 'the same speed as the high speed train . . .'

The lecturer then pointed out that putting their hands near the unguarded saw was as dangerous as standing in front of the high speed train. Then the students were directed back to work. The impression here is of a well-established 'routine' to make the safety point: and the point was certainly well made. Our field notes contain numerous examples of such teaching episodes.

Given the nature of the workshop, the machinery in it, and the nature of the youngsters who work there, safety must be a major preoccupation for the staff. The following extract from our notes may convey something of the urgency with which staff members attempt to instil safe workshop practice in the students. The workshop is noisy, and staff have to gain students' attention above the roar of the machinery.

> The manager then entered the workshop just after a lecturer had called lunch. Then he shouted everyone to gather round. But some had already

left for the canteen. The manager said 'C'mon will you all gather round.'
Just a few students who had been in the immediate vicinity remained.
Someone asked if they should fetch the others. The manager said, 'If you
could, if it's not too late.' Then he said 'I'm bringing in this machine. It's
a very dangerous machine. It may not look it but that blade can cut your
fingers off. If I ask a lecturer which is the most dangerous machine in the
workshop he'll say "this one",' as the lecturer pointed to the cutter. 'You
only have to have the handle slip down and it can take four fingers off.
We've got machines working fast in this workshop but they're not nearly
so dangerous as this because you can see how dangerous they are. I was
once working with this and the handle slipped, and the blades are very,
very sharp and it took the skin off the top of all my fingers.' The girls
went 'eugh'. 'They were only little cuts though but it was painful. Now
I'm going to put one of you on this machine this afternoon and whoever
it is I don't want you to put your fingers through there. Keep well clear of
it. And the others, I don't want you to go anywhere near the one who's
using it. Do you hear me, you've got to keep well away from whoever it is
'n I don't want to see anybody near it.'

Understandably, such warnings are not sufficient to eliminate dangerous practices altogether. Like many factory workers, the young people in the unit take
dangerous short cuts when dealing with the machinery, or they are simply
forgetful or careless. Staff supervising the workshop must therefore be on the
lookout for this, and as we have already indicated, may treat any such incident
as the occasion for a general lecture in an attempt to reinforce the basic safety
message. The lectures and demonstrations about workshop practice are often
concerned with more mundane aspects of work, such as tidiness. Such lectures
deal not only with the particular event or action which sparks them off, but
many also include more general advice on good workmanship and relations
with future employers. For instance, in the following example, the operation of
a simple task like sweeping the floor can become the occasion for general
advice on employers:

The cleaning up operation began and one of the charge-hands, Rhian,
went around collecting the ear protectors. Apart from that particular
piece of work the two charge-hands were doing nothing different from
the others. Most were busily brushing down benches, stacking timber
and two were sweeping the floor. The manager then stopped the cleaning
up operation and asked everybody to gather round Colin who was
sweeping the floor. He stated to everyone: 'I have shown you how to
sweep up haven't I? Look what I just saw this boy, Colin, doing.'
    He proceeded to sweep in a straight line from one point to another, he
then went back and swept in a straight line adjacent to the one he had
just swept. He then finally demonstrated the correct way of sweeping, i.e.
all around a particular spot. The manager concluded by pointing out that
'An employer wants to see results. He wants to get value for money.
Employers don't like people who insist on time wasting. They're not
worth paying', or words to that effect. I happened to be standing next to

one of the other lecturers at this point who stated to me, 'I don't know what's the matter with that boy. He always works untidily and I can't get him to work any better.'

This last example from the field notes illustrates how a topic of workshop practice can be expanded into a talk on 'good workers', and how students should behave in order to impress or please their future or potential employers. This is a central theme to a good deal of the more formal teaching which goes on in the unit. There is a good deal of instruction which is concerned with general matters of social and personal behaviour, and much of this is directed at how students can 'make the most of themselves', and hence make the most of their employment opportunities. We describe this component of the training as 'social and life skills'.

This aspect of the unit's work is not designated 'social and life skills training' as such by the staff, but it seems useful to describe some of the teaching that goes on under this heading. The description is that given to a major component of a great deal of comparable work training and experience for young people. As with most of the teaching, this is not necessarily a prescheduled part of the work but staff members normally capitalize on particular occurrences to make some general point to the students as a group. All the workshop staff contribute to teaching of this sort. The teaching normally takes the form of lectures to the students; the topics covered include issues relevant to students' work and employment prospects and to general social and personal behaviour.

TRAINING FOR WORKING LIFE

The sort of topics that have been taken up include: 'motivation', 'attention span', 'confidence', 'appearance', and 'smoking'. By and large the staff identify personal attributes or habits among the students which they regard as undesirable for working life.

Often a particular student is singled out to exemplify the undesirable trait, and his or her 'shortcomings' are generalized upon. A common strategy is for the lecturer to suggest that some supposedly undesirable characteristic is liable to give employers, or potential employers, a poor or false impression of the student. They therefore attempt to point out the undesirability of such behaviour and exhort the students to adopt more acceptable characteristics. In tone, then, these lectures are partly punitive, in drawing attention to a particular student and 'showing up' him or her. They also have the air of moral homilies and exhortations to self-improvement.

The following extract from the field notes exemplifies a lecture of this sort:

The machines had been switched off four times that morning for the manager to cite an incident that he had noticed, and to indicate the things that had been going wrong. Once more the manager walked over to the main power switch. 'Will you gather round,' he called. Students wandered halfheartedly from their respective positions in the workshop towards the place where the manager was now standing. The manager turned to Clive and said: 'Will you Clive walk over to the door and then walk back.' Puzzled looks appeared on students' faces and one or two voiced the complaint: 'What for?' The manager said: 'You'll see in a moment.' Clive looked up at the manager and then walked over to the door and back. The manager then asked Stuart to walk over to the door and back. Stuart arrived back and was asked to repeat the procedure. One further student was asked to complete this procedure.

The manager made a joke about the slovenly way in which the students walked about.

Several students laughed at this remark. The manager continued: 'I particularly noticed you, Stuart, walking earlier, you were straight. You looked as if you were going somewhere, as if you knew what you were doing, but you didn't do it then. Most of you slouch around, all down and out as if you couldn't care a damn. When I saw Stuart walking straight I thought to myself, he's got a purpose; he knows what he's doing. Most of you look as if you don't know what you're doing. An employer would think that you were a good worker if you were walking straight. Yes, you may know this, people can only judge us on appearances and the way we walk is very important. Don't you agree?' At this point Geraint entered into an argument with the manager:

Geraint: 'People don't just think of the way we walk.'
Manager: 'Well how else can an employer tell what we're like?'
Geraint: 'Not just by the way we walk though' (laughing as he said it).
Manager: 'People do make these impressions on the way we walk and our general attitude when we first meet.'
Geraint: 'But that's not right.'
Manager: 'You're deliberately misunderstanding me you are. Does anybody think that I'm talking through the back of my head?'
Geraint: 'Yes.'
Manager: 'What about the rest of you? Do you think that I'm talking through the back of my head?'
Stuart: 'No.'

This question was then posed to most of the students in turn. Only three students actually disagreed with him.

This particular lecture is a typical instance of how the staff members take a particular youngster's personal characteristics as the starting point for more general homilies and maxims. It is also characteristic of this teaching approach that the students are allowed, even encouraged, to 'answer back' and agree or disagree with the points that have been made. These lectures are a particularly characteristic feature of the teaching strategy and training content of the unit.

In such ways the students were exhorted to mind their demeanour and appearance so as to create the most favourable impression with employers. In various ways, images of the 'good worker' are presented to the students, who are exhorted to behave in a manner which conforms to such a view. This is amply illustrated in the following extract from our notes:

> The manager then went over to the main power switch and asked every-one to 'gather round'. He stood at the top of the workshop by the barrier which separated most of the metal working jobs from the woodworking machinery. He asked: 'What do we need to get by in life, what are the basic necessities?' One boy, Dennis, said 'food'. Another one, Stuart, said 'shelter'. A further one said 'money'. The manager then said: 'What about sex, do we need that?' Someone shouted that 'it makes you feel tired'. The manager said, 'It doesn't do that for me', at which there were a few approving giggles from the kids. He then said: 'What about this one, not many people realize this but we all like to be important: you may not have thought of it before but it's true. Everyone needs to feel import-ant in some ways. The point is there are all sorts of ways of being important.'

The manager then mentioned people wearing 'punk' clothing such as chains, earrings and rubbish bags to make themselves feel important. He went on:

> 'What they don't realize is that the only people they impress are children and others who do the same. Most people just laugh at them. An em-ployer wouldn't give them a job if they came to an interview like that, he'd think they were loonies.
>
> 'Well what I'm saying is that we all like to feel important but there are some ways of feeling important or trying to be important that are better than others. The outrageous ways, such as wearing black rubbish bags, are not going to get you a job nor help you keep that job. But you can be important by being a good worker, and that is better because you're then important to the man who pays your wages.
>
> 'Anyway that's all I wanted to say. Jeremy when are you going to get your hair cut?'
>
> Jeremy: 'I don't know' (laughing as he said it).
>
> Manager: 'You need to buck up a bit my lad.'

On such occasions, some students' personal habits will be commented on adversely, and general maxims on their 'self-presentation' offered. In the fol-lowing example, the stress on 'importance' seems to be carried through, in the lecturer's choice of 'role models' for the students to emulate:

> At this point Geraint noticed the manager writing on the board. He indicated that I should look. I laughed with him. He then shouted across to Daniel, 'look what he's writing'. On the board the manager had written:
>
> How do you know if someone is an idiot?
> Harold Wilson
> Raquel Welch
> _____
> Esther Rantzen

The manager gathered all the students together again and said something to the effect that: 'C'mon this is a serious question. How do you know if someone is an idiot? Well, from the way they behave. Are Harold Wilson, Raquel Welch or Esther Rantzen idiots?' Someone answered 'No'. 'We tell that by the way they behave, by what they do. I bet you've never seen any of these on the television biting their nails or leaving their mouths hanging open. That's one way that people will definitely know you're an idiot. We only know people are idiots if we see them acting like idiots.' (Geraint gave a glance across to Deirdre, accusing her of being the nail-biting culprit.) 'These people don't bite their nails on the television.' Geraint commented, 'They could do', but the manager ignored the remark and concluded. He said, 'I bite my nails sometimes but I don't do it where anybody can see me. I make sure nobody's watching and I do it in the car. So if you have to bite your nails make sure you do it when nobody can see you and then they won't think you're an idiot. Go on have your lunch.'

As they all filed past to go to lunch the manager said to Tina, 'Did you know who I was talking about then?' (jokingly). Tina said, 'Me.'

It is noticeable in this example how the lecturers use colloquial speech forms to produce an informal, relaxed atmosphere. These lectures to the students exhorting them to self-improvement also include injunctions to improve their general attitude, their concentration and motivation.

SOCIAL TRAINING

Again, these lectures arise as specific responses to particular incidents in the workshop. In such cases the students concerned are particularly likely to be singled out and named in the course of the lecture to the whole group. The lecturer will often attempt to demonstrate the negative consequences of the behaviour in question and provide advice on how to avoid such behaviour in the future. These lectures are particularly concerned with the students' social relationships and their general behaviour. As the manager has put it, it is a matter of 'teaching them how to get on with each other'. Clearly there can be no hard and fast distinction between such general 'social' skills, and the work-related concerns mentioned above. It is not a distinction made by the staff themselves and the two are necessarily closely related. Both kinds of lecture have to be delivered amid the machinery for lack of a classroom. The following report provides a representative example of this sort of intervention by a member of staff and of the sort of lecture it can give rise to.

The manager had observed Geraint and Frank arguing as they were returning to the workshop after loading a van. The manager asked everybody to assemble together at the front of the workshop in readiness for a lecture. The manager began: 'Before I start I want you two to shake hands and make friends. Will you do that now?' Frank moved forward to shake hands with Geraint who was sitting on a milk crate opposite to him. Geraint's head was held low and he looked up at Frank approaching and immediately looked down again. The manager continued: 'Did you notice that gesture? He's adult enough to say, "let's forget it". There's nothing worse than walking around with poison in your stomach which is what you two had. And he's not adult enough to shake hands. If you have a bit of difficulty with somebody, if they're getting on your nerves, you just go up and tell him. It's terrible if you can't get on with the people you work with. So if you have to have a row you'll have to remember to make it up. You two, each of you had poison in your stomach. When you get older you just can't do that, because what happens, you talk to somebody and then you call them names, and then you go and talk about how horrible he is to somebody else. Then that person thinks you're a great bloke and then you get on his nerves . . .'

The moral here was that quarrelling led to loss of friends and hence loneliness.

The following incident is very similar, in that an event relating to workshop practice and discipline is turned towards a concern with interpersonal relationships:

Geraint had been instructed to plane down some wood on the planer. He began to run the machine and Tony noticed that some dust was blowing out of the air bags of the waste collector. From where he was working on the rear circular saw he shouted to a lecturer who was standing just in front of the bench saw, and indicated the blowing dust. The lecturer ran and switched off the planer and shook hands with Tony for the deed he had performed. The lecturer then instructed Dennis and Geraint to repair the canvas bag. The air had been seeping from the seal between the bag and the machine. Presumably the metal band which was fitted to the bag like a belt with saw teeth fastenings had worked loose, allowing the bag to ride up. The lecturer instructed them how to unleash the band . . . The two boys then replaced the band and went over to switch on the machine again. However, the bag began to leak again and Geraint turned the planer off, and he and Dennis raced over to the bag. As they began to ply the metal band and pull at the canvas in order to replace the broken seal, the lecturer approached them. He said to Geraint, 'Oh you've put it back on wrong haven't you?' Dennis then answered 'No, it was me.'

The lecturer then shouted everybody to gather round and began to relate what Dennis had just done. He said: 'Y'know what he just did? I accused Gerant of making a mistake and Dennis said to me, "No, it was my fault". It takes a brave man to admit when he's in the wrong.' At which point the lecturer beckoned Dennis nearer and held his hand out for him to shake it. As they shook hands he said 'congratulations'.

Sometimes these incidents are basically matters of 'telling off' students who are misbehaving in some way. One day the lecturer called everybody together and said:

'I've just overheard Stuart telling Rhian to shut up. That's not the way to get on with each other, it's a childish way to talk. What happened?' he said to Rhian. She said, 'He was throwing things at me.' The lecturer's eyes returned to Stuart who said with his head held down, 'She started it.' The lecturer said 'There's no need for you to sulk, stop sulking and tell me what happened.' He said, 'I'm not sulking, she started it.' The lecturer went on, 'I was praising you for being so grown up this morning and now look how childish and stupid you are. This calling each other names and saying "she started it" and telling people to shut up is not the way to get on with each other. Honestly it's just so stupid and childish. Get back to work, and you two stop fighting.'

In addition to the lectures we have just described where working relations are stressed, general topics of demeanour and self-presentation are sometimes emphasized:

Immediately on returning to the workshop the lecturer began with a lecture on swearing. He proceeded to say something to the effect that you've got to be careful when you're swearing. 'I don't mind swearing at all. But don't do it in public where other people can hear you because they might not like it. You might get done for obscene behaviour. The other thing is, don't swear in front of girls because they may not like it either. Don't swear on buses and other public places.'

TRAINING FOR ADULT LIFE

This training is less concerned with changing students' immediate behaviour, and is more informative in character. Lectures are aimed at providing students with knowledge which the staff regards as potentially important for adult life in general. These lectures, unlike the first two types, are not necessarily triggered by particular incidents of poor behaviour or workmanship. In fact, unlike the other training, they are routinely provided at fixed points during the day – before students begin work in the morning, or immediately after the lunch break.

It did appear, however, that as with other components of 'social' training, the content of these talks was rather *ad hoc*. There was little evidence of any preplanning or sequencing of topics and so on. The result was a somewhat disparate series of topics. Over the fieldwork period, the topics covered were: 'capitalism'; 'democracy'; 'advertising'; 'literature' and 'classical music'; 'mortgages'. In style and tone these sessions differed little from those we have already described. They tended to take the form of 'improving' lectures from members of staff. The students had little or no active part to play, and the presentation of the topics was not always grounded in the students' own immediate experiences. The students were not involved in any practical activities, and no attempt was made to make use of such techniques as role playing and so on.

We reproduce here the notes on just one session of this sort. The first example shows how the students were introduced to topics 'out of the blue'. It is also revealing about some of the distinctive social and political views of the staff members themselves. The emphasis on self-help and the moral virtue of work is a theme which runs through a good deal of the unit's work. It is a recurrent theme in what we can only describe, metaphorically, as 'homilies'.

The capitalism lecture

Everybody had just started back to work and Jeremy was leaning on the bench with eyes half closed. The manager had looked over towards him, and that seemed to spark off the lecture he gave. He switched off the machinery and invited everybody to stand over by the blackboard. He began by saying something like, 'Did you know that we live in a capitalist society?' (as he wrote the word *capitalist* on the blackboard). 'What that means is that machinery and factories are owned by capitalists. This is not just one person, it's a lot of people, and they run factories to make a profit. Most people are workers and the trouble is we depend on each other for a living. The worker gets his pay at the end of the week and the capitalist gets his profit. But when workers are lazy or continually make high pay demands a lot of employers go broke and then the workers lose their jobs. Like British Leyland. So employers can't afford to carry lazy workers as passengers. Now, you're all passengers now, and you've de-pended on your parents for most of your lives. People on the dole, they are passengers, they take their living from people who are working. If you're very lucky you may go to college and become a passenger for a lot longer. But you'll all hopefully get a job and you won't lose it for laziness, with one or two exceptions.' The telephone rang and he instructed another lecturer to continue.

The lecturer began by saying, 'What he was saying about passengers is that when you leave here and get a job you won't be a passenger any longer. There are too many people today who think they're owed a living. So you've got to try to be independent, to look after yourselves and stop being passengers.'

STAFF EVALUATIONS OF STUDENT ABILITY

In organizing the day-to-day activities of the unit, and in assessing the suit-ability of students for particular tasks, the staff members base their decisions on evaluations of students' ability and motivation: these are based on their observation of the students rather than the use of standardized tests. It seems that the staff feel themselves qualified to make such assessments of students' skill, character and personality.

During the early period of fieldwork it became apparent that the students were being evaluated according to two basic dimensions. The first of these reflected the assessment of a given student's relative intelligence; it boiled down to whether they were seen as 'bright' or 'dull'. The second evaluative dimension reflected their ability and orientation with respect to work; that is, whether they were 'good' or 'bad' workers. In addition to these two basic categorizations, students were characterized in terms of their personal characteristics – sometimes their personal or social shortcomings, sometimes their more 'endearing' qualities. Examples from the field notes include:

She's ever so dull but she's a very nice kid though.

He's a nice kid but he's so shy.

He's a good lad this one only he lets himself go.

The informal assessment of students' abilities is of considerable importance for the running of the unit, and it seems to be the case that the identification of students as 'bright' or 'dull' (able or unable) is reflected in the tasks they are given and in the way they are treated. As we have just suggested, some jobs – such as the use of the woodwork lathe – were reserved for students who were regarded as 'good workers'. The evaluation of a student as a 'good worker' does not rest on *ability* alone. In practice, a major criterion of 'good work' is a student's willingness to conduct tasks for relatively long periods of time, on his or her own, without disruptive contact with other students. A good worker, then, can be left to get on with his or her work, without needing constant supervision, and without upsetting the work of other students.

Since 'good' workers are given 'good' jobs, and may be left to get on with it, there is an inbuilt bias against any systematic attempts to introduce students to progressively more demanding tasks, or to rotate students through a large range of available jobs. Rather, there is a tendency for students to be allocated to their perceived level of competence, and then for them to stop there. Of course, we do not wish to suggest that there is absolutely no fluidity and movement between jobs. Nevertheless, there is a tendency for students to spend long periods of time at the same task, and hence to work constantly at the same level, in terms of the demands made on them, intellectually and manually.

The staff's impressions of students not only have some bearing on the training they receive, but also on the types of employment they are considered suitable for. In general they are considered to be destined for manual and semi-skilled work. Occasionally, when a student shows 'promise' he or she may be steered towards a particular skill in the hope that employment in that line of work may become available. It does appear that the students so assessed and selected have a passive role, although they occasionally object to the work they are steered towards. Such objections may be that they 'want to work with their friends' or that they have unrealistic expectations of wages elsewhere. It was also suggested to us that students might object to particular sorts of employment by virtue of inaccurate assessment of their own abilities (as lower than the staff's evaluations of them).

There were, for instance, two boys who were regarded as exceptionally 'bright'. They were routinely given relatively skilled carpentry jobs to perform, and were eventually channelled into relatively skilled employment of this sort. After 'proving' their ability in routine work they were rarely allocated to repetitive tasks. In contrast, two of the girls were assessed by the staff as particularly 'dull', and as likely candidates for the adult training centre. They were provided with what the staff themselves regarded as simple, routine, uninteresting work. The manager has pointed out to us that he regards such work as necessary, in that it closely approximates the kind of work the least able students would be likely to find in open employment.

As we have already remarked, the most obvious categorization of students is on gender lines, and this overlaps with the assessment of student ability. Most of the girls are allocated work in the sewing room, except those whose ability is regarded as too low to cope with the sewing machines. When the sewing room is not in operation (approximately eight hours a week, because of timetabling problems), the girls are allocated to the more simple tasks in the workshop. Only rarely do they operate woodworking or metalworking machinery, although in theory they may do so if they wish. The manager attributes the gender differentiation to the girls' preference for the more 'congenial' atmosphere of the sewing room. There is a consensus among the staff that certain of the metalworking jobs – simple drilling and tapping operations – are safe and simple, and therefore particularly suitable for the less able student. When the girls have to leave the sewing room for varying periods of time they are given such metalworking jobs, along with the least able boys. One of the boys who was regarded as one of the 'least able' and was also seen as 'troublesome' spent most of his time conducting simple metalwork operations. He frequently complained that he would be 'dreaming of these brackets' in his sleep.

The criteria on which staff opinions are based appeared to include: attendance, timekeeping, and evidence of working ability (e.g., judged by the number of components made). But these aspects are mediated by a global impression of less tangible matters, such as aspects of students' personality. Guidelines for student assessment are explicitly included in a *Readiness for Work Chart*, which forms part of the student's record. But staff rarely articulate their assessments in terms of these explicit criteria, but rather in terms of students' personal idiosyncracies and characteristics. Thus those students who seem unable to conform to the standards expected, or who appear to possess less favourable or likeable attributes are often those who benefit least from their stay at the unit, in that they will not be considered for placement if a work vacancy arises.

Although many of the students may have extremely low IQs they may not be regarded as exceptionally dull or relatively bright unless their performance at the unit confirms or disconfirms such an impression. Thus, attempts at training on tasks and at inculcating work speeds may prove to be difficult, and may thus reinforce prior categorizations. In other words, IQ is not considered to be particularly important in itself. Appearance, demeanour and a willingness to accept subordinate roles and discipline have a far greater influence on staff impressions, and may be influential in obtaining jobs for these students.

More important, however, is the implicit notion of 'work readiness' which the staff adopt. Unless jobs are actually sought after for particular students, who are thought to have 'shown improvement', it seems to be the case that most of the student body are regarded as 'not ready' for such work. Of course, the seeking out and finding of jobs does not necessarily depend on their being 'work ready', but more importantly on other factors such as the availability of work, the geographical location of students' homes, their length of stay at the unit, and the point at which their course terminates. In other words, there are various contingencies involved in finding jobs for students, the most pressing of which is the need to find work at the end of a course or before long college holidays.

However, categorization of students as outlined above is rarely articulated fully. The staff seem to glean their impressions of who are the better students from conversations between each other. Thus, one student was regarded as particularly annoying and the following was heard during a break-time conversation in the staffroom:

> 'Oh she gets on my nerves she does. She's always wanting to organize everything.'

It would appear that others concur in this particular evaluation of the student: we have learned that the employers who subsequently took on this girl have found her unsatisfactory, not least because of her 'attention seeking'.

Perhaps the most illuminating area in which these non-articulated categorizations are elicited is in connection with job opportunities that arise. In such instances the staff would suggest particular students as suitable for that employment. Thus, the following exchanges occurred:

> A: 'I've got these two apprenticeships at —— joinery.'
> B: 'But what are we going to do about the interview?'
> A: 'Oh I'd forgotten about that, we could put somebody else in.'
> B: 'What about Stuart?'
> A: 'Oh that would be an improvement.'

and also:

> A: 'They've got a vacancy up there for a good lad, one like they had before. But I told them I don't think we've got anybody ready.'
> B: 'What about ——?'
> A: 'He's not been here long enough.'
> B: 'His attitude's not right.'

One student was found a job and the staff kept him back because they were afraid that he might 'mess up another student's chances'. Thus, when the decisions finally had to be made two members of the staff consulted:

> A: 'What are we going to do about Geraint?'
> B: 'He'll only mess up James's chances.'

In this case the staff members felt that while one of the boys would work well, together they could be 'troublesome'.

Another example relating to the problem that students present is as follows:

Staff: 'What would you do with somebody like that?'
Researcher: 'Well he works alright doesn't he?'
Staff: 'But there's a communication problem somewhere. You can't just get through to him.'

In other words, the students are categorized as having particular problems which mitigate against their consideration as 'work ready'. It seems to be the case that the problems which the students present during early training are either reinforced or not according to the problems they present on a daily basis. Although the staff may operate an implicit conception of work readiness this is subject to shifting criteria in response to day-to-day contingencies. Thus, the age of students, the imminence of their course termination, their length of stay at the unit, are all aspects that may be taken into account when decisions as to finding employment are made.

Some of the features of the staff evaluation of student ability can be illustrated by the following case study of one student, Tina. Tina was regarded as particularly dull and immature. She was normally allocated to the most simple and undemanding of tasks: drilling and tapping, and sorting springs. (This last job involved unwinding tangled springs – something which was also being done by adult workers in a nearby factory.) She was often referred to as being suitable for the adult training centre, and was given tasks which did not involve her in any potential danger. Unlike most of the other girls she was not allowed to use the sewing machines, except on rare occasions under close supervision.

Of course Tina was assigned to other tasks during her long period at the unit, but during the fieldwork period she was only provided with the opportunity of attending for one interview. This was for sheltered employment at Remploy, and she expressed considerable antagonism at this chance of employment.

Although Tina did not seem to present the staff with any particular problems that were required to be discussed among them, she was consistently allocated to the most simple tasks and was sometimes reprimanded for particular misdemeanours. The most common of these misdemeanours was that if she was assigned sitting next to Kevin, they would spend considerable periods of time telling jokes and hence Tina would end up in prolonged spasms of laughter. This laughter led on several occasions to a lecture by the manager on 'not speaking up above the machines since that may indicate that an accident has occurred'. It also led to members of staff having to instruct her to 'get on with her work'. (It seemed to be the case that often most of the misdemeanours Tina committed could be regarded as petty and in no way antagonistic.)

It would appear that the manager's view of Tina's abilities was not wholeheartedly shared by other members of staff who claimed that despite 'immature' behaviour, she had 'work rhythm', which might enable her to survive in selected open employment. The manager regards admittance to the ATC as a 'backward step to be avoided if at all possible'. During one incident during the early fieldwork, Tina was heading for lunch; she jumped down the last four stairs to the locker room and shouted 'Geronimo'. The manager turned to the fieldworker and remarked that she was likely to wind up in the ATC. It seemed to be the case that most of the tasks that she was assigned to reflected this estimation of her. That is to say, there was no conception of her progressing or improving and she was destined for sheltered employment.

There may be something of a paradox in the way in which most of the students are found jobs. That is, jobs are often found by the manager of the unit, using the network of informal relationships he has built up in local firms. As we have suggested, students are selected for vacancies which arise in line with the staff's evaluations as to their 'readiness' and suitability. Hence there is a built-in bias against the students looking for jobs themselves. It is also apparent that they are not usually aware of the nature of the staff assessments of them (although they may be made aware of particular areas of perceived 'weakness'). The resulting overall impression is that jobs are 'rewards', allocated by the manager, on the basis of compliance, good behaviour and hard work. This is not necessarily a matter for criticism in itself. The process may well be a reasonable approximation of how such youngsters might find work anyway: through the intervention of a parent, relative or elder brother or sister, rather than through formal agencies. Nevertheless there does seem to be a tension between the way jobs are found and allocated, and the professed aim of the unit's training, in fostering a degree of self-reliance and competence in the students when it comes to the world of work. Our strong impression as a result of the fieldwork so far is that the students are very *passive* in the process whereby they are channelled towards jobs. They rarely object to jobs which are found for them and are generally acquiescent.

CONCLUSION

In this chapter we have been able to touch on just some aspects of the organization and working of an industrial training unit. As we remarked at the outset, we advance no claims as to the 'typicality' of the unit we describe. It does, however, exemplify a number of themes which are generic to contemporary programmes to ease the transition from education to working life.

The work of the unit interweaves 'formal' and 'informal' components. At the level of its overt, official aims and objectives, the unit is intended to provide the young people with specific skills and competencies which will enhance their chances of finding and keeping a job in a shrinking labour market. At a more informal level, the day-to-day training is couched in terms of the model 'good worker' and the values of 'good work'. The unit's activities are pervaded by a distinctive work 'ethos' or 'ideology'.

As we have described, the industrial training unit is not run in accordance with a set 'timetable' or 'curriculum', in the sense usually used in educational settings. The work is organized primarily in terms of the production process of the unit's contract work. Many of the instructional episodes we have exemplified stem directly from threats to production, or 'failures' of workshop practice. Other types of instruction stem from staff members' perception of students' failure to live up to the model worker, in terms of deference and demeanour.

For the most part, it is not at all clear that the students' skills are significantly changed, in terms of their competence with industrial machinery. There is little or no sense of their progressing through graded tasks, and of measurable improvement in performance. Rather, the students find a level at which they work satisfactorily, and stick to it. There is also little to suggest that the actual skills and tasks mastered in the workshop correspond to those most appropriate for the available sectors of the labour market. Training in carpentry may be unlikely to produce directly marketable skills.

As high levels of youth unemployment persist, the number of projects of the kind described here appear to be increasing sharply. Those directed purely at the needs of the slow learner are in the minority, but share with other innovations a concern with work preparation in the broadest sense. Evaluations of such projects abound; in particular the Manpower Services Commission is concerned that its schemes be scrutinized. What such studies appear to lack, however, is a questioning of the aims and objectives of the schemes themselves. In this chapter we have attempted to draw out into the open some of the implicit assumptions that projects set up to ease the transition process for slow learners appear to make.

ACKNOWLEDGEMENTS

The handicapped were identified by the Council of Ministers as being particularly at risk when youth employment rates rose throughout the European Community in the early 1970s. The Industrial Training Unit described in this paper, which was set up to prepare slow learners for working life, is an associated project of the European Community Action Programme on the Transition from School to Work set up in 1977. It is one of many such innovative projects throughout the Community being evaluated for the Commission. We are grateful to IFAPLAN, the social research institute in Cologne coordinating the evaluation of the Community Action Programme, for funding the work reported here through Professor Alan Little of Goldsmith's College, London, the UK evaluator.

We are also indebted to numerous organizations and individuals in Wales for their support and cooperation, in particular the manager, staff and students of the unit. Finally our thanks are due to Dr Sara Delamont of the Department of Sociology, University College, Cardiff, for her comments upon an earlier draft.

NOTES

1. The observer was later told that the manager was seeking the boy's permission to use the incident as a teaching example.

REFERENCES

Department of Employment (1977) 'Attitude and personality lose young people jobs', *DE Gazette*, October, p. 1127.

Gregory, D. (1980) 'Current trends in the local labour market of Mid Glamorgan', Report No. 6 of Evaluation of Industrial Training Units, Sociological Research Unit, Department of Sociology, University College, Cardiff.

Gregory, D. and Markall G. (1982) 'State intervention – assumptions and programmes', in P. Atkinson and T. L. Rees (eds) *Youth Unemployment and State Intervention*, Routledge & Kegan Paul.

Hudson, B. (1977) 'Time to rethink policy for forgotten jobless', *Health and Social Services Journal*, pp. 1702–04.

Manpower Services Commission (1980) 'The Sheffield and Rotherham Labour Market Survey', MSC.

FURTHER READING

Lane, D. (1980) *The Work Needs of Mentally Handicapped Adults*, published by the Disability Alliance (1 Cambridge Terrace, London NW1).

Jackson, R. N. (1978) 'Are we unrealistic about jobs?' in *Special Education – Forward Trends*, Volume 5, number 1, pp. 11–13.

Rogers, J. (1979) 'The Prospects for ESN(M) School Leavers', in *Special Education – Forward Trends*, Volume 6, number 1, pp. 8–10.

The ESN(M) School Leaver – Transition to What? Report of a Joint Conference of the National Elfrida Rathbone Society at the Centre for Educational Disadvantage, July 1980, Manchester.

2

EARLY EDUCATION: MULTIRACIAL PRIMARY SCHOOL CLASSROOMS

C. Wright

BACKGROUND TO THE STUDY

In recent years there has been much written on 'race', ethnicity and education yet, somewhat surprisingly, little material has been based on observational studies. I wish to argue that, if we are to understand fully the workings of the education system (particularly its influences on black[1] children's educational outcomes), we need to consider both the problems and solutions which are experienced and created at the 'chalk-face'. Indeed, practitioners, academics and the black communities have criticized research projects, government inquiries and local initiatives which omitted to address problems at the school level (Troyna, 1987). The value in conducting research into school processes and the resultant effects is borne out by the numerous studies which have looked at aspects within schools, and have revealed the influences which individual schools can have on the progress and academic achievement of their pupils (e.g. Rutter et al., 1979; Gray et al., 1983; Mortimore et al., 1988).

More recently there has been an increasing amount of observational work conducted in multiracial schools. Most of the research has been carried out in secondary schools (Driver, 1979; Wright, 1987; Mac an Ghaill, 1988; Gillborn, 1988). Observational studies in this field have yielded insightful accounts of black children's experience of secondary schooling. The finding to emerge consistently from the studies is that black and white pupils experience schooling differently. For example, compared with their white peers, Afro-Caribbean pupils typically experience greater amounts of criticism and conflict in their relationships with white teachers. Consequently, as a group, Afro-Caribbean pupils are likely to be disadvantaged within the secondary school setting.

The few studies available on black children's primary schooling show Afro-Caribbeans to be already disadvantaged at this stage of their education. The most detailed study of black children's primary schooling was conducted by Peter Green in seventy multiracial primary and middle school classrooms. Green's findings revealed that in the classroom, in comparison with other pupil groups, Afro-Caribbean pupils (especially boys) received more criticism, and experienced relatively more authoritarian and negative relationships with their teachers (Green, 1985). Whilst providing insightful accounts of life in multiracial primary school classrooms, this work gives little indication of the processes responsible for the classroom life experienced by the different pupil groups. Indeed, the lack of attention given to the underlying processes which generate the different classroom experiences documented for the multiracial context has led some commentators to argue that the disproportionate amount of control and criticism experienced by Afro-Caribbean pupils may simply be a consequence of these pupils' classroom behaviour (see for example, Foster, 1990).

THE CONTEXT OF THE STUDY

This article aims to examine black children's experiences within the primary classroom, focusing particularly on their relationships with their teachers and classmates. Black children's day-to-day classroom experiences are examined through the use of classroom encounters drawn from my 1988/89 ethnographic study of four inner-city primary schools.[2]

The selection of the four schools was based on two major criteria:

1. that they should have a substantial proportion of children of Afro-Caribbean and Asian origins, and
2. that they should contain both working-class and middle-class areas in their catchment zones.

However, schools falling in middle-class areas in the city failed to meet criterion (1) which was the overriding criterion. Four schools (A, B, C and D) were selected that *came closest* to reaching the two criteria. Schools, A, B and C are nursery/infant schools (3–8 years, two multiracial and one predominantly white); school D is a multiracial middle school (8–13 years).

According to census figures, the catchment area for school A contains 6 per cent of the city's black population, originating from the following areas of birth: West Indies 12 per cent; Pakistan and Bangladesh 8 per cent; India 4 per cent; and UK 76 per cent. This is an area of mixed council and private housing.

The catchment area for schools B, C and D contains 16 per cent of the city's black population, originating from the following areas of birth: West Indies 22 per cent; Pakistan and Bangladesh 18 per cent; India 10 per cent; and UK 50 per cent. This area is mostly a large post-war council housing estate, with over 80 per cent of children entitled to free school meals. The staff and student characteristics of the four schools are shown in Table 1.

Table 1 Staff and student characteristics of the study schools

School	Afro-Caribbean	Asian	Mixed race	White	Other
Teaching staff					
A	0	0	0	9	0
B	0	0	0	12	0
C	0	0	0	10	0
D	0	0	0	13	0
Support staff					
A	0	0	0	0	0
B	1	1	0	1	0
C	1	0	0	1	0
D	0	0	0	1	0
Nursery: teaching staff[3]					
A	0	0	0	1	0
B	0	0	0	2	0
C	0	0	0	2	0
D	—	—	—	—	—
Nursery: support staff[3]					
A	0	0	0	2	0
B	1	1	0	2	0
C	2	1	0	2	0
D	—	—	—	—	—
School pupils					
A	12	5	3	153	0
B	41	65	38	131	2
C	32	37	22	79	0
D	23	37	14	111	3
Nursery children					
A	3	1	1	15	0
B	12	21	8	3	2
C	6	8	7	44	0
D	—	—	—	—	—

METHODOLOGY

The ethnographic approach is characterized by a concern to chart the realities of day-to-day institutional life. During the study close observation of classrooms and schools was undertaken. Approximately 970 pupils and 57 staff (which included teachers, nursery nurses and other support staff) were observed in the classroom.

The specific research methods used were:

1. Classroom observations of pupils and staff. These were documented via note-taking, case studies, tape recordings and verbatim descriptions of events.
2. The same methodology was used in recording interactions in other school settings.
3. Informal interviews with all teachers observed, most support staff and headteachers.

4. Informal interviews with most pupils observed in the classroom.
5. Personal interviews with either one or both parents from the following sets of parents: six white, four Afro-Caribbean and four Asian from school A, and eight from each of these groups for schools B, C and D.
6. The use of attainment test scores completed for schools B, C and D. These were not available for school A.

This methodology of intensive observation and interviews is thought to be the most suitable for eliciting the views of teachers, pupils and parents on the widest range of issues relating to the schools. This approach is also sensitively disposed to capturing school experience in its entirety.

My own ethnicity, as an Afro-Caribbean, produced a variety of attitudes. For some white teachers this was a source of insecurity and antagonism. This varied with the level of acquaintance with the teacher. The black pupils often held me in high esteem and frequently used me for support when they felt stressed and under threat. Throughout I remained empathetic to everyone and non-judgemental. This rapport generated considerable co-operation from teachers and pupils.

TEACHER–PUPIL RELATIONS

Primary education is generally assumed to be rooted in a child-centred ideology (Alexander, 1984). The quality of interpersonal relationships and experiences offered to the child at the school level is fundamental to such an approach. Regardless of whether the primary ideology is as widespread as claimed, the first impression of the schools in the study was that a pleasant atmosphere and a constructive relationship existed between teachers and children. There was an emphasis on providing caring support and a friendly and encouraging environment for all children. This approach was also reflected in the schools' pedagogy. There was a degree of sensitivity to the needs of the different groups of children as shown by some use of multicultural materials and images. The vast majority of the staff (e.g., teachers and support staff in the classroom) seemed genuinely committed to ideals of equality of educational opportunity.

However, classroom observation revealed subtle differences in the way white teachers treated black children. Differences in teachers' treatment of these children were observed both within the nursery and junior classrooms.

THE ASIAN CHILD IN THE CLASSROOM

In the nursery units children came together as a group each day for 'story time' and (English) language work. Through effective discussion and questioning, the teacher encouraged the children to extend their spoken English – through talking about stories, songs, objects and so on.

In these formal sessions, the Asian children were generally observed to be excluded from the discussions because of the assumption that they could not understand or speak English. On the occasions when the Asian children were encouraged to participate in a group discussion, teachers often communicated with them using basic telegraphic language. When this strategy failed to get any response the teachers would quickly lose patience with the children and would then ignore them.

This was also the observation of the black nursery nurses working in the nursery units, as the following comment from school B reveals:

> They [white teachers] have got this way of talking to them [Asian children] in a really simple way . . . cutting half the sentences 'Me no do that' sort of thing . . . and that is not standard English. And they've [teachers] got this way of saying words 'That naughty' and they miss words out and it really does seem stupid . . . I feel that it's not my place to say 'Well that's a silly way to speak to children . . .' I worry about what it tells the white children who think that the Asian children are odd anyway.

Teachers often expressed open irritation or frustration when they believed that the Asian children's poor English language skills interfered with their teaching. The scenario below illustrates experiences common to the schools observed.

> *In a classroom in school A, 5–6 year olds are working on a number of activities. The class teacher calls children out individually to listen to them read. She asks an Asian girl, recently arrived from Pakistan and in the school for less than a term, to come to her desk.*

Teacher: (*to Asian girl*) Right, let's see what you can do. (*Teacher opens a book, pointing to a picture.*) This is a flower, say flower.

> *Rehana[4] nods nervously, appears a little confused.*

Teacher: This is a flower. After me, FLOWER.

> *Pupil doesn't respond.*

Teacher: (*Calls for assistance from one of the Asian pupils.*) Zareeda, would you come here a minute. (*Zareeda walks over to the teacher's desk.*) What is the Urdu word for 'flower'? (*Zareeda fidgets nervously.*) Tell her in Urdu that this is a flower.

> *Zareeda looks very embarrassed, refuses to speak. A few children gather around the teacher's desk. Zareeda hides her face from the children who have gathered around the teacher's desk.*

Teacher: Come on Zareeda, what is the Urdu word?

> *Zareeda refuses to co-operate with the teacher, stands at the teacher's desk with head lowered, looking quite distraught.*

Teacher: Zareeda, if you're embarrassed, whisper the word to me.

Zareeda does not respond.

Teacher: *(Visibly irritated)* Well, Zareeda, you're supposed to be help-
             ing, that's not the attitude in this school, we help our friends.
             You're supposed to be helping me to teach Rehana English
             . . . *(To the Asian girls)* Go and sit down, both of you . . . I'll
             go next door and see if one of those other Asian children can
             help me. *(Teacher leaves the room.)*

*The incident has attracted the attention of the whole class.
Whilst the teacher is interacting with the Asian girls, the white
children are overheard making disparaging remarks about
'Pakis'.*

In the classroom many of the Asian children displayed a quiet and controlled
demeanour; in comparison with other children they appeared subdued. There
was a sense in which the Asian girls seemed invisible to the teachers. They
received the least attention from the teacher in the classroom. They were rarely
invited to answer questions and take a lead in activities in the classroom.
Interestingly, for children of this age group, greater classroom co-operation
was observed between Asian boys and girls than was the case for other pupil
groups. In the classroom these children operated as a closed group.

Initially, such a reaction to their classroom experience was in itself perceived
to be a problem by some teachers, as reflected in this comment from a teacher
at school B:

The Asian children tend to be self-isolating. I have to deliberately separate that group. They tend to ignore all other children – are not too
happy sitting next to anybody else and see themselves as their own little
group. They tend to converse in their own language. I'm afraid I have to
say 'Now come on, stop'.

When asked to explain why Asian children conversing in their mother tongue
in the classroom was a concern, she pointed out:

Because I don't know what is being said. It could be something against
the other children in the class. I mean, I've no idea what is going on.
Often one [Asian child] will come up to me and say 'Miss he's swearing',
that kind of thing. They always tell on each other of course. But no, I
don't encourage that, at least not in the normal classroom situation. They
[Asian children] do go as a special group to Mrs Reeves [English as a
second language support teacher] and she does special stories in Urdu
with them.

Among the negative responses to Asian children expressed by teachers was also
open disapproval of their customs and traditions, often considered to pose
problems for classroom management. Such disapproval added to the negative
experiences of school of some of these children, precisely because of the con-
tradictory expectations of home and school.

Preparing for physical education lessons, for example, posed some difficulties for the Asian girls because pupils were required, particularly at the nursery school, to undress in the classroom. The girls employed a number of creative measures to acquire some privacy, such as hiding behind chairs or under desks. The teachers often showed total disregard for the feelings of these children, openly disapproving of what they considered was over-sensitive, modest behaviour on the part of the Asian girls. At the end of the PE lesson the Asian girls were the recipients of teachers' sarcasm – 'Well, don't you wish you were all as quick getting undressed?

The anguish experienced by the Asian girls was expressed by these 7 and 8 year olds at school A:

Parvin:	We don't like PE. I get a headache when we do PE.
Rashida:	I don't like it because we are not allowed to do it.
Researcher:	Why?
Parvin:	Because it's like my mum and dad said, her mum and dad, if you do PE you get Gonah.[5]
Rashida:	We go to mosque and if you do PE and you just go to mosque like that, you get smacked from that lady. That's why we don't like to do PE. We don't want trouble from God for doing PE.
Parvin:	Because we don't allow other people to see our pants, so we hide behind the table when we get changed for PE.
Researcher:	What does the teacher say when you hide behind the table?
Parvin:	Sometimes she shouts.
Researcher:	Have you told the teacher about your feelings?
Parvin and Rashida:	No no.
Researcher:	Why?
Rashida:	Because we're scared.
Parvin:	Because we don't like to, she would shout.

The girls are expressing a fundamental conflict between the perceived expectations of their background and the requirements of the school. However, they were reluctant to share their feelings with the class teacher, because of the fear of being reprimanded. Thus, the teacher was perceived as being unsupportive.

Another example of teacher insensitivity in dealing with Asian pupils is illustrated by the following scenario at school D. The teacher was distributing letters to the class to take home to parents to elicit their permission for a forthcoming school trip. The teacher commented to the Asian girls in the class 'I suppose we'll have problems with you girls. Is it worth me giving you a letter, because your parents don't allow you to be away from home overnight?'

The cumulative effects of teachers' attitudes towards Asian children was to create a sense of insecurity for these children in the classroom. Moreover, the attitudes of the teachers influenced the Asian children's social disposition among their classroom peers. They were extremely unpopular, especially among their white peers. Indeed, children of other groups would refer to the very same features of the Asian children's perceived character deficiencies (which the class teacher had previously drawn attention to in the classroom) to tease and harass them.

Such responses tended to counteract the positive attempts by teachers to address multicultural issues and led to an ambivalence from Asian children on curriculum topics or school celebrations focusing on aspects of their traditions or customs. On the one hand, they expressed some pride in having aspects of these acknowledged by the school. Yet on the other they were concerned that this often exacerbated the teasing, ridicule and harassment which they felt they received daily, particularly from the white children.

THE AFRO-CARIBBEAN CHILD IN THE CLASSROOM

As with the Asian child, the Afro-Caribbean child carries a range of expectations of their behaviour and educational potential, right from the nursery class. While the Asian child may experience a pattern made up of assumed poor language skills and negativity towards their cultural background alongside expectations of educational attainment, the Afro-Caribbean child's experience is often largely composed of expectations of bad behaviour, along with disapproval, punishment and teacher insensitivity to the experience of racism. Some Afro-Caribbean children of Rastafarian origin also experience a cultural disapproval.

An example of such assumptions revealed at a very early stage took place in a nursery group of 4 year olds in school C:

Teacher:	Let's do one song before home time.
Peter (white boy):	Humpty Dumpty.
Teacher:	No, I'm choosing today. Let's do something we have not done for a while. I know, we'll do the Autumn song. What about the Autumn song we sing. Don't shout out, put your hand up nicely.
Mandy:	*(Shouting out)* Two little leaves on a tree.
Teacher:	She's nearly right.
Marcus:	*(Afro-Caribbean boy with his hand up)* I know.
Teacher:	*(Talking to the group)* Is she right when she says 'two little leaves on a tree'?
Whole group:	No.
Teacher:	What is it Peter?
Peter:	Four.
Teacher:	Nearly right.
Marcus:	*(Waving his hand for attention)* Five.
Teacher:	Don't shout out Marcus, do you know Susan *(white girl)*?
Susan:	Five.
Teacher:	*(Holding up one hand)* Good, five, because we have got how many fingers on this hand?

Whole group:	Five.
Teacher:	OK, let's only have one hand because we've only got five leaves. How many would we have if we had too many? Don't shout out, hands up.
Mandy:	*(Shouting out)* One, two, three, four, five, six, seven, eight, nine, ten.
Teacher:	Good, OK how many fingers have we got?
Marcus:	Five.
Teacher:	Don't shout out Marcus, put your hand up. Deane, how many?
Deane:	Five.
Teacher:	That's right, we're going to use five today, what makes them dance about, these leaves?
Peter:	*(Shouting out)* The wind.
Teacher:	That's right. Ready here we go.

Teacher and children sing: 'Five little leaves so bright and gay, dancing about on a tree one day. The wind came blowing through the town, whoooo, whoooo, one little leaf came tumbling down.'

Teacher:	How many have we got left?
Deane:	*(Shouting out)* One.
Marcus:	*(Raising his hand enthusiastically)* Four.
Teacher:	*(To Marcus)* Shush, Let's count, one, two, three, four.
Teacher:	How many, Deane?
Deane:	Four.
Teacher:	Good, right, let's do the next bit.

Teacher and children sing the next two verses.

Teacher:	How many have we got left, Peter?
Peter:	Don't know.
Mandy:	Two.
Teacher:	I know that you know, Mandy.
Marcus:	Two.
Teacher:	*(Stern voice)* I'm not asking you, I'm asking Peter, don't shout out. We'll help Peter, shall we. Look at my fingers, how many? One, two. How many, Peter?
Peter:	Two.
Teacher:	Very good. Let's do the next bit.

Teacher and children sing the next verse; at the end of the verse:

Teacher:	How many have we got left, Susan?
Susan:	One.
Teacher:	Good, let's all count, one. Let's do the last bit.

Teacher and children sing the last verse; at the end of the verse:

Teacher:	How many have we got left?
All children:	None.
Teacher:	That's right there are no leaves left. Marcus, will you stop fidgeting and sit nicely.

Marcus was frequently the recipient of teacher control and criticism. He was often singled out for criticism, even though several pupils of different ethnic origins were engaged in the same behaviour.

In a conversation about the above observation, the Afro-Caribbean nursery nurse attached to the unit commented:

> Marcus really likes answering questions about things. I can imagine he's quite good at that because he's always got plenty to say . . . but they [white teachers] see the black children as a problem here.

Black nursery nurses in another nursery unit of school B also expressed concern about the attitudes of white colleagues towards Afro-Caribbean boys in particular. One of them pointed out:

> The head of the nursery is forever saying how difficult it is to control the black children in the nursery, because they only responded to being hit . . . there is an attitude that they all get beaten up at home and they're all used to getting a good slap or a good punch. There are one or two [black children] that they are quite positive about . . . they happen to be girls. I think it is a very sexist nursery. That black girls, they are positive about, are thought to be clean, well spoken, lovely personalities. As for the boys, I think boys like Joshua [Rastafarian] and Calvin who have recently moved into the reception class, they were labelled disruptive. When Fay [Afro-Caribbean nursery nurse] was there she really got these two children to settle, because they had somebody to relate to, that understood them, realized that they weren't troublemakers. They just needed somebody to settle them, especially Calvin, he related to her really well. Then just when he was settling down, they upped and took him [transferred to the reception class] . . . He went right back to stage one, he sat outside the classroom for the first few months of school apparently . . . all he used to do was sit outside the classroom. I used to go over to speak to him, I'd ask him what had happened. He used to say 'The teacher said, I've been naughty, so she's put me outside.'

In contrast to the lack of attention which the Asian children often faced, Afro-Caribbean boys received a disproportionate amount of teachers' negative attentions. For example, there was a tendency for Afro-Caribbean and white boys to engage in task avoidance behaviour in the classroom, to fool around when they should be working and to be generally disobedient. Teachers were observed to be more inclined to turn a blind eye to flagrant breaches of normal classroom standards when committed by white boys, or to be lenient in their disapproval. By contrast, similar conduct on the part of Afro-Caribbean boys was rarely overlooked by the teachers. Furthermore, Afro-Caribbean boys were sometimes exclusively criticized even when peers of other ethnic origins shared in the offence. Disapproval was usually instant. The punitive sanctions employed by the teachers included verbal admonishment, exclusion from the class, sending children to the headteacher, or withdrawal of privileges. Afro-Caribbean boys were regularly the recipients of these punitive measures, which were often made a public matter. Such reprimands often went beyond discipline to become more of a personal attack on the individual concerned, as in the following example from school B:

> *A class of 7–8 year olds settle down to work after morning break. The children are seated four to a table. The classroom noise varies from low to medium level. The teacher, seated at her desk marking the children's work, keeps a vigil on a table where the following four children sit: one Afro-Caribbean boy (Carl), two white boys and one white girl. Every time the classroom noise level increases, the teacher looks at the Afro-Caribbean boy, who works effortlessly at the task set him, stopping occasionally to converse with the white boys seated at his table.*

Teacher: Carl get on with your work.

> *The Afro-Caribbean boy gives her a disparaging sideways glance. Attends to his work.*
>   *The classroom noise decreases temporarily. The classroom noise rises again. The teacher looks up from her marking and sees that Carl and the white boys seated at his table are engaged in task avoidance behaviour.*

Teacher: *(Shouting)* Carl stop disrupting the class!
Carl: It's not only me, *(pointing to his peers)* they're not working.
Teacher: *(Shouting)* Carl leave my class, go and work outside. I'm not having you disrupting the class.

> *Carl picks up his book and leaves the room, giving the teacher a disparaging sideways glance.*

Teacher: *(Addressing the class)* Look at that face *(referring to Carl)*. Go on outside. The trouble with you is that you have a chip on your shoulder.

Carl spent the remaining school day outside the classroom, working in the corridor.

In a conversation with the class teacher, she admitted that she had excluded Carl from the classroom on other occasions, against the policy of the school. The teacher appeared not to be concerned that Carl's exclusion from the classroom meant that he could not participate in the lesson.

> Teacher: He stops me doing my job. I mean my job isn't a disciplinarian, or a perpetual nagger, my job is to teach and I'm not able to do that because of him constantly interrupting. If I'm not looking at him he'll do something terrible to make me.

Researcher: Have you shared your experience with the headteacher, for instance?

Teacher: Yes . . . I mean she has been very supportive but is unaware of the constant stress factor in the classroom, you know where you feel you need to eject that child from the classroom. But we're told not to put them outside, so the next thing is to send them to Mrs Yates [headteacher]. I got to the point on Friday . . . that last half hour, I just thought there's no way – he'd get the better of me. So I sent him down to Mrs Yates and I hadn't realized that Mrs Yates wasn't in. So he sat there with the secretary all the time, which I mean is a plus as far as that is concerned, my class gained the benefit of his absence. Carl's behaviour is a shocking problem. Now there are other children in the class with problems, a lot of it's behavioural, ever so much of it is learning difficulties and then you've got all that plus a bright one like Carl, you know it's not a very good teaching/learning situation.

Afro-Caribbean boys' experience of public reprimands were not confined to the classroom, however. This experience extended to other formal settings, for example assemblies. Consider the following example from school C:

> Four classes in school C (approximately 70 children) gathered in a large hall with their class teachers for morning assembly. The children are seated in the middle of the hall in a semi-circle (except for one class who stand up to sing to the rest of the children). Seven teachers sit around the semi-circle. The class finishes singing to the assembly.
>
> The teacher conducting the assembly waits until the children are sitting down and then endeavours to engage the assembly in a drill which is frequently used in the classroom to settle the children and focus their attention.

Teacher: Look this way, right children. Hands on heads. Hands on shoulders.

Teacher: (Shouting in anger) Stop everyone! Calvin stand up, go to the back of the hall!

There is total silence. Then Calvin, the 5 year old Afro-Caribbean boy referred to by the nursery nurse above, stands up slowly, looks around in embarrassment, and defiantly slithers across the hall with his hands in his pockets. Everyone's eyes, including the teachers', follow Calvin as he makes his way to the back of the hall some eight yards away. The teachers look on disapprovingly as do many of the children. When Calvin eventually arrives at the back of the hall he stands with his face to the wall.

Teacher: (Shouting in anger) Turn around and face this way Calvin.

> Calvin shrugs his shoulders defiantly and refuses to turn around to face the teacher and the rest of the assembly.

Teacher: *(Shouting very irately)* Come here Calvin!

Calvin turns around and faces the assembly and slithers back to his seat, looking extremely dejected, confused and defiant. He stands where he was sitting previously. All eyes are on Calvin.

Teacher: *(Disapprovingly)* Tut, tut.

Teacher: *(Sarcastically)* So you can hear me – sit down! Right children, let's try again. Hands on heads, hands on shoulders. *(Looking at Calvin)* Calvin, pay attention and do as you're told! I don't want to pick on you but I can't help noticing that you are not doing as you are told. *(Looking at the rest of the children)* And it's not only Calvin who is not paying attention, there are other children not listening to what I'm saying.

At the end of the assembly the children are instructed to return to their classes.

Teacher: Children, I want you to very quietly make your way to your classroom. *(Pointing to three children)* You three stay behind! I would like to talk to you.

The children all leave the hall except for these three, a white girl and two white boys. The teacher takes them to the back of the hall, out of earshot.

Teacher: *(To the three children)* You saw me telling Calvin off for not sitting still and paying attention. You three behaved as if this was not also expected of you. You too are expected to sit still and pay attention.

After the three pupils had been told to return to their classroom, the teacher made the following comment to me about the incident:

Poor Old Calvin. I don't mean to pick on him, but he's one of those children who just can't conform. He's not very bright you know.

When I spoke to Calvin about his feelings regarding the above and other incidents, he said: 'It makes me feel sad when teachers tell me off for nothing.'

From the teachers' staffroom conversations it would appear that both Calvin and his friend, Winston (another 5 year old Afro-Caribbean boy) had poor reputations in the school, acquired when they were in the school's nursery, where they had been described as 'very disruptive'.

Experiences such as these led Afro-Caribbean boys to identify their relationships with teachers as a special difficulty. Samuel, a 7 year old Afro-Caribbean child at school B, talked of what he perceived to be the teachers' unfair treatment of other Afro-Caribbean pupils:

Samuel: I always get done and always get picked on . . . I want to go to a black school with all black teachers, it's better. I want to go to a school with just black people.

Researcher: Why?

Samuel: Because when you go to a school with white people they give you horrible food and you're always picked on when you don't do nothing. When it's white people, they just say stop that and stop doing this.

Researcher: Are you saying that you would like some black teachers here [in the school]?

Samuel: Yes.

Researcher: Have you ever told anybody this, have you ever told the teachers?

Samuel: I haven't said that to any of the teachers . . . because they'll be cross and say the white people just treat black people the same as other people. And one time someone hit Sandra [Afro-Caribbean child] and she was crying, and if it was a white person and I said 'Miss she's crying', she would have went there straight away but when it was Sandra, she [the teacher] just ignored me. And she said 'Get in the line' [join the queue] and I said 'You only think about white people'. Then she told Mrs Johnson [head-teacher] and Mrs Johnson started shouting her head off at me.

Researcher: So you felt that the teacher didn't do anything because Sandra was black?

Samuel: Yes, because if it was a white person, she would say 'What's the matter', and then she would have said, 'What's up?' And when you hit 'em, if someone said it didn't hurt, she just say 'Stand against the wall.'

Researcher: Do you think that the teacher treats black children differently to white children?

Samuel: Yes.

Researcher: In what ways?

Samuel: Because when it's black people, and they just run down the stairs. I mean when Martin [white boy], he ran off, she said 'Come back, stop at the door' and Martin didn't hear, Martin ran off. And then Richard told me that the teacher want us to come back to the classroom, so I walked back. Then I told on Martin, and Miss just told me to shut up, she said, 'Be quiet'.

Researcher: What about the Asian children, the Pakistani children, how do the teachers treat them?

Samuel: Treat them the same as black people.

Researcher: In what way?

Samuel: It's just that they treat Pakistani people a little better than black people.

Researcher: Can you just tell me why you say that?

Samuel: Because every time everything goes wrong in the class, and everyone's messing about around the carpet, they call out me, Rick and Delroy [both Afro-Caribbean] and that. But they don't call out the white people and the Pakistani.

Researcher: How does this make you feel?
Samuel: *(Long thoughtful pause)* Sad.

This view was also echoed by older children. Benjamin, an 11 year old Afro-Caribbean child at school D, said:

Benjamin: My teacher can be all right, but other teachers irritate me a lot. This teacher called Miss Lucas irritates me. When everybody's making a row in the hall, they call my name, instead of other people's . . . they don't like black people.
Researcher: What makes you say that your teachers don't like black people?
Benjamin: They don't, because there's a girl in my class, Raquel. There is only me and her in the class that's black. Miss Smith, she's always involving Mr Jones [the headmaster] a lot. Always going to see Mr Jones. It's always black children getting done. You know Raquel's brother, he was in trouble a lot, and it was always because of other kids, white kids . . . This white boy pushed Raquel down the stairs. Now if it was me, I would have got detention. That boy never got detention. He went in the head's room for about three minutes and came back out. The girl [Raquel] was curled up on the floor in pain. You should have seen all her legs, cut up. And there's this prejudiced dinner lady that don't like blacks.

In addition to their perceived regular experience of reprimands, children felt that the other teachers discriminated against them in the allocation of responsibility and rewards. A 9 year old Afro-Caribbean child at school D said:

In the first school the teachers were really prejudiced. There was quite a lot of coloured people in the class and Miss Butler . . . she'd never picked any coloured people to do a job and nearly all the white people got a biscuit, but the coloured people never. Like if a white person wanted to go to the toilet, she'd say yeah, but if a coloured person wanted to, she'd say no.

A teacher at school D expressed her objection to being accused by the older Afro-Caribbean children of being prejudiced:

I was accused of doing several things last year. 'I didn't like blacks.' 'You are only saying that because I'm black.' 'You wouldn't be picking on anyone else' – this came particularly from Delroy, who has got a big chip on his shoulder. I think it's because his dad left and there is a lot of emotional instability there. But I objected to that . . . I am not saying that I am not *me*, I am sure that I respond to things in a very unfavourable way, but I am fighting it. I am not saying I am pristine and my halo is glowing, but at least I am aware of my own shortcomings and I do make positive steps to overcome what has been instilled in me for years. Whether or not things come out sort of unconsciously without me knowing. I am sure that if I knew things were coming out, then I would take positive steps.

THE RASTAFARIAN EXPERIENCE

One group who seemed to be particularly prone to experiencing prejudice were the Rastafarian children. Here too, expectations seem to have emerged even in the nursery class.

An Afro-Caribbean carer at school C expressed her considerable distress at the responses of white colleagues to Levi a 3 year old Rastafarian child who was having difficulty adjusting to the nursery environment. Levi, on occasion, would lash out in frustration. She felt that her white colleagues were reluctant to accommodate his needs as they would normally do for a white child in a similar situation. As she states:

> When Levi first came in [to the nursery], he did things. I got the feeling that Maureen [white teacher] resented him. Because he took up too much time. He had only just turned 3. She used to say 'Well, I'm not going to waste my time like that.' And if Levi messed about, I think sometimes the way she handled him, made him do things. If a child is going to bite you or scratch you, you'd make sure they didn't. You'd hold their hand or you would stop them. She didn't, she just let him do it, then she'd flare up and walk across [to the school] and tell the head. In the end the head said 'We've got to keep a record of his behaviour, write down incidents.' I just didn't write anything down. He's lashed out at me . . . he's come back to me the next day and said sorry about what he's done. And I think 'Fair enough. He's only a child.' I just think Maureen blows it up. I don't see him as a problem. Confidential notes are kept on him. I don't think his mother knows. What upsets me about it is that when this first happened, the reason why the head said that she wanted to keep records on things that he'd done was in case he ever needs statementing.[6] She would have the evidence. I was really upset, he's 3. I'm really glad that Levi behaves the way he does, he says sorry whenever he does things . . . Only bad things goes in this book . . . I never write in this book. I don't agree with them [colleagues] because you don't know who's going to see it or where it's going to go.

By the time they were older, Rastafarian children were seen by some teachers as a particular threat to classroom management:

> I would say that probably the black children, particularly the Rastafarian children, are taking the lead in quite a lot, they are making the running quite often, but not in all cases. Those children I'm sure are being made particularly aware by their parents as regards racism. And there is a problem of a small child trying to negotiate a world which they have been made aware is a racist one. You know, they've got to watch out – and actually finding out that their teacher is one. A teacher faced with such children is quite vulnerable. I think it is very complex, because they're sort of getting their own back from a racist white world.

An example of this was given by the headteacher of school C recounting her experience with a 4 year old Rastafarian boy. As with the teacher quoted above, she expresses a sensitivity to the child's experience of racism, but an apparent incomprehension in knowing how to tackle this.

> He was in his first term in school so he was under 5, and he was vulgar in class. He had this habit of running wild and hurting other children and we actually removed him from the class before he actually hurt other children. So he had been removed and he came into my room where he didn't want to be and he was angry and he just screwed up his face and said, 'I hate you, I hate you, you are white . . . and you're not a Rasta'. He felt that I was getting at him because he was black, I think it was the first time I had actually confronted the issue and that's what I feel with several of the Rastafarian children in particular, that's what they see. So there is this enormous barrier because of who we are.

MULTICULTURALISM IN THE CLASSROOM

In all the schools individual teachers were observed to be genuinely trying to take the multicultural nature of the classroom into account in curriculum application. A common practice was to draw on the resources provided by the children themselves. Unfortunately, the teachers' efforts were not always immediately rewarded and their sincerity was often questioned by the ethnic minority children concerned. The teachers' efforts often only served to make the ethnic minority children feel awkward and embarrassed.

This situation was observed to occur for two fundamental reasons. First, the teachers often appeared to lack confidence, basic factual knowledge and understanding of the areas or the topic they were addressing. More significantly, the teachers also clearly communicated this lack of competence to the class. For instance, teachers frequently mispronounced words or names relevant to the appropriate area or topic. This frequently got laughter from white children, but floods of embarrassed giggles from the black children. This situation unintentionally served to make topics or areas of knowledge associated with ethnic minority values and cultures appear exotic, novel, unimportant, esoteric or difficult. Moreover, the intended message of the teacher's approach was often at variance with the black children's experience of racial intolerance in the school.

The black children's responses to the sincere intentions of individual teachers to use them as a resource were essentially to refuse publicly to cooperate with the teacher, dissolve into giggles or lower their heads with embarrassment, deny or conceal skills or knowledge. The white children, on the other hand, often laughed, ridiculed, taunted or looked on passively.

The lesson reported here, in a class of 10 years old in school D, highlights aspects of this observation. As part of its language work, the class was looking at the linguistic composition of the school.

The teacher was using a text printed in two languages – Urdu and English – as a resource.

Teacher:	Last time we talked a little about the different languages we speak at home and in school, and we made a list on the board, and I said that we would talk about this book that I found in the library *(holds the book up to the class)*. Rehana and Aftab might be able to help me. It is an unusual book. Can you tell me why? *(Holds book up for class to inspect.)*
White girl:	It's got funny writing.
Teacher:	It's written in two languages. English and . . . can you tell me Rehana?
White boy:	Jamaican.
Rehana:	*(Shyly)* Urdu.
Teacher:	Is that how you say it? Urdeo?

Rehana laughs, embarrassed. White pupils snigger.

Teacher:	*(To Rehana)* Say it again.
Rehana:	Urdu.
Teacher:	Urdeo.

Asian pupils laugh, embarrassed.

Teacher:	Say it again.
Rehana:	Urdu.
Teacher:	Urdeo.

Asian pupils laugh, embarrassed.

Teacher:	Say it again.
Rehana:	Urdu.
Teacher:	*(Mimicking Rehana but showing signs of defect in the pronunciation, laughs)* Urdeo.
Teacher:	*(Laughingly)* How do you say it, Aftab?

Aftab holds his head down, refuses to respond.

White boy:	It's Pakistani language.
Teacher:	Can we write it on the board. *(Teacher writes the word 'Urdu' on the board.)* Because you see what we've been saying. We pronounce things differently. But not just to lots of other countries. We pronounce things a bit differently than everywhere else apart from 'Hometown'. Paula [white girl], where do you come from?
Paula:	Portsmouth.
Teacher:	How long have you been living in 'Hometown'?
Paula:	Don't know.
Teacher:	Since you were little. So Paula has lived most of her life in 'Hometown' but Paula's dad has lived most of his life in Portsmouth and all over the place. And he doesn't talk like me. He doesn't talk like Paula. He's got what we would call an accent. A quite different accent. He pronounces lots of things quite differently. You are fortunate really, because lots of your teachers

come from different parts of the country. I come from 'Hometown'. I've lived in 'Hometown' all my life, Mrs Mason comes from 'Hometown', Miss Robinson comes from 'Hometown' I think that's it . . . I don't think none of the other teachers do. They come from all over the place, all over the country. When you live in a different part, not just of the world, but England, you pick up different accents. Now an accent is when you pronounce words differently. One word that I would pronounce differently is 'Urdeo'. I know that 'Urdeo' is completely wrong. *(Looks over to the Asian pupils.)* Is it spelt like that in Pakistan *(pointing to word 'Urdu' written on the board)*

Rehana: *(Shyly)* No.

Teacher: No, it's not spelt at all like that because that is not 'Urdeo' writing or *(with a grin)* 'Urdoo'. A lot of the things in 'Urdeo', as we found a lot of things in Ancient Egypt, cannot be translated exactly, because there are some words that come in Egyptian, that we haven't got in English, some words in English that we haven't got in Egyptian, and there are some words in English that we haven't got in Arabic. That's why I told you that some parts of the Bible are quite difficult to translate because they were not written in English but . . .?

Afro-Caribbean
boy: African.

White boy: Welsh.

Teacher: *(Laughing)* No, not Welsh.

White girl: Jewish.

Teacher: Arabic, originally written in Arabic. It can't be directly translated. It's the same with this book. This can't be directly translated. *(To Asian boy)* Can you read that? *(Boy bows his head.)* I think he's shy, that's fair enough. Well I can't read it, I might even have it upside down, I don't know. *(To Asian girl)* Can you tell us about 'Urdeo', is it written like that *(pointing left to right)* or written like that *(pointing right to left)*?

Rehana: No, that way *(pointing right to left)*.

White pupil: Backwards.

Teacher: It's written from right to left?

Rehana: Yes.

Teacher: No, it's not backwards. It's English that's written backwards.

White pupil: *(Exasperated)* Is it?

Teacher: Don't forget that when the Ancient Egyptians and lots of Eastern countries were writing, we were still swinging in trees and living in holes in the ground.

Pupils laugh.

Teacher: And living in caves. We couldn't write, and they could
                        write in hieroglyphics. The Egyptians wrote down-
                        wards. The Chinese write down from top to bottom.
                        I'm not sure where, but I think there's somewhere
                        which actually writes upwards, is it the Japanese? Bot-
                        tom of the page to the top of the page. We wouldn't
                        get Aftab to read this book because he's a little bit shy,
                        I know he can read it . . .

TEACHER VIEWS

So far I have concentrated on both Afro-Caribbean and Asian pupils' relationships with teachers from the nursery to infant classroom. I have focused on the
pattern of classroom interaction, in particular how this is mediated by the
children's ethnicity. In both cases pupils' ethnicity was shown to adversely
influence their relationships with teachers. Classroom observation indicated
that teachers tended to treat Afro-Caribbean children (especially boys) in a
more restrictive way than other pupil groups. For instance, issuing orders
rather than encouraging them to express their ideas. Asian children, on the
other hand, received less individual attention; in other words, they tended to be
overlooked or underestimated by teachers. These children were also frequently
the recipients of teachers' expressed annoyance and frustration. Reflected in
these patterns of classroom interactions would appear to be teachers' expectations and 'typing' of these pupil groups. In order to explore this further it is
necessary to examine teachers' expressed views or adopted perspectives on
both Afro-Caribbean and Asian pupils.

Classroom observation studies in a variety of settings suggest that, on the
whole, teachers categorize or develop typifications of the children they teach
(see, for example, Rist, 1970; Leiter, 1974; Hargreaves *et al.*, 1975; Sharp and
Green, 1975). It is recognized that the use of typifications is a normal part of
interaction in many social situations (Burrell and Morgan, 1979). However,
the classroom context is a particularly significant one in which the teacher has
to face and cope with a relatively large number of children. Given the teacher's
occupational reality, typing is a means of reducing the complexity or, as Schutz
(1970) states, 'making the world of everyday life "cognitively manageable" '.
Thus the teacher simplifies by classifying. Related to the typification that
teachers develop of pupils is the 'ideal pupil' model. The notion of the ideal
pupil is a construction which is drawn primarily from the lifestyle and culture
of the teacher concerned.

The ideal pupil for teachers is likely to be a child who acts in ways which are
supportive of teachers' interest-at-hand, who enables them to cope and so on.
Work by Becker (1952) and, more recently, Sharp and Green (1975) has
suggested that teachers differentiate between pupils according to how closely
they meet the ideal pupil criteria. Children, therefore, tend to be classified and

typed by the ways in which they vary from the ideal. For instance, social class factors have been found to be reflected in teachers' 'specifications' of the ideal pupil. Classroom observations reported above suggest that ethnic differences also influenced the way in which teachers viewed their pupils.

Teachers' views in relation to their experience of the classroom were concerned with the children's motivation and adjustment to the learning situation. Their views of the children's educability revealed extremely complex feelings. Often these revealed an ambivalence about their working conditions. Yet they generally exhibited personal and professional concern for the children.

The teachers' main concerns about classroom life related first to their perceptions of the children's competence and, secondly, to their behaviour in the classroom. The levels of competence across all groups of children were considered by the majority of the teachers to be relatively poor. But certain skills were recognized to be poorer in the white children, as this teacher from school C explained:

> In all the groups, the speech, language, listening, the concentration, are low, generally at lack of competence levels. There is also low energy levels, tiredness, lassitude . . . poor responses to requests and a lack of compliance that goes across the board. If I were referring children for special needs, they would be more likely to be white. In fact, for language development they would be more likely to be white than Asian, because relatively speaking the Asians are making progress given that you take into account that English is a second language. These children are more competent in English than the children who had been exposed to English . . . from English parents. That is when you really get worried, because you realize that the level of competence is deteriorating.

However, the majority of teachers, as this one from school A, considered all the children positively disposed to most aspects of classwork:

> Generally speaking the children do have, within limitations, a good attitude to work. They have limited concentration skills, but within those parameters they do actually do their best. The attitude to work is one of 'I will do my best to do this'. I would say a child who doesn't try is fairly rarer than the ones who do . . . I think most of them have a strong desire to please and are also proud to please . . . They like the idea of doing their best, if you say, 'Would you like to try again?' If you don't make an issue of it, they will do it again.

Further probing showed that children were differentially categorized on the basis of their orientation to work. For instance, white girls and Asian children, particularly boys, were considered to be the most motivated groups. On the other hand Afro-Caribbean children were often considered to reveal the lowest motivation, a view expressed by the teacher below:

> I would say that the Asian boys, in general, are the most individually motivated in that it seems to come from within, from whatever input they have had at home, but they are much more determined to succeed, they

know their work and they listen, they have the greatest listening skills in my class and this is very generalized overall . . . The difference between white boys and Afro-Caribbean children is that there is no difference. If they have been to bed early, then they might do well that day. If something happened in the playground, they are not going to. They don't seem to have any incentive or deep urge to want to succeed in that educational way that the Asian boys do . . . I do sometimes feel though, especially last year that some of the children, Afro-Caribbean, felt like they were underachieving and consequently because of that they wouldn't try. They would get to a point . . where if they reached a problem like a stage in maths which they hadn't come across and they were stumped, they would get very upset about it, over the top, dramatic, upset about it, rather than just, 'I can't do this – how do you do it?' It was like 'I can't do it, because I am hopeless'. I had two children in particular last year who reacted in this way.

Teachers regularly reported the prevalence of problem behaviour in the classroom and around the school. The problems commonly referred to by teachers were aggressiveness, disobedience, distractability, overactive behaviour, teasing, quarrelsome attitude, children being overdemanding, conflict with peers, having temper tantrums and emotional problems.

Boys were considered to be more of a problem than girls and Afro-Caribbean children were seen as being of a greater problem than white. Asian children were less associated with behaviour problems. On the other hand, Afro-Caribbean boys were generally associated with aggressive, disobedient and distractable behaviour. Teachers frequently talked about feeling worn down by the sheer number of teacher–pupil interactions which involved some element of control or response to acts of indiscipline, particularly on the part of the Afro-Caribbean children. Furthermore, teachers felt that a succession of disruptive moments in the classroom often led to a change in the nature of their interactions with the children. Thus a point articulated by a teacher:

I would say some days I fulfil virtually nothing. Quite seriously, some days it's a battle. Some days you are quite happy at the end of the day, I feel I have achieved quite a lot, it all depends really on the temperament of the children. And I mean the powerful children in the class, their temperaments really do dictate the mood of the class, which is quite sad in a school like this, 'cause it means that the new children and the quiet children get swallowed up, that worries me. They don't get the attention at the time that they should have. These quiet children are likely to be girls, more girls than boys, but I do have some boys who will just get on with what they have to do and don't hassle me at all . . . I have one little Asian girl who I would like to spend more time with her, because she has got a lot to offer, she just sits there and gets on with what she has to do and doesn't bother me at all. I think that is how they are brought up, don't you? To be quiet and get on with it, and they are not troublemakers at all, they are very nice children. They are swallowed up definitely, which is sad. Delroy and Vincent [two Afro-Caribbean boys] are the trouble, very disruptive. I have to admit I like Delroy, I don't think I would have survived if I hadn't liked him. I mean quite seriously as well, there is something very appealing about him. At times I could strangle him, he's a very nice boy, he's got a very nice nature, he's very kind. You get him on your own, you know, in the right place at the right time, he can be kind. Vincent, I have to be careful with because I find him very difficult to relate to. I mean possibly I could spend more time with them all, but at the moment I can't. I am afraid my attitude tends to be negative and I have to think 'Come on now, be positive.'

An examination of teachers' classroom logs, where daily experiences were recorded, showed a tendency for some teachers to direct their frustration at the Afro-Caribbean children.[7] This was reflected through the nature of the teachers' written comments, which often ranged from negative stereotyping to insults.

For example, this recording on Justin (age 6), an Afro-Caribbean boy:

I think Robert [fellow pupil] may be in little pieces by the morning. He had an argument with Justin today and I've seldom seen a face like it on a little child. The temper, rage and marked aggression was quite frightening to see. I wouldn't be surprised in years to come if Justin wasn't capable of actually killing someone. When he smiles he could charm the birds off the trees, but when he's in a temper he is incapable of controlling himself. He has an extremely short fuse, is a real chauvinist and to cap it all he's got a persecution complex. He has to be handled with kid gloves.

A comment on the behaviour of Ruth (6 years old), an Afro-Caribbean girl, was in a similar vein:

What a thoroughly objectionable little bitch, she's intelligent enough to egg others on and seem totally innocent herself. She pinches, nips and uses her brain to impose her will on others. She's one of those children who can't bear others to have friends – she likes to break-up friendships (and is very good at it). If she were to use her brain in the way a normal child would, she would be bright by any standards.

Not all the teachers' comments recorded in their classroom logs relating to Afro-Caribbean children were as harsh and intemperate in tone. None the less, the illustrations presented were symptomatic of the feelings of some of the teachers. Overall, the teachers' view showed a general tendency to associate Afro-Caribbean children (particularly boys) with behaviour problems.

In contrast, teachers in their general conversation, as well as in their interviews with me, often cited Asian children as a group being a 'pleasure to teach'. However, classroom logs revealed certain contradictions in their attitudes. Some teachers were less favourably disposed to those Asian children who were perceived as having learning problems arising out of language difficulties; those who were perceived as operating as an exclusive group; and those who tended to converse in their 'mother tongue' in the classroom. In general, teachers showed greater approval of those Asian children who were perceived to be socially integrated in the classroom and proficient in the English language.

PEER RELATIONS

An aspect of the 'primary ideology' is a form of pedagogic folklore which, *inter alia*, views childhood as an age of innocence. Regarding issues of 'race' and ethnicity, the popular belief still exists among teachers that young children are 'colour-blind'. Moreover, primary teachers assume that young children, whilst capable of unacceptable behaviour, remain free from the malign influences of individual racism.

In the nursery classroom, children reflected their awareness of racial and ethnic differences in conversations with both teachers/carers and peers, and attributed value to these differences. A dialogue between Charlene, a 3 year old Afro-Caribbean girl and Tina, a 4 year old white girl during creative play in school C illustrates this perfectly.

> *Charlene:* *(Cuddling a black doll)* This is my baby.
> *Tina:* I don't like it, it's funny. I like this one *(holding a white doll)* it's my favourite. I don't like this one *(pointing to black doll)*. Because you see I like Sarah, and I like white. You're my best friend though, you're brown.
> *Charlene:* I don't like that one *(pointing to the white doll)*.
> *Tina:* You're brown aren't you?
> *Charlene:* I'm not brown, I'm black.
> *Tina:* You're brown, but I'm white.
> *Charlene:* No I'm not, I'm black and baby's black.
> *Tina:* They call us white, my mummy calls me white, and you know my mummy calls you brown. When you come to visit if you want . . . She'll say 'hello brown person . . .' I like brown, not black. Michael Jackson was brown, he went a bit white.

Observations also suggest that children at this early age were showing a preference for members of their own racial/ethnic group and a desire to mix and play with them rather than with others. This 'own-group' preference did on occasion reflect antipathy towards children of other skin colour or cultural groups.

The children's preference for members of their own racial/ethnic group is corroborated by an Afro-Caribbean Child Care Assistant at school B:

> The white children, particularly a set of white children, even though they relate to me and Tazeem (Asian carer) all right, they won't play with anybody else, when I say with anybody else I mean black or Asian children. There are a couple of black children that won't play with Asian children but they won't play with white children either. I've noticed that the Asian children play very well and they play well amongst themselves

and alongside each other but they don't mix themselves as well . . . But I think there is an attitude in the school that makes the Asian children feel negative about themselves as well.

Even at this early age, white children tended to be extremely negative towards the Asian children in both their attitudes and behaviour. They often refused to play with them and frequently subjected them to threatening behaviour, name-calling and hitting.

An example of this is shown in the incident below in school B:

A group of four white boys (aged 3–4) were collaboratively building a tower block out of the building blocks. An Asian boy walked over with the thought of participating. Two of the boys were heard to say vehemently, 'No, Paki, no, Paki'. Another boy pushed the Asian boy aggressively. The Asian boy wandered off looking quite dejected.

The nursery teachers/carers were also aware of similar incidents of this nature. As an Afro-Caribbean carer at school B points out:

Peter . . . [the] blond headed boy, I notice that he used to go up to the Asian children in a really threatening way, just threatening behaviour. He wouldn't say anything. If the Asian children had anything he would take it off them. The Asian girls, they'd leave things, by just the way he looked at them. They'd leave something if they were playing with it. He would look at them and they would drop it.

In the classroom, white children engaged in persistent racist name-calling, teasing, jostling, intimidation, rejection and the occasional physical assault on black and ethnic minority children. Aspects of this behaviour are illustrated in the following incident from school A:

I was in a classroom observing and working with a group of six white 6 year olds on English language and number tasks. Taseem (an Asian girl) came over to the group, and with a rather desperate look on her face asked me to help her.

Taseem: 'Miss Cecile, can you help me do times by?'

Taseem was working on a multiplication exercise which she did not fully understand. The ten sums she had completed for this exercise had been marked as incorrect by the teacher and she had been asked to do the exercise again. I spent some minutes explaining the exercise to Taseem. The children in the group were very resentful of the fact that I had switched my attention from them to Taseem and also that she had joined the group.

Researcher: *(After having finished explaining the exercise)* Taseem, do you understand how 'times by' works?

Jane (a white girl):   No, she won't understand, she's a Paki.

Taseem is very upset by this comment and is on the verge of tears.

Researcher:	*(To Jane)* What do you mean?
Jane:	Because she's a Paki.

The other children in the group are sniggering.

Researcher:	And why should she not understand multiplications because she is a Pakistani?
Jane:	Because she's not over us and she's not in our culture.
Michael (a white boy):	She's Paki! *(Laughs)*
Researcher:	What is our culture?
Jane:	England.
Researcher:	She is in England, she lives in England.
Jane:	Yeah, but she comes from Pakistani.
Alice (a white girl):	Yeah, Pakistani, she was born in Pakistan she means.
Taseem:	*(Dejected but in protestation)* I wasn't, I was born here.
Jane:	She couldn't understand, that's what I think because she speaks Paki.
Other children:	*(To Taseem)* Where were you born?
Researcher:	Yes, just because she speaks 'Pakistani' it does not mean that she can't understand how to multiply.
Jane:	Because when I say something, she doesn't know what I say. And when it were assembly they were doing a Paki dance.
Researcher:	Taseem was born in England, her parents are from Pakistan, but she was born in England. Her parents are from Pakistan but she was born in England.
Taseem:	My parents are here.

The researcher continues to assist Taseem with her number work. The other children become increasingly resentful.

Jane:	*(Sharply)* Will you help me now?

Some of the children take to taunting and name-calling Taseem. However, sensing my disapproval of their behaviour, they adopt a strategy of name-calling by sounding out the letters.

Jane:	P-A-K-E, P-A-K-E!
Alice:	*(Quietly spoken, but so I would hear)* She's a Paki!
Researcher:	What does P-A-K-E mean?
Jane:	*(With a mischievous grin, whispering)* She's a Paki!
Taseem:	*(Visibly distraught)* Miss, I want to go out to play.

Echoing of P-A-K-E from the other children.

Alice:	She's a Paki, that's what it means.

This encounter not only highlights the existence of racism in the very young, but it also shows that the children are well aware of its taboo status. On recognizing my displeasure with their remarks, they endeavoured to disguise their intent. The teachers, with only a few exceptions, mentioned that racial intolerance was prevalent among the children. Indeed, the white children's attitude and behaviour towards the Asian children was a concern for the majority of teachers. A teacher at school A explains:

> The Asian children are getting so picked on, it's awful. In the playground the Asian girls never leave the teacher's side. One little girl last week, they [white children] never left her alone, she was really frightened. I mean she really did need protection . . . but we can't stand next to her all the time. Every time I looked, somebody was at her.

One strategy for avoiding expressions of racial intolerance was to separate children of different ethnic groups. The following teacher's comment was typical of many that were expressed to me:

> I have to think very carefully when I select children to work together be-cause, more often than not, white children will refuse to sit next to or work with a Pakistani. You have to bear this in mind so as to avoid any nastiness.

In their view on aspects of school, many of the white children volunteered particularly vehement feelings towards the Asian children. Some also ex-pressed a certain abhorrence at the prospect of being taught by a black teacher. The example below from school D pointedly illustrates these views:

Jason (white boy, aged 12): I don't like the Pakistani children. I call them Pakis. Mostly Zahid, he's about the best one in the school.

Researcher: Why do you not like the Pakistani children?

Jason: Don't know. Like blacks because I've got a lot of black friends. Most of me friends are black anyway. I've got more black friends than I have white.

Researcher: What have the Asian children done for you to dislike them?

Jason: Got me in trouble with the police, and that . . . They blame me for going in houses . . . Saying that I've been smashing the windows and that.

Researcher: Did you?

Jason: (Long pause, smirk) No.

Researcher: Do you think that it is really right for you to dislike people for no reasons?

Jason: (Defiantly) Yes.

Researcher: What's right about it?

Jason: They're buying all shops and all that . . . There's only one shop what's in't a Paki shop round our way. And they're not going to let Pakis take it. Mr Smith round our way, he's white.

Researcher: How do you know he's not going to let this happen?

Jason: Because he's told me mum and that the rest of the shops been taken over by Pakis. Its not right for white people. Everytime they walk into a shop they see a Paki.

Researcher:	What's not right about it?
Jason:	Don't know, I don't like it.
Researcher:	Providing there are the things in the shop that you wish to buy, does it matter who owns it?
Jason:	*(Angry)* I don't go to Paki shops.
Researcher:	It could be said that you're racially prejudiced?
Jason:	If I'm prejudiced, I wouldn't like blacks at all, but I do like blacks. Some of me friends are black . . . there's no black shop owners on our road, they're all Pakis except for one.

It is interesting to note the complex nature of Jason's reasoning. On the one hand he expresses hostile attitudes towards Asians. At the same time he hastens to add that he cannot be considered 'racially prejudiced' because he has black friends.

Many of the white children expressed a definite view against being taught by black teachers. My discussion with two young children in school B, Samantha (aged 7) and Claire (aged 6), encapsulates this view:

Samantha:	Ranjit is the best behaved [in the class].
Researcher:	Why is she the best behaved?
Samantha:	Because she helps – she works here.
Researcher:	Who is Ranjit?
Claire:	She's that lady.
Samantha:	She's that lady.
Researcher:	Can you describe her to me?
Samantha:	She's got long black hair, she's got a striped jumper on and she's got black eyes . . .
Researcher:	And is she a teacher?
Samantha:	No, she helps Mrs Moore [class teacher], helps us.
Researcher:	How do you know she's not a teacher?
Samantha:	Because she's not here all the time – she only comes Wednesday, Thursday and Friday mornings . . .
Claire:	. . . and a little bit . . .
Samantha:	She's brown.
Claire:	She's yellower than Zahra [an Asian girl in the class].
Researcher:	Have you ever been taught by a brown teacher?
Samantha:	No.
Researcher:	Would you like to be taught by a brown teacher?
Samantha:	*(Aghast)* No.
Researcher:	No? Why?
Claire:	I don't like it.
Researcher:	Why don't you like it?
Claire:	I just like talking with . . . I like talking with white teachers and *(under her breath)* I don't like talking in Paki's language . . .
Samantha:	In Urdu.
Researcher:	Why don't you want to be taught by a brown teacher?
Samantha:	Because we don't like her because . . . she speaks Urdu.

Researcher:	Why don't you like people speaking in Urdu?
Samantha:	Because Urdu people are from Pakistan and nobody knows what they're talking about . . .
Claire:	. . . and we don't want to learn Urdu . . .
Researcher:	So you don't want a brown teacher?
Claire and Samantha:	*(Together)* No!
Samantha:	I'd like a French teacher . . .
Researcher:	You'd like a French teacher? Why would you like a French teacher?
Samantha:	So I could go to France when I grow up and I'd know the language . . .
Researcher:	But wouldn't you like to go to Pakistan when you grow up?
Claire and Samantha:	*(Together – aghast)* No way!
Researcher:	No way? Why?
Samantha:	Because it's too far and I might get sunburnt because it's always sunny there and *(under her breath)* the people . . . and sometimes it doesn't sunshine . . .
Researcher:	You don't like the sun?
Samantha:	Sometimes I do.
Researcher:	So you wouldn't like to have a brown teacher then?
Claire and Samantha:	No.
Researcher:	Don't you think a brown teacher would be a good teacher?
Samantha:	No.
Researcher:	No? Why?
Samantha:	She is sometimes, but sometimes she'd speak in Urdu to the other children because some children like the Urdu and don't understand English and she'd speak in Urdu.
Researcher:	And wouldn't you like her to do that?
Samantha:	No. Because we'd think she wasn't listening to us because she wasn't . . .
Claire:	Because we'd think she's playing [not being serious with them].

CONCLUSION

In this article I have examined the pattern of classroom interaction experienced by both Afro-Caribbean and Asian children, from the nursery to the upper primary classroom. I have focused in particular on the ways in which their ethnicity is reflected in their relationships with classmates and teachers.

Both Afro-Caribbean and Asian pupils faced negative teacher interaction in the classroom. In both cases this teacher response occurred when these children were seen by the teacher as an apparent threat to classroom management or teacher effectiveness. The teachers' response reflected to some extent their perception of what constituted appropriate pupil behaviour or, put differently, their notion of the 'ideal pupil'. The kinds of behaviour exhibited by Asian pupils which elicited a negative teacher response were shown to be different from those which produced a similar teacher response towards Afro-Caribbean pupils.

Ostensibly, the Asian pupils (particularly the younger ones) were perceived as a problem to teachers because of their limited cognitive skills, poor English language and poor social skills and their inability to socialize with other pupil groups in the classroom. However, teachers' expressed views revealed images of Asian pupils and parents which were not always negative. Teachers expect pupils of Asian origin to be industrious, courteous and keen to learn. They also tend to assume that Asians are well-disciplined, highly motivated children from family backgrounds where educational success is highly valued.

Afro-Caribbean pupils by contrast (especially boys) were always among the most criticized and controlled group in the classroom. Perhaps of most concern, in addition to the frequency of critical and controlling statements which Afro-Caribbean pupils received, was the observation that they were likely to be singled out for criticism even though several pupils of different groups were engaged in the same act or behaviour. Just as they did in relation to Asian children, teachers often held generalized images of Afro-Caribbean pupils. However, in contrast to the Asian pupils, teachers' images of Afro-Caribbean children tended to be negative; more significantly, teachers' negative expectations transcended their judgements of these children's ability.

The evidence provided on the relationships between the children themselves within the classroom shows that victimization was a common experience for many Asian pupils. Racist name-calling and attacks from white peers was a regular, almost daily, experience for Asian children. Teachers were aware of the racial harrassment experienced by Asian pupils, but were reluctant to formally address this issue. Thus the treatment they received from white peers proved to be a further source of classroom insecurity for the Asian children.

This article has highlighted the complexity of classroom life in the multiracial context; moreover, it confirms the analysis of Parekh (1985) and others concerning the fallacies which often underpin debates regarding the existence of racism in schools. As black pupils, children of Afro-Caribbean and Asian origin experience school in similar but also in very different ways, some of which are highlighted above. In both cases, the pupils' ethnicity influenced their interaction with teachers and their experience of teacher expectations. Only in the case of the Asian pupils did ethnicity appear to be a direct influence on their relations with their classmates.

It is generally accepted that the foundations of emotional, intellectual and social development are laid in the early years of formal education. The kind of education a child receives at this stage, therefore, is considered to be of greatest importance. From the evidence gathered in connection with this project, it could be argued that some black children are relatively disadvantaged at this stage of their education.

NOTES

1. 'Black', as used throughout the article, refers to those of South Asian or Afro-Caribbean parentage.
2. This study was conducted as part of a CRE-funded research project.
3. It was common practice in the schools for the nursery units to be staffed by one or two teachers and several nursery nurses. In the schools, the nursery nurses (often referred to as Care Assistants) worked as support staff in the classroom.
4. All names used throughout the article are pseudonyms.
5. 'Gonah' is a term used by Moslems to mean sin (in the eyes of Allah).
6. Statementing is a formal assessment of a child's cognitive and behavioural development, normally undertaken by the school and the Psychological Service.
7. Classroom logs were used by teachers in all four schools as a systematic way of recording facts and incidents relating to pupils. They were available for consultation by other staff.

REFERENCES

Alexander, R. J. (1984) *Primary Teaching*, London, Holt, Rinehart and Winston.
Becker, H. S. (1952) 'Social class variations in the teacher–pupil relationship', *Journal of Educational Sociology*, 25, pp. 451–65.
Burrell, G. and Morgan, G. (1979) *Sociological Paradigms and Organizational Analysis*, London, Heinemann Educational.
Driver, G. (1979) 'Classroom stress and school achievement: West Indian adolescents and their teachers', in Khan, V. S. (ed.) *Minority Families in Britain: support and stress*, London, Macmillan.
Foster, P. (1990) 'Cases not proven: an evaluation of two studies of teacher racism', *British Educational Research Journal*, 16(4), pp. 335–50.
Gillborn, D. A. (1988) 'Ethnicity and educational opportunity: case studies of West Indian male–white teacher relationships', *British Journal of Sociology of Education*, 9(4), pp. 371–85.
Gray, J., McPherson, A. F. and Raffe, D. (1983) *Reconstructions of Secondary Education: theory, myth and practice since the war*, London, Routledge and Kegan Paul.
Green, P. A. (1985) 'Multi-ethnic teaching and the pupils' self-concepts', Annex to Chapter 2 of *Education for All*, the final report of the Committee of Inquiry into the Education of Children from Ethnic Minority Groups, London, HMSO.
Hargreaves, D. H., Hester, S. K. and Mellor, F. J. (1975) *Deviance in Classrooms*, London, Routledge and Kegan Paul.
Leiter, K. C. W. (1974) 'Ad hocing in the schools' in Cicourel, A. V. (ed.) *Language Use and School Performance*, New York, Academic Press.
Mac an Ghaill, M. (1988) *Young, Gifted and Black: student–teacher relations in the schooling of black youth*, Milton Keynes, Open University Press.
Mortimore, P., Sammons, P., Stoll, L., Lewis, D. and Ecob, R. (1988) *School Matters: the junior years*, Wells, Somerset, Open Books.
Parekh, B. (1985) 'Background to the West Indian tragedy', *Times Educational Supplement*, 22 March.
Rist, R. C. (1970) 'Student social class and teacher expectations: the self-fulfilling prophecy in ghetto education', *Harvard Education Review*, 40, pp. 411–51.
Rutter, M., Maugham, B., Mortimore, P. and Ouston, J. (1979) *Fifteen Thousand Hours*, London, Open Books.
Schutz, A. (1970) *On Phenomenology and Social Relations: selected writings*, Wagner, H. R. (ed.), Chicago, Chicago University Press.

Sharp, R. and Green, A. (1975) *Education and Social Control: a study in progressive primary education*, London, Routledge and Kegan Paul.

Troyna, B. (ed.) (1987) *Racial Inequality in Education*, London, Tavistock.

Wright, C. (1987) 'Black students – white teachers', in Troyna, B. (ed.) *Racial Inequality in Education*, London, Tavistock.

3

THE MAGIC OF *GODSPELL*: THE EDUCATIONAL SIGNIFICANCE OF A DRAMATIC EVENT

P. Woods

INTRODUCTION: CRITICAL EVENTS

During recent work on creative teaching (Woods, 1990a), my attention was drawn to certain outstanding events in the schools of my research. These events had won wide acclaim from teachers, other professionals, pupils, parents, academics, advisers and other members of the public. Some of them had won an award. Initially I was interested in them, individually, as exciting educational events. Eventually, however, it became clear that they had common properties, and that they were all examples of the same kind of activity, which I came to call 'critical event'. The musical play *Godspell*, produced at Roade Secondary School in 1989–90, was one of these. In this article, I shall examine its qualifications as a critical event, and its educational significance.

Since events can only be seen to have been critical after they have occurred (Kelchtermans, 1991), a historical approach was used, involving qualitative methods aimed at exploring meanings and understandings, and recreating cultures and contexts in the evocative manner typical of ethnography (Eisner, 1991). The chief methods were extensive and in-depth interviewing; use of documentary evidence such as audio- and video-tapes, film, reports, all made at the time of the event; and visiting scenes. A measure of observation was involved, for example attending the final production of *Godspell*. Analysis then followed the procedures recommended by Strauss and Corbin (1990). Following the identification of a core category (critical event) from the comparison of cases, I sought to specify the conditions which give rise to it, the context in which it is embedded, the strategies by which it is handled, and the consequences of those strategies.

The main features of these critical events were as follows (see Woods, 1993, for a full account).

Radical change

They promote children's education and development in uncommonly accelerated ways, be it in terms of attitudes towards learning, the discovery of
hitherto unsuspected abilities, understanding of the self, relationships with
others, acquisition of knowledge or development of skills. As with Nias,
Southworth and Campbell (1992, p. 74), 'teachers were overwhelmed by the
realisation that children were able to achieve standards of which they had
never before thought them capable'. This contrasts with the gradual cumula-
tion of learning and development that takes place at other times, which both
consolidates and is informed by critical events.

These events are also critical for teacher development. They are the 'great
moments of teachability' (McLaren, 1986, p. 236), when things are 'set alight'
and 'take fire' (Connell, 1985, p. 127), when teachers 'transcend the contradictions of the job and achieve the "peak experience" . . . and become aware of
their full identity' (Nias, 1989, p. 200). So the teacher also learns and develops
in fulfilling ways, either as pedagogue in understanding of children's learning
and refinement of teaching methods; or as self, in relation to one's own knowledge, powers, aptitudes and abilities. As well as change, however, these events
can have an important preservation and confirmatory function for teachers,
helping to maintain a particular definition of reality and identity against the
pressure of contrary forces (Berger and Kellner, 1964). They can be the salva-
tion of high ideals.

Relevant learning

So much apparent learning is not relevant to students' own concerns in the
sense that it is not about their education but the structures and processes in
which it is embedded. Thus children learn about 'classroom culture'
(Hammersley, 1977), the structure of questions rather than their content
(Mehan, 1986), 'procedural display' (Bloome, 1987), and 'pleasing the
teacher' (Woods, 1990b). In relevant learning, the artificial controls of traditional schooling are removed. The central concern is pupils' own needs, and
the framework is their existing cognitive and affective structures. There is a
strong emphasis on reality, on a real problem or issue of importance or value,
on real rather than 'mocked-up' (Atkinson and Delamont, 1977) experiences,
on using real professionals, on collecting first-hand evidence and materials, on
doing things oneself, and having a realistic aim. The learning theory is constructivist, wherein the teacher is facilitator, helping children construct their
own learning, negotiating its construction with them, and paying particular
attention to social circumstances such as the context in which learning takes
place and the opportunities made available for interaction and co-operation
among others (Vygotsky, 1978; Wood, 1986; Edwards and Mercer, 1987).
Relevant learning is holistic in the sense both of regarding world as school and

of interrelating rationalist, algorithmic modes of thinking with aesthetic experience (Hargreaves, 1982; 1983) and 'poetic' thinking (Bonnett, 1991).

Communitas

Exceptional relationships are developed during critical events. The teachers involved have similar values and aims, and are deeply committed. Nias *et al.* (1989) have shown the nature and benefits of 'collaborative cultures' in primary schools. Nias, Southworth and Campbell (1992) describe how 'a sense of unity' developed during the production of a school concert: 'the whole staff and sub-groups worked together, people learnt more about one another's strengths and talents, everyone was valued for his/her particular contribution . . . [and] their sense of collective purpose was strengthened'. Similarly, collaborative work among pupils has many benefits. Research shows they learn from each other, work at their own pace, lose the fear and stigma of failure, improve their self-image, learn respect from others, and gain confidence (Galton and Williamson, 1992). In critical events, teachers and pupils come together to form a highly integrated and productive group, which develops its own distinctive identity and culture. It has something of the spirit of what Turner (1969) calls 'communitas'. Here, individuals are liberated from the constraints of status and role, and develop bonds that produce a 'state of undifferentiated, homogeneous human kindness' (McLaren, 1986, p. 259). Latent or suppressed feelings, abilities, thoughts, aspirations are set free and new persons born. Uncommon excitement and expectations are generated. All know that this experience is something special.

A distinctive structure

Critical events appear to go through fairly well-defined stages. First, there is conceptualization, when the initial idea and spark of enthusiasm is born and developed. Preparation and planning follows, involving clarification, briefing, resourcing and enskilling. There is, then, 'divergence', an 'explosion' stage, when pupils are encouraged to be creative and innovative, experiment with different media, explore opportunities and stretch their abilities. This stage may seem rather chaotic and anarchic. However, soon, the products are examined, differentiated and integrated to serve the aims of the enterprise in the subsequent 'convergence' stage, and further 'consolidated' in the writing-up, performance, picture-mounting or whatever medium is being used. The event concludes with a 'celebration', such as an exhibition, a concert, play, film, launch of a book. The celebration brings to a peak the accomplishments and offers them to a wider audience, signals the end of the event and serves as a rite of passage back into the normal routines of school life. A period of consolidation within the pupil's whole scheme of learning typically follows the end of the event. Critical events may not occur very often, since it is difficult to sustain such high levels of intensity. They are peaks of activity – but they must be connected to the basic general structure of learning if the full benefits are to be achieved. Testimony from students several years after some of the events indicate their long-term effects.

Learning proceeds through these stages with a certain rhythm and flow, 'periods of equilibrium preceding sudden disequilibrium' (Prawat, 1992, p. 357). Learning spirals and accumulates and becomes more complex as the event unfolds (Gershman, 1988). It resembles a qualitative research study, wherein initial conceptions prompt data collection, the primary analysis of which prompts more data collection, which fills out and refines ideas, and so on. The creativity is thus founded on an increasingly solid basis, which, in turn, promotes creativity of a higher order. It is similar to the 'positive cycle of teaching and learning' identified by Pollard (1985, p. 239).

Favourable conditions

The critical events researched all took place in 1988–9 before the National Curriculum took effect. Most of the teachers involved say they have been unable to launch similar projects because of the scale and nature of the new requirements. The rationalist frame of these requirements, the behaviourism of the assessment, the market-led orientation of other reforms and the sheer weight of mandatory activities are not conducive to this kind of teaching (Pollard, 1991; Campbell *et al.*, 1991). On the other hand, a reading of programmes of study and attainment targets would suggest that critical events would be highly appropriate. It remains to be seen in the gradual implementation of the Act over the years whether they are feasible. Whatever the result, the prime condition is legitimation within the curriculum structure.

At institutional level, teachers are supported by whole-school policies informed by compatible learning theories (Nias, Southworth and Yeomans, 1989). This ensures the support of colleagues, and particularly the headteacher. Apart from the moral and resource value of this, the expansive and holistic nature of the events and the need for them to be integrated within the pupils' general learning would seem to require it. It would be difficult to see such events occurring in schools which lacked this support, or where the emphasis, for example, was on behaviourist or instructionalist approaches, or primarily on the functions of selection and control.

At the centre of operations, generating and developing the ideas, gathering the resources, arranging the context, setting up the collaboration, encouraging, inspiring and co-ordinating, is the teacher – the critical agent. These are highly creative people, who have themselves and others 'bubbling like a hot spring' (Nias, 1989). They are visionary, but also strongly disciplined. Too much 'divergence' might yield an insubstantial product; too much convergence an unimaginative one. The skill comes in securing the balance between the pleasure of inventing and the pain of application. They also practised a range of methods with a basic fitness-for-purpose policy, but also with the view that variety promotes productivity, and offer more 'ways in' to different children's abilities, interests and motivation.

There were also critical 'others' – non-teachers, who none the less played a key role in the event, like professional experts (for example, architects, archaeologists, authors) or interested citizens (like the villagers in a film about the community). They added to the charisma of the proceedings. They do this, first, by being 'other'. Like Schutz's (1964) stranger, critical others challenge the taken-for-granted, introduce novelty and new perspective, cut across routines. They bring new ideas to teaching. They also present new role models for students, offering alternatives and dispelling myth and mystery about what they do. Second, those selected have qualities of self-inducing trust, faith and inspiration. Third, as experts within their field they contribute towards the authenticity of teachers' work and towards relevant learning. They do this by the provision of verisimilitude ('living history', a real book, a community film of real worth, etc.); by contributing to the integrity of knowledge both within itself and with the learner's self. This integrity is encouraged by, and reflected in, the holism of space, time and personnel; by providing and fostering information skills and communication skills; and by validating teachers' and pupils' work as genuine endeavours within their field of discipline.

This model was derived from studies of primary schools. In seeking to extend its generality, I want now to consider a particular activity in a secondary school as a critical event. I shall be concerned with two main questions: How does the model of critical event assist our understanding of the activity itself? How does the activity, in turn, help to refine the model?

GODSPELL AS A CRITICAL EVENT

In September 1988, Roade Comprehensive School in Northamptonshire began rehearsals for the rock musical *Godspell*. Five performances were given at the school in December 1988. It was selected for the 34th National Students' Drama Festival, held in Cambridge in March 1989. Selection was an honour in itself, but there, against competition from older students, it won a top award. A final performance was given to the general public in Northampton in October 1989. At all points the production won high praise, from drama experts, inspectors, teachers, parents, students, audiences. But it was more than 'a brilliant interpretation' (drama review) and 'the best school production I have ever seen' (local drama inspector). I studied the event through viewing of the play; through interviews with the cast, including several with the producer; and through a variety of sources of documentary evidence, including marked scripts, director's notes, reviews, audio-cassettes, videos, letters and poems. I concluded that it was a critical event of some magnitude. Like other such events, it brought about radical change; established communitas; used constructivist learning theory; took place in typical conditions; and showed the distinctive structure. I shall examine each in turn.

RADICAL CHANGE

Of particular note here were personal and emotional development.

Personal development

Several students spoke of their increased confidence and control. Samantha Jane found it a 'really brilliant experience'. She was 'more confident in herself'. Before, she had been 'very loud and blurty and scatty', but she had learned to control that because she 'had to be more mature and work with my group'. Chris felt that he grew with each performance, being very nervous over his lines to begin with, but enjoying them at the end. Josie thought 'you gained so much more from that experience than you ever could from sitting in a classroom . . . You gained more confidence in yourself which obviously makes you more confident in the classroom, because you felt totally secure and totally part of something.'

Part of this new-found confidence was reflected in a heightened sense of control. Johanne at first 'couldn't accept criticism', but found that now 'she could handle things because I know I can change to suit situations'. She had learned how to 'personally adjust' (Becker, 1964), and to manipulate the self to protect its essence. Ian, who had to be angry at certain points in the play, at first could not control himself, and 'would shout and be really angry'. Then he was told, 'You've got to be angry, but compassionate'. He had not read that into anger before, but it occurred to him that 'that was what teachers did'. His colleagues attested that his performance went up to new levels during the career of the play. He – and they – learnt that indispensable art of the actor, namely 'achieving that absolute contradiction – the control of spontaneity' (Barrault, 1972, p. 31).

Their creative abilities had been sharpened, notably through the demands for spontaneity and intuitive powers of improvisation. Here, actors 'have to "ad lib" to turn to experiences which are not performed and ready-made, but are still buried within them in an unformed stage. In order to mobilise and shape them, they need a transformer and catalyst, a kind of intelligence which operates here and now' (Moreno, 1972, p. 138). There are many examples of successful and ingenious improvisation in *Godspell*: Kate's adaptation of the first parable, Ian's developing charisma until in the final performance, 'he commanded the stage'; the 'sparks of inspiration' deriving from their strong identification with their characters; the musicians' contributions . . .

These developments brought about a new realization of self in some instances. Sara, at 18, was the oldest student in the *Godspell* cast. She started at the school in the third year and felt that she 'never belonged there properly'. During the production period of the play, she underwent a transformation, mainly through the intensity of the experience and the many caring relationships that she found. Matthew felt it had been a maturing experience. He was 'more calm and rational . . . a completely different person . . . I learnt more about myself at Cambridge than about drama itself'. As Heathcote (1970, p. 1080) observes, role-taking 'may surprise persons by a constant confrontation to them of their own thinking and behaving'.

Emotional development

The play aroused strong emotions, and for a time these were uncontrolled. Matthew, for example, after the second performance 'had a guilt complex. I just couldn't get to sleep . . . It all got so on top . . . the massive emotional outlet when we're all shouting and screaming. I just broke down . . . It was awful.' Sara became so involved that she would 'often find myself shaking during a performance. It was almost as if I'd lost touch with reality, could not wake from a dream.' Sally (the director) reported that, on returning from the prize-winning performance at Cambridge, 'We were absolutely in floods of tears the whole day, and it was very, very difficult to control . . . I was just as bad as them, and all you can do is try and bring some rationality to it but try to maintain the feelings as well.'

There is recognition here of a rare worth in the profound emotions. They contain a truth seldom touched upon, expand the self in ways not previously suspected. Yet for the moment they are out of control, not understood. Ross (1978, p. 43) argues that the purpose of self-expression in the arts is 'the elaboration and development of an emotional life, of our capacity to make sense in feelings of the subjective world of feeling, our capacity to feel intelligently, to find our way among feelings by feeling.' The *Godspell* cast eventually 'found their way'. In developing their role they 'became the part', but also developed the ability to recognize that very process and to de-role. Thus Ian (the Jesus figure) told of their initial self-consciousness at hugging each other (especially one of them being a teacher) on the departure of the Jesus-figure, but 'You go on and you go on, and . . . it all slots in. You hug, and you don't just hug because it's a direction – you hug because you'll never be seeing these people again'. Matthew discovered a new stance, legs astride, hands behind back, straight back, that once he had it, it always made him feel powerful and in control. He watched a video, listened to his voice, made it deeper in places, more threatening, getting spite into it. Chris (sailor) and Samantha Jane (tatty doll) had to grasp each other at one point, against their real characters, but worked on 'bits of their selves' and eventually totally lost their embarrassment. Sara reported that

> We had created a kind of truth in the play. You believed in everything, and by the time Matthew was about to betray Jesus you could see

genuine regret on his face. It was so genuine, you totally believed him. It wasn't that we were meant to believe him. We actually did believe.

The play thus provided opportunities for a range and depth of emotional expression; and, almost ironically, it provided experience in searching for truth, and for what is genuine, rather than theatrical, emotion. Rather than 'losing touch with reality', as Sara felt she was doing initially, the experience eventually brings you *closer* to reality. Stanislavski (in Hodgson, 1972, p. 94) writes, 'Truth on the stage is whatever we can believe in with sincerity, whether in ourselves or in our colleagues . . . Each and every moment must be saturated with a belief in the truthfulness of the emotion felt . . .'. Such belief is promoted by depth and lucidity. Bolton (1984, p. 119) argues that participants are concerned with 'tapping their own reservoirs of emotional memories to find within themselves a sophistication, subtlety or depth of emotional engagement so that in concentrating on the character's actions, a wider, deeper range of emotions may be released'. Lucidity, Collingwood (1966) argues, comes as actors explore their own emotions by means of gesture, speech and other forms of expression, thus discovering emotions of which they were previously unaware, and 'by permitting the audience to witness the discovery, enable them to make a similar discovery about themselves' (p. 47). Perhaps this is why Kevin's granddad was so impressed:

> He was one of the first to stand up and shout 'Encore! More! More!' He's a conservative-type person, but he was up there cheering. He'd had a heart attack previously. We thought that he was going to have another one! Anyway he was yelling and everything, and afterwards he said he'd never been so moved in 40 years of going to the theatre.

Teacher development

Critical events also bring about radical change in teachers. In a letter to the cast after the final performance, Sally (the 'critical agent') said, 'I shall quite simply never forget this show. I have also had to come to terms with the fact that there will never be another show like it for me, and I shall never be quite the same person again'. How, exactly, had she changed? This was her answer:

> It's dominated a whole year of my life. You can't be the same person after that. I feel much more vulnerable in some ways as a person because it opened up whole ranges of emotion that I hadn't experienced to such depth before. It gave me tremendous faith, obviously, in young people. It's given me some very wonderful friendships with some of them. It's given me those people to care for and it's made me happier really. It just gave so much more meaning to life. It was so wonderful to see that on stage and it just made me very, very happy to have thought I'd created that and, of course, very proud. It's given me much more confidence in myself. There's knock-on effects. Clive Wolfe, the guy who runs the National Students' Drama Festival, has now asked me to direct a produc-

tion in Edinburgh next year. So practically speaking it's changed my life because it's led to other things and probably will continue to do so. It's given me an insight into what we see at more professional theatres. It's just made me feel more relaxed. It gives you so much hope when you see young people working like that, and you see what they get out of it, and it suddenly makes everything worth while . . . I suppose it's the ultimate production for me, the most satisfying. I had the chance to work on something and develop it as fully as is probably humanly possible within the job that we do. I don't think I've learnt to employ many new skills or developed that much as a teacher because of it, except that I feel much more positive about life in general . . . You're constantly striving to get that feeling again in other situations with other productions, in other lessons – and it does seem much more attainable now purely because of my attitude. I'll go into lessons and expect the best. I suppose in that sense the work actually has improved. I never even thought of it like that, but that's probably exactly what's happened, and that's one of the reasons why I'm so pleased with my teaching over the last few months.

This seems to be a kind of ultimate in teachers' experience. It is perfect in its own terms. It reaches heights unthought of in the initial conception, brings out hidden or dormant qualities in the self and opens up new educational possibilities.

COMMUNITAS

Personal development was matched by social development. The *Godspell* cast experienced the sense of 'oneness with humanity' (Musgrove, 1977, p. 9) and with each other; 'the magic and spontaneity of life outside "structure" ' (ibid., p. 209), and the freeing of 'the imagination for the discovery of what is new' (Holmes, 1973, pp. 63–4). They had the features of what Cooley (1964) calls a 'primary group', characterized not by the functional relationships of the more common secondary groups (MacIver, 1937), but by 'intimate face-to-face association and co-operation. They are primary chiefly in that they are fundamental in focusing the social nature and ideas of the individual . . . one's very self, for many purposes at least, is the common life and purpose of the group' (Cooley, 1964, p. 311). Self and group are bound together, therefore, in a mutual advancement that produces such unexpected and delightful results that it seems like 'magic'. What, then, does it consist of? *Godspell* exhibited the following features.

A special culture developed by the group, and strong affective ties

'You've got this big thing in common that outsiders just don't really know about' (Sara). There was 'so much contact and closeness', which was 'developed' not 'fabricated' (Kevin). 'It was really the group that brought across the atmosphere' (Adam). 'You find yourself walking by somebody who was in the cast, and you both smile, and you both know what you're smiling about because there's something between you and it's just special' (Chris). When Kevin looks back on *Godspell*, 'I feel warm inside, I don't know why, I just do'. There were many such expressions of camaraderie, love, caring, and it applied to the whole group. If one of the 47 were missing, it didn't seem right. Thus when one missed the final performance, Chris commented, 'That felt strange to me . . . Even though I probably didn't say anything to her on the actual performance, I felt there was something missing.'

Discovering others

Barriers were broken down. People discovered new things about themselves and others. These relationships were special for they were forged, released almost, by the discovery of a new truth and sincerity. Thus Sam had thought the older Sara 'a real snob, but I got to know her, and she's really lovely, totally different from what I expected'. For her part, Sara 'never knew Sam before this . . . but we got so close because of the play'. Adam found it 'difficult working with Sean and Ivan to begin with', because as Sally said, 'they're unruly and cynical and witty'. This, however, was turned to advantage in the development of the tin soldier group as the smaller, officious commander struggled in vain to control his squad. Matthew emphasized the 'special' friendships he had made. For Johanne, it all began to work and come together '. . . when the relationships between the actual actors came. The characterizations just came from those sort of tangents from the relationships.' This sometimes carried surprises. Thus, Martin told how he was 'surprised by Ian Robson' on one of the nights he had to play the part of Chief Clown. He 'took over brilliantly'.

Levelling

Pupils of different ages, backgrounds and sexes, and teachers, were all one in co-operative unity. Previously, impressions of others had largely been formed by perceptions of institutional roles and barriers, or typification of people on slender evidence. Matthew now talks to fourth year students, which is 'unheard of' for the lower sixth. He was even pleased his sister was in the play. Martyn was the only teacher in the cast. He thought 'one of the amazing things was that there weren't any barriers of any sort . . . We were putting ourselves into the same sort of role and we were just on the same level.' After some initial strain on their part, students, too, accepted Martyn as one of them. It was as if he passed through a magic screen. To Matthew, 'He ceased to be a teacher when he got on stage. He was Martyn, Martyn the Clown, not Mr Glass, the French teacher, and now it's rubbed off.' Thus even teachers were transformed by the experience into 'persons' (Blackie, 1980).

Mutual support

Communitas is empowering to the individual who gathers strength from the support of the group. As mutual trust and self-confidence developed, so they were encouraged to experiment, and to take risks in the interests of finding what worked best and what capabilities they possessed. This rapport helped draw the best out of them, to profit from mistakes (turning them into natural developments if they occurred in the play), and to boost confidence. The main thing, for Sara, was 'to have so many people supporting you . . . I felt that I could just go for it and do whatever I wanted to do.' Kevin also said, 'The other actors were brilliant. When people are having a hard time they do encourage you . . . that really did help me build up my confidence.' Early counter-indications, like a sense of competition, were shown in the end to be counterproductive. Chris felt 'he was having to keep up with everybody else to begin with' but eventually 'it was unity, which was superb.' For Martyn, it was the religious message that was so binding. For Matthew, it was the fact 'that we were showing that people can work together'.

Contagiousness

The benefits of communitas reach out to others, rather than being inwardly directed in the creation of a differentiated group or élite. The sense of community included the audience. They became part of the oneness, embraced by the spirit emanating from the stage. Their ecstatic reaction to the performance was more than appreciation of a good show. The play had a cathartic influence on them (Moreno, 1964). The audience had been 'purged of their personal anxieties and [purified], reassured, revitalised, tranquillised by what seems a dispensing of justice' (Barrault, 1972, p. 25). This is why Kevin's granddad was so excited. In turn, audience reaction had an energizing effect on the cast. Ian G—— noted that 'After "Prepare You" there was the most massive roar of applause you ever heard. It was amazing, it was so uplifting!' Several mentioned what a great thrill it was to give other people so much pleasure.

LEARNING THEORY

Clearly there are several ways in which the educational outcomes can be represented as relevant learning. There are the truths connected with emotional development, with the discovery of propensities, abilities and sensitivities of the self, and of others. However, I wish to concentrate here on the one aspect of truth that is most difficult to describe, that of aesthetic appreciation. It is this, above all, I would argue, that lies behind the 'magic' of *Godspell*.

A 'traumatic theory of learning'

We can usefully approach this through David Hargreaves's (1983) 'traumatic theory of aesthetic learning'. Following some informal research among adults and their experience of art, he suggested that their illuminating experience of aesthetic recognition (which he calls 'conversive trauma') had four main characteristics (ibid. p. 141): (1) the 'powerful concentration of attention'. One is 'totally absorbed and fascinated' and becomes 'lost in the art object'; (2) a sense of revelation, of 'new and important reality'. There is a sense of 'entering a new plane of existence which is somehow intensely real.' There is 'profound emotional disturbance', and also 'a feeling of discovery as if some already existing core of the self is suddenly being touched and brought to life for the first time'; (3) inarticulateness. 'The affective elements can be so powerful that, as it were, feelings drown the words'; and (4) the 'arousal of appetite' – the desire to continue or repeat the experience.

Hargreaves argues that the trauma is the first step in initiation. It leads to motivation for more experience of that nature; exploration to find it; discrimination between experiences as one's understanding grows; and a search for background knowledge. *Godspell* provides a good opportunity to test Hargreaves' theory using a different art form (drama), different subjects (students), in a different situation (school). The results suggest a confirmation of the traumatic features, with some refinements, but the need to contextualize the trauma within a more general theory. I will consider these in turn.

The traumatic experience

The first three of Hargreaves' features of trauma were evident in *Godspell*. I have no evidence on the fourth, though we might reasonably assume that this also applied. The 'powerful concentration of attention' is akin to what, in drama, Slade (1968, p. 12) refers to as 'absorption' and Heathcote (1972) as 'living through'. This is accompanied by a sense of 'timelessness', where students 'own' the time, time passes quickly, 'dissolving' into whatever activity the students are doing, with each moment being richly rewarding (Hall, 1984; McLaren, 1986). There were frequent expressions from students of how they 'put their whole selves into it', how it 'took over their lives', how you 'left the outside behind you when you put on the costumes', how they were 'caught up in the creation of another world', and how it was 'so hard to leave behind'.

A sense of 'new and important reality' is clear in the frequent expressions of the discovery of new truths, of moving up 'levels' and of reaching ultimates. The quality of these revelations is such that they assume a magical character. Ross (1982, p. 80) writes that profound aesthetic experience 'occasionally reaches the state of rapture and ecstasy . . . It always implies some degree of standing outside the merely mundane and the sensing in some degree of something infinite, of the heart's leaping in wonder as expectation and longing are somehow felt to be satisfied – beyond our dreams and hopes.' Several spoke of the magic of the experience in the sense of it continuously producing unexpected and startling results, leading to new peaks of excellence. *Godspell* was 'great fun', 'like nothing on earth – it's so difficult to explain', 'the morale was just incredible. It was like this electric burst as we were about to go on stage'. They were caught up in 'the creation of another world. It's so difficult to describe, it's magic'.

Closely associated with the feeling of magic was the sense of achievement – clearly important when you participate in the construction of a work of art. As an experience, this came top of most people's list. For Sally-Ann, 'So far it's the best experience I've had at school.' For Jo, 'It's something you never forget – a once-in-a-lifetime chance.' Ian G—— could feel that he had done something worth while, 'whatever you have done of any importance'. It was hard for Johanne to leave behind, because 'You're special then – you've done something for other people'. For Matthew, in his school career to date, 'Emotionally it comes top. Mentally it comes joint top along with my GCSE results' (he achieved 9 As in these). Claire said 'the last fourteen months have been the best months of my life.' Sally spoke for them when she said that they could feel 'that was incredible, and that was a wonderful achievement.'

Hargreaves' third feature was 'inarticulateness'. Clearly this was relevant to *Godspell* from the earlier discussion, though with important modifications. My interviewees were mostly very articulate, and gave detailed and vivid accounts of their experiences. However, some parts, usually the essence of the 'magic', they found difficult to explain. They could describe appearances and events, but certain parts of their experience were beyond words. You have to *feel them.* Interestingly they tried to convey this by a special use of words, such as repetition of superlatives, statements of wonderment accompanied by gestures and facial expressions, tone of voice and above all by a warmth and spirit which I took to be typical of the feeling generated by the play and which was generously ex-tended to me. Much of this, of course, is missing from the transcript. They successfully conveyed this to me, especially with the build-up of testimony as I moved through the interviews, to such an extent that they were almost recreating and reliving the experience, and engaging me in it. They *wanted* to talk about it and sustained a sense of excitement at the prospect. They wanted to recapture the experience, perhaps find out new things about it (the possibilities had still not been exhausted), explore, rehearse, share it universally in a different way from performing. Their talks with me were in a sense a continuation of the experience. They did find ways, therefore, of expressing their feelings. Prominent among these were those indicating warmth and *love*. This feature, and indeed any other to do with relationships, is missing from Hargreaves' list.

Contextualizing the trauma

Hornbrook (1991) has argued that trauma is embedded within more general cultural experiences. Consequently, it can be represented as 'the experience of an instant in time when elements of this internalised sensibility suddenly coincide with their representations in the culture itself and burst vividly into our consciousness' (p. 37). I would argue, further, that, as an educational experience, conversive trauma – if it is to be fully conversive – needs situating within a more gradual, cumulative theory of learning. In considering the evidence for this in *Godspell* we shall see that some of the conditions typical of critical events are embodied within this theory.

View of pupil

First, there is emphasis on students' presenting behaviour. All students are seen as having relevant cultural capital (Bourdieu and Passeron, 1977); they all have abilities, and they all have an aesthetic faculty (Read, 1966). The task is to cultivate them to recognition of this, chiefly through the encouragement of confidence. Read (1966, p. 264) writes

> It is only fear that prevents the child from being an artist – fear that its private world of fantasy will seem ridiculous to the adult, fear that its expressive signs and symbols will not be adequate. Cast out fear from the child and you have then released all its potentialities for emotional growth and maturation.

We saw earlier how students gained in confidence, and how they discovered new abilities in themselves and in others.

Teacher style

Teacher style was directed towards this, following constructivist principles. The teacher in this model is a skilled orchestrator, co-ordinating what is, at times, a great deal of disparate, and in the early stages apparently unconnected and conflicting, activity. Like the best orchestral conductors, her approach is firm but sympathetic, containing a sure touch that becomes hidden in the performance. Sara, for example, said that obviously they had a lot of direction from Sally, but they were encouraged to do 'what came natural to us in our parts so that we weren't forcing anything . . . You became so engrossed in it, you almost forgot you were being directed.' Sally saw her role as creating a situation, devising a structure and inspiring the participants. If all that went well, the cast could almost 'lead' themselves in working out the detail. But she was there as a guide and consultant on their creative endeavours and, since the complicated whole needed a central point of integration, the final arbiter.

Charisma

As well as a cultivated style, the agents at the centre of this event had a natural charisma. They had commitment, vision and faith. The commitment is to an ideal representing their cherished values and beliefs; to teaching as a vocational professional activity in helping others appreciate the ideal; and to students. Vision sees beyond the known, recognizes possibilities, initiates outcomes, evaluates risk. It appreciates unpredictability, and that the self is such a complex organism that 'we do not know what wonders it is capable of' (Mead, 1934). The faith is in her own abilities, those of the students, the medium and methods, and the potential product. An important part of the teaching is conveying these qualities to others. For example, at the worst moment of the trauma, when they were breaking down uncontrollably, Sally had to counsel her cast: 'Look, trust me, I know what I'm doing. It will come.' Sometimes when 'things didn't go right', according to Sara, 'you had to be shouted at. But because she [Sally] got it right somewhere along the line everyone accepted everything she said.' They admired her dedication and energy so that 'everyone felt that they owed it to her to be the same . . . and to be loyal to her and the play'.

The cast thus found Sally's direction inspirational. She was supported, at one difficult phase, by a 'critical other'. The point in question was that following the school performances, when inspiration had to be rekindled for the Cambridge performances. A drama expert associated with the NSDF, Nick Phillips, visited the school for a weekend and introduced new ideas and fresh enthusiasm. Members of the cast attested that 'he tightened bits up', 'put a little bit of polish on the numbers', helped them 'find the energy we thought we'd lost', made the show 'a bit more flowing and professional', made them 'feel good about themselves', gave them renewed confidence. He thus enhanced the role of the teacher with his own brand of charisma.

View of pedagogy

There were four prominent features informing Sally's pedagogy:

1 *Context* Creative arts has its own purpose-built block in the school. Within this, attention could be given to group alignments and arrangement of props to secure appropriate definitions of the situation (Stebbins, 1975). Once an appropriate situation is constructed, it generates its own momentum. The provision of a stimulating learning environment is even more important, in Rowland's (1987) opinion, than the teacher acting as instructor. The wider context is also important. *Godspell* was aided by the strong investment of the school in the creative arts. In this sense, the production belonged to the whole school, as a result of whole-school policy.

2 *Co-operation* The context was designed to serve the principle of co-operation. That teamwork was paramount in *Godspell* is clear from the discussion of communitas earlier.

3 *Content* The vehicle selected to assist students' journey to the aesthetic experience is obviously important. It has to have certain qualities as a work of art, has to be accessible, but also challenging. *Godspell* has its critics as a play,

but it provided a framework for an inspired adaptation. Sally's interpretation embraced more students than the original production (45 as against 12), provided for the generation of unity among them, capitalized on the qualities of youth, remained faithful to the basic text and, above all, provided its own impetus for further multiple individual and sub-group interpretations within the overall plot. In short, it enabled the cast to go through the process of 'remaking' the play themselves, bringing to it 'their own experience of life . . .' (Protherough, 1983).

4 Grounded and open inquiry   Learning is grounded in the student. It is open in the sense that it is expansive. The emphasis is on inquiry, and students finding their own way. Multi-methods are used both in a 'fitness for purpose' sense, and with a view to opening up the route to all students. In *Godspell*, a range of techniques were used to break down the blockages and inhibitions induced by normal, everyday life, and to open up the participants to the reality of the play. Once inspired, individuals and teams developed their own momentum and imported their own methods. Kevin, chief teddy bear, for example, had got all the teddy bears he could find and watched how they moved. He imagined how they would talk. At the dress rehearsal he suddenly found 'this voice came along. It was weird, it just came, it's kind of inspirational. It came from within.'

The case of *Godspell*, therefore, adds some confirmation to Hargreaves' 'traumatic theory of aesthetic learning'. It suggests, however, the need for it to be contextualized within a more general theory which embraces preparation (important for appreciation to occur), and follow-up (necessary for full consolidation of the educational gains). The trauma is the catalyst, the sensitizing change-agent that raises levels of awareness and sensitivity.

STRUCTURE: A MULTI-CRITICAL EVENT

Godspell shows the distinctive structure of critical events. Sally had done the play before using some of the same concepts, but at a simpler level. She wanted to develop the ideas:

> It took three weeks originally to think of the idea of the nursery. I can remember every day in the car thinking 'I've got to find a format for *Godspell*', and just running through ideas and eventually I hit on the nursery idea. Then everything followed. I wanted toys, and I wanted groups of toys . . .

There followed auditions and assembling of the cast, readings of the script, provision of props, costumes, and other resources, recruiting of stage-crew, front-of-house staff, make-up personnel, lighting team and so forth – all the elements of preparation and planning. It also included some fairly general directions as to movements and positions. Within these directions there was scope for each group to create their own activities in the divergence stage. This blended into convergence in the three-and-a-half months of 'night after night' rehearsals – 'We gradually built up the reactions and all the little details to add to the central storyline. This was then consolidated in the dress rehearsals, and finally celebrated in the actual performances.'

It is nothing unusual, of course, for a production in drama to follow this course. Hornbrook (1991, p. 73 *et seq.*) outlines a roughly similar framework. The remarkable thing about *Godspell*, rather, was that it was not only a critical event, but a multiple one. There were three events, in fact, each building on the one preceding and each showing the same basic internal structure. The first event lasted from September to December, culminating in the performances at the school. The second phase, from December onwards, was a repeat of the first, but on a higher plane. They could not repeat phase one in exactly the same circumstances. Such events are unique. How to pick up the traces again, therefore, was a serious problem. Two things were distinctive. First, the circumstances were different. The first phase was a 'school career', geared for presentation to pupils and parents at the school. Phase two was a 'national career' requiring fine-tuning for competition with the best student drama in the country. The process was the same, but the intensity was greater. To launch them on this second phase required the services of a 'critical other'. Nick Phillips 'did the trick', and helped to set them on course for their triumph. During the second phase they 'went up a level'. Not only did they reach new heights in their own performance, they encountered new learning experiences. The whole week they spent at Cambridge brought them in touch with what Kevin described as 'more subtle and particular analyses'. Also the Cambridge experience had aided their integration by the process of differentiation from other groups, who were not only in competition with them but where also, apart from one, senior to them in age and experience. Again, therefore, they stood out, and their reception confirmed their distinctiveness. By the time they arrived at Northampton's spacious Derngate, they had become thoroughly professional. Sara was sure 'we could not have achieved it if we'd had just five nights of performance. We could never have reached the height of feeling that we did in just a week's production, because it's just this process of learning, a gradual mutual understanding and appreciation of the play.'

Essentially, therefore, *Godspell* as an educational event was a mixture of trauma and incrementalism. This applied both within the event, and more broadly and long term outside it. Much of the high point of growth and development within the period, I have argued, was due to the elevating effect that occurred, almost serendipitiously, as they went from one set of performances to another, each with a distinctive and different purpose. In a real sense, they went from strength to strength. From a longer-term perspective and a wider view, *Godspell* might be regarded as a critical educational event that does not merely sit atop the everyday routine, but actually informs and enhances it. Routine is enhanced by peaks that lift it from the commonplace, give it meaning, establish its relevance, motivate and inspire. Schools cannot do a *Godspell* every year. But they can aspire towards it – as *Godspell* itself was an aspiration. Nobody dreamt at the beginning that it would turn out as it did. The search for quality is made and achievement judged by degree of closeness to the ideal. The conjunction of factors do not always permit the ideal to be achieved. When it does, however, the results are extraordinary. The mundane is elevated, and imbued with new meaning. Different, better, people emerge from the experience than went with it.

Those who took part in *Godspell* will always remember it. It will figure among the high peaks of their achievements. In giving people a sight of the ultimate, an indication of possibilities, some hitherto undreamt of, and new views of themselves, it established a platform for even greater endeavours.

REFERENCES

Atkinson, P. and Delamont, S. (1977) Mock-ups and cock-ups: the stage-management of guided discovery instruction, in P. Woods and M. Hammersley (eds.) *School Experience*, Croom Helm, London.

Barrault, J. L. (1972) Best and worst of professions, in J. Hodgson, (ed.) (1972) *The Uses of Drama*, Eyre Methuen, London.

Becker, H. S. (1964) Personal change in adult life, *Sociometry*, Vol. 27, no. 1, pp. 40–53.

Berger, P. L. and Kellner, H. (1964) Marriage and the construction of reality, *Diogenes*, Vol. 46, no. i, pp. 1–23.

Blackie, P. (1980) Not quite proper, in S. Reedy and M. Woodhead (eds.) *Family, Work and Education*, Hodder & Stoughton, London.

Bloome, D. (1987) Reading as a social process in a middle school classroom, in D. Bloome (ed.) *Literacy and Schooling*, Ablex, Norwood, NJ.

Bolton, G. (1984) *Drama as Education*, Longman, London.

Bonnett, M. (1991) Developing children's thinking . . . and the National Curriculum, *Cambridge Journal of Education*, Vol. 21, no. 3, pp. 277–92.

Bourdieu, P. and Passeron, J. C. (1977) *Reproduction in Education, Society and Culture*, Sage, London.

Campbell, R. J., Evans, L., St J. Neill, S. R. and Packwood, A. (1991) *Workloads, Achievements and Stress: Two Follow-Up Studies of Teacher Time in Key Stage 1*, Policy Analysis Unit, Department of Education, University of Warwick.

Collingwood, R. G. (1966) Expressing one's emotions, in E. W. Eisner and D. W. Ecker (eds.) *Readings in Art Education*, Xerox College Publishing, Lexington, Mass.

Connell, R. W. (1985) Theorizing gender, *Sociology*, Vol. 19, no. 2, pp. 260–72.

Cooley, C. H. (1964) Primary groups, in L. A. Coser and B. Rosenberg (eds.) *Sociological Theory*, Collier-Macmillan, London.

Edwards, D. and Mercer, N. (1987) *Common Knowledge: The Development of Understanding in the Classroom*, Methuen, London.

Eisner, E. W. (1991) *The Enlightened Eye: Qualitative Enquiry and the Enhancement of Educational Practice*, Macmillan, New York, NY.

Galton, M. and Williamson, J. (1992) *Group Work in the Primary Classroom*, Routledge, London.

Gershman, K. (1988) Surviving through time: a life history of a high-school drama production, *International Journal of Qualitative Studies in Education*, Vol. 1, no. 3, pp. 239–62.

Hall, E. T. (1984) *The Dance of Life*, Anchor Press/Doubleday, New York, NY.

Hammersley, M. (1977) School learning: the cultural resources required by pupils to answer a teacher's question, in P. Woods and M. Hammersley (eds.) *School Experience*, Croom Helm, London.

Hargreaves, D. H. (1982) *The Challenge for the Comprehensive School*, Routledge & Kegan Paul, London.

Hargreaves, D. H. (1983) The teaching of art and the art of teaching: towards an alternative view of aesthetic learning, in M. Hammersley and A. Hargreaves (eds.) *Curriculum Practice: Some Sociological Case Studies*, Falmer Press, Lewes.

Heathcote, D. (1970) How does drama serve thinking, talking and writing? *Elementary English*, Vol. 47, December, pp. 1077–81.

Heathcote, D. (1972) Drama as challenge, in J. Hodgson (ed.) *The Uses of Drama*, Eyre Methuen, London.

Holmes, U. T. (1973) Revivals are un-American: a recalling of America to its pilgrimage, *Anglican Theological Review*, supplementary series, no. 1, pp. 58–75.

Hornbrook, D. (1991) *Education in Drama*, Falmer Press, Lewes.

Kelchtermans, G. (1991) Teachers and their career story: a professional development, paper presented at the Fifth Conference of the International Study Association on Teacher Thinking, Guildford, 23–7 September.

MacIver, R. M. (1937) *Society*, MacMillan.

McLaren, P. (1986) *Schooling as a Ritual Performance*, Routledge & Kegan Paul, London.

Mead, G. H. (1934) *Mind, Self and Society*, University of Chicago Press, Chicago, Ill.

Mehan, H. (1986) What time is it Denise? Asking known information questions in classroom discourse, in M. Hammersley (ed.) *Case Studies in Classroom Research*, Open University Press, Milton Keynes.

Moreno, J. L. (1964) *Psychodrama*, Beacon House, New York, NY.

Moreno, J. L. (1972) Drama as therapy, in J. Hodgson (ed.) *The Uses of Drama*, Eyre Methuen, London.

Musgrove, F. (1977) *Margins of the Mind*, Methuen, London.

Nias, J. (1989) *Primary Teachers Talking: A Study of Teaching as Work*, Routledge, London.

Nias, J., Southworth, G. and Campbell, P. (1992) *Whole School Curriculum Development in the Primary School*, Falmer Press, Lewes.

Nias, J., Southworth, G. and Yeomans, R. (1989) *Staff Relationships in the Primary School: A Study of Organizational Cultures*, Cassell, London.

Pollard, A. (1985) *The Social World of the Primary School*, Holt, Rinehart & Winston, London.

Pollard, A. (1991) The child's place in a conflict of interests, *ASPE Conference Papers*, University of the West of England.

Prawat, R. S. (1992) Teacher's beliefs about teaching and learning: a constructivist perspective, *American Journal of Education*, Vol. 100, no. 13, pp. 354–95.

Protherough, R. (1983) *Developing Responses to Fiction*, Open University Press, Milton Keynes.

Read, H. (1966) The aesthetic method of education, in E. W. Eisner and D. W. Ecker (eds.) *Readings in Art Education*, Xerox College Publishing, Lexington, Mass.

Ross, M. (1978) *The Creative Arts*, Heinemann, London.

Ross, M. (ed.) (1982) *The Development of Aesthetic Experience*, Pergamon Press, Oxford.

Rowland, S. (1987) Child in control: towards an interpretive model of teaching and learning, in S. Pollard (ed.) *Children and Their Primary Schools*, Falmer Press, Lewes.

Schutz, A. (1964) The stranger: an essay in social psychology, in A. Brodersen (ed.) *Collected Papers, II*, Martinus Nijhoff, The Hague, pp. 91–105.

Slade, P. (1968) *Experience of Spontaneity*, Longman, London.

Stanislavski, C. (1972) Emotional involvement in acting, in J. Hodgson (ed.) *The Uses of Drama*, Eyre Methuen, London.

Stebbins, R. (1975) *Teachers and Meaning: Definitions of Classroom Situations*, E. J. Brill, Leiden.

Strauss, A. and Corbin, J. (1990) *Basics of Qualitative Research: Grounded Theory Procedures and Techniques*, Sage, Newbury Park, Ca.

Turner, V. W. (1969) *The Ritual Process*, Routledge & Kegan Paul, London.

Vygotsky, L. S. (1978) *Mind in Society: The development of Higher Psychological Processes*, Harvard University Press, London.

Wood, D. (1986) Aspects of teaching and learning, in M. Richards and P. Light (eds.) *Children of Social Worlds*, Polity Press, Cambridge.

Woods, P. (1990a) *Teacher Skills and Strategies*, Falmer Press, Lewes.

Woods, P. (1990b) *The Happiest Days? How Pupils Cope with School*, Falmer Press, Lewes.

Woods, P. (1993) *Critical Events in Teaching and Learning*, Falmer Press, Lewes.

4

TIME AND TEACHERS' WORK: AN ANALYSIS OF THE INTENSIFICATION THESIS

A. Hargreaves

Whatever else might be said about teaching, few would disagree that the nature and demands of the job have changed profoundly over the years. For better or worse, teaching is not what it was. There are the needs of special education students in ordinary classes to be met. Curriculum programmes are constantly changing as innovations multiply and the pressures for reform increase. Assessment strategies are more diverse. There is increasing consultation with parents and more communication with colleagues. Teachers' responsibilities are more extensive. Their roles are more diffuse. What do these changes mean? How do we understand them? For those who perform the work of teaching, is the job getting better, or is it getting worse?

While there is wide agreement about the extent of change in teachers' work, there are differences regarding the meaning and significance of this change. Two contending explanations are *professionalization* and *intensification*. Arguments organized around the principle of professionalization have emphasized the struggle for and, in some cases, the realization of greater teacher professionalism through extensions of the teacher's role. Teachers, especially those in elementary schools, are portrayed as having more experience of whole school curriculum development, involvement in collaborative cultures of mutual support and professional growth, experience of teacher leadership, commitment to continuous improvement, and engagement with processes of extensive schoolwide change.[1] In these accounts, teaching is becoming more complex and more skilled. What Hoyle calls extended teacher professionalism, and Nias more cautiously terms bounded professionality, is, in this perspective, both an emerging reality and a point of aspiration.[2]

A second line of argument is broadly derived from Marxist theories of the labor process. This highlights major trends towards deterioration and deprofessionalization in teachers' work. In these accounts, teachers' work is portrayed as becoming more routinized and deskilled, more and more like the degraded work of manual workers and less and less like that of autonomous professionals trusted to exercise the power and expertise of discretionary judgment with the children.[3] Teachers are depicted as being increasingly controlled by prescribed programs, mandated curricula, and step-by-step methods of instruction.[4] More than this, it is claimed teachers' work has become increasingly *intensified*, with teachers expected to respond to greater pressures and to comply with multiplying innovations under conditions that are at best stable and at worst deteriorating. Under this view, extended professionalism is a rhetorical ruse, a strategy for getting teachers to collaborate willingly in their own exploitation as more and more effort is extracted from them.

This article takes a critical look at the second of these competing perspectives: the intensification thesis. It does so through the voices of teachers themselves – through their own words about their world and their work. This is important because the evidence for the intensification thesis has so far rested on a rather small number of single- or two-teacher case studies. Empirical support for the thesis, while mounting, can still be regarded as no more than slender. The time is ripe, therefore, to open the intensification thesis to more detailed empirical scrutiny. Drawing on a recent study of how elementary teachers use newly provided preparation time in the school day, this article examines the implications of what appears to be a critical case for the intensification of teaching – the scheduling of additional statutory release time for elementary teachers from classroom responsibilities. First, though, it is important to identify the propositions and claimed empirical generalizations that make up the intensification thesis, so that when we listen to teachers' voices, the standard of comparison will be clear.

The concept of intensification is drawn from general theories of the labor process, particularly as outlined by Larson: 'Intensification . . . represents one of the most tangible ways in which the work privileges of educated workers are eroded.' It 'represents a break, often sharp, with the leisurely direction that privileged non-manual workers expect' as it 'compels the reduction of time within the working day when no surplus is produced.'[5] This discussion contains the following claims:

- Intensification leads to reduced time for relaxation during the working day, including 'no time at all' for lunch.
- Intensification leads to lack of time to retool one's skills and keep up with one's field.
- Intensification creates chronic and persistent overload (as compared with the temporary overload that is sometimes experienced in meeting deadlines), which reduces areas of personal discretion, inhibits involvement in and control over longer-term planning, and fosters dependency on externally produced materials and expertise.
- Intensification leads to reductions in the *quality* of service, as corners are cut to save time.

- Intensification leads to enforced diversification of expertise and responsibility to cover personnel shortages, which can in turn create excessive dependency on outside expertise and further reductions in the quality of service.

Discussion of the intensification of *teachers'* work draws extensively and often directly on Larson's broader analysis of the labor process.

In works by Michael Apple, intensification is particularly evidenced in teachers' work in the growing dependence on an externally produced and imposed apparatus of behavioral objectives, in-class assessments and account-ability instruments, and classroom management technologies. This, he says, has led to a proliferation of administrative assessment tasks, lengthening of the teacher's working day, and elimination of opportunities for more creative and imaginative work – a development that has occasioned complaints among teachers.[6] In his analysis with Susan Jungck of the implementation of com-puterized instruction, Apple points to one particular effect of intensification on the meaning and quality of teachers' work – reduction of time and opportunity for elementary teachers to show care for and connectedness with their stu-dents, because of their scheduled preoccupation with administrative and as-sessment tasks.[7] In addition to the insights they draw from labor process theory, Apple and others point to two additional aspects of intensification that are specifically grounded in education and teaching.

First, there is the implementation of simplified technological solutions to curriculum change that compensate 'teachers for their lack of time by provid-ing them with prepackaged curricula rather than changing the basic conditions under which inadequate preparation time exists'.[8] Scarce preparation time, that is, is said to be a chronic and persistent feature of intensification in teachers' work. Solutions to change and improvement focus on the simplified translation of externally imposed expertise rather than complex evolution of internally developed and shared improvements, along with the time needed for their creation.

Second, Apple reports that the employment of technical criteria and tests makes teachers feel more professional and encourages them to accept the longer hours and intensification of their work that accompany their introduc-tion: 'The increasing technicization and intensification of the teaching act . . . [is] misrecognized as a symbol of their increased professionalism.'[9] In an anal-ysis of two elementary teachers and the place of intensification in their work, Densmore notes that 'out of a sense of professional dedication, teachers often volunteered for additional responsibilities', including after-school and evening activities. One teacher is described as working 'quickly and efficiently so that she could include creative supplementary lessons once required lessons were finished. Her own sense of professionalism together with parental pressures for additional effort, propelled her to increase the quantity of lessons taught.' The way that such teachers voluntarily consort with the imperatives of intensifica-tion, it seems, means that 'the ideology of professionalism for teachers legiti-mates and reinforces . . . intensification'.[10]

There are therefore two additional claims about intensification in teaching to add to the earlier list:

- Intensification creates and reinforces scarcities of preparation time.
- Intensification is voluntarily supported by many teachers and misrecognized as professionalism.

Let us now listen to some teachers' voices and compare them with these claims. What do these voices say about teachers' work? And how might they serve as more than echoes for preferred theories, instead leading us to question these theories, however uncomfortably, by having authenticity and authority of their own?

PREPARATION TIME: A CRITICAL CASE

In September 1987, elementary teachers in Metropolitan Toronto school districts took strike action in support of their claim for a guaranteed minimum of 180 minutes per week of preparation time. Throughout the province of Ontario, contract negotiations before, during, and after this time centered around increased preparation time as a key bargaining issue. At the time of writing, elementary teachers in most Ontario school districts now have a guaranteed minimum of 120 minutes or more of preparation time per week.

Such guaranteed time for elementary teachers away from class is unusual in Western schooling systems, yet this has long been advocated as a desirable – indeed, necessary – condition for increased collegiality among teachers, for opportunity to commit to and get involved in change, and, more recently, for restricting the process of intensification in teachers' work. A study of the uses of increased preparation time therefore constitutes a critical case for examining the nature and conditions of teachers' work. Does scheduled preparation time lead to fundamental changes in the nature of teachers' work and in the relationship teachers have with their colleagues? Does it generate closer and more extensive collaborative relationships between teachers and their colleagues? Or are the uses of preparation time defined and absorbed by prevailing patterns of work within the teacher culture of a more individualized, classroom-focused nature? Moreover, does the provision of increased preparation time halt or restrict the encroaching intensification of teachers' work? If only in this one geographical region, does it constitute an important empirical and theoretical challenge to the intensification thesis?

In 1988 and 1989, my colleague Rouleen Wignall and I interviewed twelve principals and twenty-eight teachers in a total of twelve schools in two school boards (six schools per board). Using a semi-structured schedule, we collected data on the uses and perceptions of preparation time among these teachers, and also on their broader understandings of their work as elementary school teachers outside their scheduled class responsibilities. We asked questions about teachers' working relationships with their colleagues and about perceived changes in their work and their working environment over the years. Thus, while at the outset we were more interested in exploring propositions concerning the relationship of time to the culture of teaching than we were in testing the intensification thesis, the nature of our questions and of teachers' responses to them yielded data that were highly pertinent to that thesis.[11]

TEACHER TIME AND INTENSIFICATION

The first set of issues arising from our data concerned the changes, the pressures, the increased expectations that many teachers had experienced in recent years – changes that in a broad quantitative sense would seem to offer some support for the intensification thesis.

One teacher described some of the ways that teaching had changed for her:

> Teaching is changing so much. There's so much more social work involved in your job now than there ever was before. So many problems, behavioural and social problems, that are sitting in your classroom that have to be dealt with before you can ever attempt to start teaching. I don't think a lot of people realize that . . . it's really a changing job. This is my fifteenth year, and since I started teaching, you can really see horrendous changes . . . and I don't think a lot of people who've never been in a school and seen a school run know exactly what a person puts up with in a day. Then they say: 'What do you need two months off for?'

The effects of special-education legislation and the mainstreaming of special-education students into regular classes were areas of concern for several teachers – in terms of both their implications for classroom discipline and their demands on the teacher to provide more diversified programs.

> T: I know in the beginning, during prep time, there were more teachers who at least had time to take a break, which is sometimes necessary. And now you rarely find a teacher taking a break.
> I: So how do you explain that?
> T: I find my workload now is much heavier than it used to be. I just think that although there are times that I know I need to stop, I can't. I have to get things done. So I think that part of it is the changing expectations of teachers. Large class sizes – I have 29 – and when you figure that goes from a Special Ed kid, to enrichment, to ESL, it's a lot of kids that you always seem to be on the tear. I think there's more and more social work going on. If we were to write teachers' descriptions ten years ago, twenty years ago and now, they're vastly different. I think there just isn't the time now for us to sometimes sit down and recuperate.

This teacher went on to describe a number of children in her class who might previously have been retained in a segregated unit. 'You've got all these kids that you never used to have,' she said. Nor is it simply a matter of containing them, of maintaining discipline. 'We're to meet the individual needs of the kids. Kids don't fail today, really, so we have to keep adjusting the programme.'

An additional problem for some teachers was what they perceived to be scarce and possibly declining in-class specialist support and assistance to help them cope with and prepare programmes for the new special-needs students. One teacher commented that he had 'a very large class', 'a low-average class' with two students who were repeating grades, which was 'very tough, very demanding' for him. The reason for this concentration of ten to twelve 'needy' children in his class, he believed, was that 'it's easier for the people in the resource department to schedule time into . . . one class, as opposed to three separate classes'. Another teacher pointed out that her para-professional in-class support had been removed because of budget cuts. Therefore she now devotes most of her preparation time to working with individual special-needs students to give them the support they need and help them 'catch up'.

The changing composition of teachers' classes over the years, then, has had implications not only for discipline and stress but for the complexity of programming and preparation too.

> You're always being told that you're constantly responsible for the children. You need to know where they are and what they're doing. You have to be able to programme for all the different abilities in your classroom. It's not a simple matter of saying – 'Today, we're going to read this story!' It's who can read this story and what am I going to do with the kids who can't? And how do I go about getting these kids to answer in complete sentences while I'm getting this child who's sitting in my Grade 4 and can only read at Grade 1 – what am I going to give this person to read, because I have to be there to read with her, but I also have to be there to help these children learn how to do this better than what they're doing.

Accountability to parents and administrators increased the sense of pressure for a number of teachers.

> Especially at this school, we have parents who are very demanding as to what kind of program their children are getting, how its being delivered, how the paper was marked, how the test was marked that you sent home – all kinds of things like that. So I find that you have to be very accountable to them as well as to the kids and to the administration too. So therefore it takes a lot of thinking through ahead of time too, as to how you're going to mark a paper or present something.

Accountability has also brought with it more paperwork – more accounting for what is being done, what has been done, and what is intended to be done, for the benefit of parents, administrators, and other audiences, as seen in the following statements of teachers:

> Fifteen years ago I didn't have paperwork. Fifteen years ago the paperwork I had, I created for myself . . .

> The paperwork we're getting I'd almost like to give it up. If I didn't enjoy it with the kids so much, I would . . . What the administration has asked us to do I don't think they have much choice in that either . . . We have to make plans for everything that we do . . . We spend so much time

sitting and writing out. Maybe that's the way we don't get ourselves into difficulty, I don't know. We have to do a lot of accounting for everything we do.

It's a lot different than 25 years ago. Paperwork has increased . . . the board's gone out with these pink forms in triplicate, class lists . . . I must spend 10 minutes each day.

I'm close to 20 years now and I find from the first year to now, the paperwork has increased.

They're forever – this year we've all said the same thing – this year seems to have been particularly bad for conferences and workshops. And they want you to attend this and they want you to attend that; there's this new program and that new program. At one point, we had so many things on our plate for the Grade 5s, we finally said 'Call a halt! Forget it!!! . . .' There was one week, I was out of the school more than I was in it!

There are people who love meetings. They live for those meetings. I live for a meeting if it's purposeful for me and if it's not, then the meeting is useless and I just cut them right off, which I have done.

These rising demands on and expectations of teachers certainly offer strong support for the intensification thesis, as does the combination of high expectations (e.g., individualized programming) with reduced support (e.g., reductions of in-class assistance).

TEACHER TIME AND PROFESSIONALISM

The high expectations and stringent demands that accompany elementary school teaching do not always clearly emanate from external sources. We observed that working hard was not simply a question of bowing reluctantly to outside pressure. Many of the demands and expectations in teaching seemed to come from within teachers themselves, and teachers appeared to drive themselves with almost merciless commitment in an attempt to meet the virtually unattainable standards of pedagogical perfection they set themselves. They did not appear to need direction or pressure from above to motivate them in their quest. They drove themselves quite hard enough.

Part of the reason for this phenomenon is to be found in the diffuse definitions and expectations that attach to teaching in Ontario and similar systems. Comparative studies of the teacher's role by Broadfoot and Osborn have indicated that in France, for instance, the teacher's role is defined tightly and clearly as being specifically concerned with academic learning and performance in school. Teachers there are consequently more certain about their role and more satisfied with their performance.[12] In other places, such as Great Britain and North America, the role is defined and perhaps increasingly being defined ever more widely, encompassing social and emotional goals as well as academic ones, concerns for the child's welfare at home as well as performance in school, and so on. Goals and expectations defined and understood in such diffuse terms become difficult, indeed impossible to meet with any certainty, yet dedicated elementary teachers strive hard to meet them. As Flinders puts it:

> More so than other occupations, teaching is an open-ended activity. If time and energy allowed, lesson plans could always be revised and improved, readings could always be reviewed again, more text material could always be covered before the end of the term, students could always be given more individual attention, and homework could always be graded with greater care.[13]

The teachers we interviewed talked a lot about their work in these terms. When describing their use of preparation time, they reeled off activity after activity, giving an urgent, frenetic sense of how densely packed, how compressed that time was. 'The time goes really fast,' said one. Others remarked that the list of what they do and what they can do 'just goes on and on!' 'Its endless.' 'You can always do more.' 'There are never enough hours in the day.' 'There's always something I could be doing because I am never finished.' In some cases, work became almost an obsession, threatening to overwhelm them. Some stayed late, until after 5:00, so they would not need to take their work and therefore their problems home with them. One had been counseled by his principal to ease up on the work and give more time to his personal life, to his leisure. Many, particularly women with families, spoke wistfully about having more time to themselves – 'time for me', as they put it.

Many dedicated teachers gave generously of their time and effort to their work, to the students in their charge. The majority took work home in the evenings. The extraordinary lengths to which their commitment stretched stands out in many individual cases. One teacher regularly stayed until six or seven o'clock, even in winter after the heat had been turned off. There was the teacher who spent over a $1,000 of her own money on materials and resources for her class. There was the teacher who came to work in his temporary classroom every Sunday and the teacher who came in on Saturday for several hours a month to sort out the staffroom bulletin boards. There was the single-parent teacher with a handicapped child who dashed home at the close of school, two days a week, to take her child for specialist help and then returned to cook supper, to read to both her children and put them to bed – finally taking out her schoolbooks to start all over again after eight or nine o'clock at night. There was the teacher who had been widowed young, had brought up her children alone, and had commonly worked from 9:00 until 11:00 or midnight after they were asleep – and who was only now, in her middle age, choosing to ease off a little, reduce her commitments somewhat as she felt she had 'paid her dues' in the past and now deserved the opportunity to develop a life with her new husband. There was the teacher who had shelves and bookcases at home packed with materials and resources that she had made and accumulated over the years. There was the teacher who spent his Sunday mornings compiling tests, quizzes, and worksheets on his word processor. There were the teachers who were taking additional qualifications in computers or visual arts or teacher librarianship; the teachers who coached sports teams and refereed House Leagues; the teachers who involved themselves with the choir or organized school charities. The list, as one of the teachers said, is endless.

The time and effort these teachers commit to their preparation and teaching comes not so much from grudging compliance with external demands as from dedication to doing a good job and providing effective care within a work context that is diffusely defined and has no clear criteria for successful completion.[14] This internally generated dedication in the context of a diffusely defined occupation seems to be grounded in what both Woods and Nias call professional and vocational commitments, commitments that are grounded in the kinds of meanings and purposes that teachers attach to their work.[15] It is churlish, and perhaps also theoretically imperialist, to dismiss these deeply held commitments and their consequences as merely belonging to a pattern of 'professionalism' that misrecognizes and legitimates the intensification of teachers' work.

In these patterns of commitment and care are to be found important modifications to the intensification thesis. The same cautions apply to the data reported here. In certain respects, intensification may be an important feature of the work of the teachers we studied, but this does not mean that all that passes for professionalism is but a ruse or a myth. Teachers' commitments and skills cannot be explained away quite that easily.

THE BENEFITS OF PREPARATION TIME

Against these tendencies toward increased workload and pressure, to which intensification has contributed significantly, the advent of preparation time has introduced a measure of compensation and easement.

Some teachers remarked that perhaps the public does not understand what teachers do with their preparation time, or how important it is to them, given the changing nature of the job. When asked if there was anything he would like to add at the end of the interview, one teacher ventured:

> The only thing that I was going to say was that – how much better it is for me now than it was. Receiving that prep time is really important. I know a lot of people – I think my mother-in-law for one of them – sort of wonder what I do during that time . . . I just think she really doesn't have any idea, because she's never in – (I don't say that meanly because . . . she knows that I have a lot of work to do) – but I think she wouldn't understand, and a lot of people wouldn't understand that it is really nice to have that time when they've been in the situation or know somebody who is.

Airing similar concerns about not being fully understood, another teacher commented: 'I just think it is very important for people to understand that . . . the job does not start at 8:40 in the morning and end at 3:30 . . . We have a lot a parent volunteers and they all say to us – but we had no idea how much you do!'

Teachers reported that increases in preparation time had conferred important benefits on the quality of their work in general and their instruction in particular. First, they pointed out that increased preparation time had been important in reducing stress. Second, it helped restore something to their lives outside teaching, enabling them to give a little more time to their families, to leisure, to themselves. Together, these two things helped improve teachers' temperament in the classroom, they argued, improving the quality of interaction they had with their classes. The following quotations give some sense of this commonly noticed relationship between stress, wider life circumstances, and classroom temperament.

> It [preparation time] eases the stresses of the job, because all of that planning or duplication would have to be done after school time when you have everybody in the school after the same machines, so you're not waiting your turn for something to become available to you.

> I feel that this year, I'm very much more relaxed. I don't get that same feeling of stress. For instance, having them first thing in the morning, if I've got something I particularly want for that day even, I have time to do it instead of coming in at 7:30, which for me is a real bonus not being an early morning person.

> I think [preparation time] is very vital, because if a teacher is too tired out, too tired and too overworked with homework you are not at your best when you are in contact with the children. Your nerves get a little short. Your children soon pick that up and it's not a good learning atmosphere. I think it's crucial to keep your mental and physical health, and having sufficient time to do the work that you have is a large component.

A third point is that in addition to relieving stress and creating space in other parts of the teacher's life – in addition to making existing work easier, that is – preparation time for many teachers also enables them to do things better. It enables them to be more organized, to be better prepared. For instance:

> I think I'm more organized, and the fact that if there is something that's coming up, I know that I have that time tomorrow to do it in, so that I can do it at that time, rather than staying after school or putting that time in after school, or doing it at a lunch time. I can do it during my prep time. It's nice.

> It's most invaluable. Phone calls. For example, you get busy lines and so on. If you're just trying to do it quickly in between classes, it's impossible. And little things like looking over your notes and seeing – looking through my files and seeing what activities I can use to help this group of kids who are having difficulty. Those are invaluable. You just don't have the classroom time to sit down and say 'Wait' to the kids while you try to find a file for somebody that evening. You just cannot use the time enough.

Preparation time, according to some teachers, also allowed them to do more things, to take on a wider range of activities than they had before. Before preparation time, said one, 'I didn't do as much. I didn't run as many House Leagues. I wasn't involved with as many activities after school because I was just so busy doing all these other things. So I think the preparation time made me a more efficient person during the day. I can get more done between 8:00 and 4:00 than I could before.'

For a number of teachers, the benefits of preparation time were to be found not in time for extracurricular activities, but in the extra investments they could make in the business of instruction within their own classes. For these teachers, preparation time helped them improve the inventiveness and appropriateness of their pedagogy. They were more able to make games to teach an idea rather than 'give a child a piece of paper to write, push a pencil around on'. Many teachers also talked about marking, about how preparation time helped them evaluate students' work more effectively.

> I don't feel I have to do quite as much rushing at lunch hour to get materials ready and get work marked. I like to mark my work at school so I don't carry big bundles of books home, for one thing. And it's nice to mark it as soon after the kids have done it as possible, so they can see what their mistakes are. If it hangs on for a day or two, it is not as effective.

> I feel it's crucial to have the children's work marked as soon as it's done. I get it back to them as soon as possible, because if you leave it two or three days – 'what's this?' It's like a week old to children.

Preparation time can be seen as a way of providing teachers with working conditions that are designed to help them catch up with the diversification and changing requirements of the job. Certainly, many teachers spoke vividly about the changes in their work and were unequivocal in their praise of preparation time as a way of helping them cope more effectively with these changes. Preparation time here seems like a clear gain for teachers – a counter to the process of intensification. This is certainly how Ontario teachers' organizations involved in collective bargaining viewed the issue of preparation time when it was in dispute. According to the president of the Ontario Public School Teachers' Federation, 'quality education for our children and teachers is what is at issue and, without guarantees of adequate preparation time, that *can't* be obtained'.[16] The president of the Federation of Women Teachers of Ontario affirmed this view when she said: 'Until we have a serious proposal [on preparation time] that addresses these needs of children, we're at a state of impasse because we as teachers care about the students we teach and we're not about to throw in the towel and give up on the students.'[17]

THE PERVERSITIES OF PREPARATION TIME

Preparation time, it seems, can alleviate stress and increase the opportunities for relaxation. It helps reduce chronic work overload and leads to opportunities for the planning and preparation of more creative work. In these respects, preparation time helps counter the effects of intensification. It may even help reverse the spiral. The very existence of preparation time, in fact, constitutes a major challenge to the intensification process. Still, the long-called-for introduction of increased preparation time for elementary teachers does not reverse all the effects of intensification and can to some extent be absorbed by them. The preparation-time study revealed four ways in which such additional time did not always lead to restrictions of the intensification process.

First, increased preparation time did not necessarily enhance the processes of association, community, and collegiality among teachers. Time itself was not a sufficient condition for collegiality and community. As I have documented elsewhere, unless there was a commitment to collaborative working relationships at the level of school or school district leadership, preparation time became absorbed by the deep-seated culture of individualism and classroom-centeredness that has become historically and institutionally ingrained in the prevailing patterns of teachers' work.[18]

The immediacy of the classroom, its centrality within the teacher's world and the multiple demands it placed upon the teacher for diversified programming and preparation that would be rationally accountable to others, made most teachers predominantly classroom-focused and classroom-centered in their actions, their thoughts, and their preferences. They were practical and classroom-focused inside their own classrooms, but in many respects outside their classrooms too, concentrating their energies on what would best and most immediately benefit their own students: preparing materials, ordering resources, marking promptly, and so forth.

Flinders remarks that 'isolation is an adaptive strategy because it protects the time and energy required to meet immediate instructional demands.'[19] The same can be said of teachers' individualistic uses of preparation time. Indeed, even within one of the boards where there was a systemwide commitment to collaborative planning, a number of teachers referred to preparation time not scheduled for consultation with colleagues as 'my time', as time they could use directly for the benefit of their own students. Preparation time was considered too precious and too scarce to fritter away on activities like relaxation or casual conversation with colleagues. These things were more likely to take place at recess. Hardly any teachers stated that they used preparation time for relaxation. There was simply no time for this. There were too many things to do. As one teacher put it: 'If you make the mistake of getting into a conversation with somebody, then [the prep time is] done.' Preparation time, therefore, did not automatically assist the process of association between teachers and their colleagues.

A second, somewhat perverse consequence of preparation time was that an important minority of the teachers interviewed stated that, while they appreciated the preparation time they now received, they probably did not want the further amounts for which their federations were fighting in order to move closer to the working conditions of high school teachers. What was at stake for these teachers was the continuity of the relationship they felt they needed with their classes and the quality of care that relationship would enable them to provide. The ethic of care was a powerful source of motivation and direction for these teachers – not surprisingly, given the importance of care as a key reason among elementary teachers for entering teaching, and given its pervasiveness as a central moral principle among women more generally.[20]

Ironically, while preparation time to a certain extent assisted a process of disintensification in elementary teachers' work, there appeared, for some teachers, to be a point where the law of diminishing returns set in – where further additions to preparation time *reduced* rather than *enhanced* the quality of classroom service provided, because this drew teachers away from their classrooms too much. The data supporting these observations have been reported extensively elsewhere,[21] but the words of two teachers capture the prevailing sentiments here:

> I don't think I would like to be away from them too much more, unless it's the same teacher. Even the one teacher that does come in, unless I specifically state what I want, the children don't work as well for her as they do for me.

> I think when they're talking about prep time – I had a letter put in my mailbox the other day and apparently there's some elementary teachers that are in quite a flap, because they are teaching ten minutes longer than the senior school teachers who are teaching [Grades] 7 and 8. And they want this justified. They want that time. And I'm thinking: 'What are you here for? Teaching the kids, or trying to find out how much time they don't have to teach them?'

A third teacher summed up the fundamental dilemma and the way she chose to resolve it: 'I wonder if I had much time away if I would feel I was losing something with the kids.'

These remarks reveal a classroom commitment to quality of care, a professional and vocational commitment that cannot be summarily dismissed as a 'misrecognition' of trends toward intensification in the labor process of teaching. On the contrary, these teachers recognize that there is a point at which it is not so much intensification as disintensification that threatens the quality of service they can provide. For these teachers, concerns about the quality of care superseded ones about the costs of time even when opportunities to improve the latter were available.

A third perversity of preparation time is to be found in the preferred arrangements for preparation-time cover. Teachers we interviewed preferred what can be called *segregated* cover arrangements, in which a colleague comes in and teaches a self-contained specialty for which he or she holds complete responsibility. *Integrated* cover, in which what is taught in preparation time forms part of a wider class program for which responsibility is shared to some degree between the class teacher and the covering teacher, was viewed much less positively. There were several reasons for this.

First, segregated cover saved time. A self-contained program required no prior preparation by the classroom teacher and no consultation with the covering teacher. It was the covering teacher's sole responsibility. In these conditions, there was no need to prepare for preparation time itself.

Second, some teachers had concerns about shared rather than personal accountability. They were worried they might not be able to provide a good or a reliable account if they shared responsibility for an 'important' subject with a covering colleague. As one teacher put it, 'One of my things that is a pet peeve is that when I talk to a parent I want to know that what I'm telling them is something I've seen with my own eyes, that I know is a truth and I've seen it. If I'm not there, I don't feel that I can comment on that, even though I've had feedback from the person [the covering teacher].'

Closely related to these concerns about accountability were those about expertise, which preparation time exposed. One principal put it like this: 'Primary teachers feel OK about handing their kids . . . across to somebody who they know can teach particular things better than they can. But what they already know they themselves can teach well, then it's trickier . . . We will all be better served,' he said, if we can provide teachers 'with a sense of comfort and satisfaction that what's going on back there (in their classes) is good and valuable.' 'We don't feel discomfort,' he went on, 'sending somebody off to French. It's just not there because its assumed competence. And it's assumed incompetence on my part if I send my kids to you.' Therefore, he argued, preparation time is best covered through specialist subjects like music, which are 'highly visible, highly valuable'.

This was certainly the preferred arrangement for preparation-time cover among teachers. They readily acknowledged the specialist expertise of particular colleagues who could teach a specialty better than they could, and they recognized the value of giving students access to this greater competence. Through exchanges of expertise, the clumsy could ensure their students had access to good quality physical education. Groaning male baritones could secure better quality teaching in singing and in music more generally. The teacher trying to improve her own visual arts expertise by upgrading her qualifications in the area could meanwhile have this part of the curriculum taught by another specialist during preparation time. Sharing classes where both teachers' expertise in the chosen subject was adequate or strong, however, exposed differences, and raised doubts about whose expertise might be weaker – doubts that teachers preferred to keep suppressed.

These problems of accountability and expertise that were exposed by the administration of preparation time sometimes led to a situation in which covering teachers who were responsible for sharing 'important' subjects like mathematics with the class teacher were assigned routine drills of a safe, self-contained nature. This did little for the quality of classroom instruction. More usually, as I noted earlier, teachers searched hard for subjects they disliked or in which they were weak, which colleagues could cover. Where expertise in the covering subject was strong, this arrangement appeared to work well. The separation of powers between the classroom teacher and the covering teacher was counterbalanced by a collegial respect for complementary subject expertise. But where expertise in the covering subject was weak, the segregated pattern of cover appeared to undermine rather than enhance the quality of instruction. In some cases, this was not perceived as a problem. Of a teacher covering for physical education, for example, it was said that the program guidelines were clear. 'It was all set up' and needed no extra preparation. Yet one wonders how such apparently slavish following of written guidelines would affect the quality of instruction. Interestingly, Apple[22] attributes such patterns of teacher dependency and technical control to the processes of intensification in teachers' work. In the context of preparation time, however, such patterns, and the shortfalls in quality that result from them, appear to come from seemingly contrary processes of disintensification.

A case of cover in health education serves as a striking example. The classroom teacher was eager for this area of the programme to be covered. It was self-contained, and in a French-immersion system, where she was involved with only half the program anyway (the other half being taught by the French teacher), finding such self-contained areas for cover was not easy.[23]

> I wanted to give the Health, because that's a whole subject in itself and it works very well into a short time period. Health lessons can be presented and completed in a 40 minute period.

Against the advantages of its being clearly bounded, though, problems arose with selecting this subject as one to be covered. For one thing, there was an apparent overreliance on published guidelines.

> There is a Junior Health Course, and most topics such as dental health, disease, whatever, are presented in Grades 4, 5 and 6, but the objectives change somewhat for each age level, although there is a fair bit of overlap. I gave them [the covering teachers] sections out of the core and I asked them to be responsible in presenting it to the kids.

In a split-grade class, especially where the teacher was strongly dependent on published guidelines, there were also serious difficulties in programming appropriately for each part of the split.

> She tries to cover it with one class. She takes the same core and she will take, depending on the unit and how delicate it is, she might take the objectives from the Grade 6 core or the Grade 5 core and try and blend them a bit. So that's probably the hardest.

In particular, avoiding duplication of the program from one year to the next with split-grade students was something achieved more by accident than design:

> The topics are the same [between grades]. It would probably be a different teacher and . . . for example, there's an objective at the top of the page and there are several different ways of attaining that objective. So the chances of them choosing those same activities to meet these same ends are quite low. So they might say to themselves – 'sounds familiar' –

but they won't be doing the same thing, and they'll be a year older and they'll be looking at it from a different perspective.

This teacher concluded, 'It's not the ideal situation' – especially, one might add, where subjects like health education address important social and emotional goals and depend on close, continuous, open, and trusting relationships between teachers and their students. Again, the perversity of preparation time is that in some cases it can lead not to improvement but to deterioration in the quality of service offered to students, and to deskilling rather than reskilling of the teachers involved.

The fourth perversity of preparation time is that while its absence inhibits association among teachers, its presence by no means guarantees such association. More than this, the kinds of association that are created in the spaces afforded by preparation time may not always be those that enhance teacher development and empowerment. Elsewhere, I have provided extensive data to show that in terms of increased association among teachers, preparation time can help create or reinforce *either* collaborative cultures *or* contrived collegiality in the school community.[24] *Collaborative cultures* are a relatively rare occurrence. They comprise more spontaneous, informal, and pervasive collaborative working relationships among teachers that are both social and task-centered in nature. They involve teachers' having high responsibility to develop things themselves as a community, the outcomes of which may be relatively unpredictable from the point of view of school and system leadership. And they entail forms of leadership that support and facilitate these collaborations on an ongoing basis, rather than controlling and constraining them. In conditions of *contrived collegiality*, teachers are scheduled and required to meet with their colleagues for administratively determined purposes such as liaising regularly with the special-education resource teacher, or engaging in joint planning of new units of work with grade partners. The purpose of collaboration here is less that of evolutionary teacher development than of implementing systems initiatives or the principal's preferred programs. Contrived collegiality is more controlled, regulated, and predictable in its outcomes. In the study reviewed here, it constituted the dominant pattern of teacher collaboration in the context of preparation time.

More important than the existence of teacher collaboration and collegiality, then, is its meaning. From the point of view of preparation time, a particular concern is that many teachers and their federations may be at risk of becoming trapped in a Faustian bargain in which, for the worldly riches of 'extra time', they ultimately trade something of their professional souls – their control and discretion over how such time is to be organized and used.[25]

CONCLUSION

What have we learned from this investigation of teacher preparation time and its relationship to the intensification thesis?

First, many of the recent changes that teachers described as occurring in their work are highly compatible with the intensification thesis and offer considerable support for it. Heightened expectations, broader demands, increased accountability, more 'social work' responsibilities, more meetings, multiple innovations, increased amounts of administrative work – all are testimony to the problems of chronic work overload documented in the thesis. Pressure, stress, no time to relax, no time even to talk to colleagues – these are effects that teachers mentioned that again are highly consonant with those of the intensification process. Particularly before the advent of preparation time, many aspects of intensification appear to have been at work in the labor process of teaching, even in what was, at the time of the study, a materially favored provincial environment.

There are some qualifications to make to this finding, of course. First, the time scale over which teachers reported changes that were consonant with intensification is a relatively short one of only five or ten years. Evidence over longer time scales is not available in this study, and even when it is inferred from other historical work, it is not always convincingly supportive. For instance, many studies of teaching in the nineteenth century indicate that in quantitative terms, teaching may have been just as hard and demanding as it is now. In qualitative terms, it may also have been less rather than more skilled.[26] Certainly, as Densmore acknowledges, claims and inferences that intensification is part of a long, linear process of degradation in teachers' work are difficult to support through longer-term historical study. The appropriate time scale for intensification and its validity claims therefore remains a matter of open debate.[27]

Second, the data of this study are reported and retrospective evidence rather than evidence collected longitudinally. Given that such evidence comes from retrospective accounts of individuals, it is also difficult to disentangle *historical* changes in the labor process from *biographical* changes in the life and career cycles of teachers over time, when maturation may bring more responsibilities, or declining physical powers a sense of reduced capacity to cope.[28]

Third, intensification may not impact on all teachers in the same way. It may be felt particularly keenly by those teachers who are, because of their own commitments or work circumstances (e.g. full-time rather than part-time), rather more work-centered than their colleagues,[29] and it may be felt less keenly by others.

Fourth, this evidence suggests that by no means all instances of broadened commitment and heightened professionalism can be explained in terms of the intensification of the labor process, or as misrecognition of that process.[30] Professional commitments to improving the quality of service for clients are often real ones, pursued by teachers themselves in a social context of growing complexity and challenge. These commitments extend far beyond processes structured to extract increased productivity from teachers' work. They are not exclusively reducible to labor process factors.

These four qualifications do not disconfirm the intensification thesis, but they do raise doubts about its scope and singularity as an explanation of changes in teachers' work, suggesting that further inquiry is needed in which other theories and perspectives in addition to those concerned with the nature of the labor process may need to be acknowledged as important for our understanding.

The second broad lesson we have learned concerns the potential of preparation time to alleviate many of the problems of intensification, and even to create some elements of disintensification. Preparation time has fulfilled some of its promise. Shortage of time to do and develop things that would enrich their work is a common complaint of teachers and is a key component of the intensification process. Teachers, in the preparation-time study saw the provision of such time as relieving stress, giving them back a personal life, allowing them to 'do more', to contribute more to extracurricular activities, and to improve the quality of their planning and instruction. If only in the short term (for we have no longer-term evidence), increased preparation time really does appear to help disintensify teaching and to help improve some of the quality of service teachers provide. Its introduction is more than merely cosmetic. In both professional and collective-bargaining terms, the benefits it confers appear to be real and worth fighting for.

But preparation time is no panacea. It issues no guarantees. It offers only opportunities. Preparation time can be used for purposes other than those intended, and the organizational contingencies surrounding its implementation can yield a range of unintended consequences that cannot easily be explained within the parameters of labor process theory. Preparation time, that is, has its perversities as well as its potentials. This is the third lesson we have learned from the study.

Beyond a certain point, increases in preparation time reduced rather than improved the quality of service provided to students, as teachers were drawn more and more away from their own classes into other areas of work. Handing over compartmentalized pieces of the programme to covering teachers could also create dependency on published guidelines and subject teachers to those very patterns of technical control that proponents of the intensification thesis ironically attribute to the absence of preparation time, not to its presence.

Last, when preparation time was used in the context of mandated or *contrived collegiality* and collaborative planning, this could create a proliferation of meetings and additional work that intensified teachers' work still further and subjected them to administrative control instead of releasing them to develop things themselves.

These perversities point to the unanticipated ironies of complex bureaucratic systems that hold within them only yet more problems for every new solution that is offered. The unintended system consequences of French-immersion programming, split-grade responsibilities, local distributions of expertise, and the like are important, are not easily predicted, and are not reducible to labor process explanations. In addition to the unanticipated consequences of preparation time, we have seen that this promising if perverse innovation can also itself serve as new terrain for traditional struggles for control between administration and teachers and between bureaucracy and professionalism more generally. In this sense, struggles surrounding preparation time and the Faustian bargains that are at stake within them may not so much solve the problems of intensification as displace the conflicts over intensification and the control of teachers' work to other levels and sites.

Preparation time can seem and has seemed an easy solution to the problems of intensification and change. Perhaps the confidence expressed in the solution of increased teacher time away from class has to some extent been a result of the perceived unlikelihood of its implementation. Sometimes, our problems really begin only when our wishes come true. This article has shown that intensification is a real and serious problem for teachers and their work. It explains many of the changes we are witnessing in teachers' work. But intensification and labor process theories more generally do not fully explain what is happening in teachers' work. Our understanding of such work cannot be reduced to labor process theory. While time as an antidote to intensification can provide some of the solutions to the problems of teacher development and teachers' work, it can be a source of further problems as well. Reform is often guided by the belief that every problem has a solution. Perhaps the real challenge of reform as a continuous process, though, is acknowledging that every solution has a problem. In this sense, intensification is an important, but not the only, source of problems with teachers' work, and preparation time is only partly a solution to it. Sincere commitments of a professional and vocational nature among teachers that amount to more than ideological misrecognition, the increasingly complex nature of society in the postmodern age and the necessarily widening demands it places on education and educators, the complexities and unanticipated consequences of large bureaucracies, and the displacement of struggles about intensification to new sites even when time has been provided as an antidote to it – these things too must be considered.

NOTES

This article was first presented at the annual conference of the American Educational Research Association, San Francisco, April 1992.

1. On curriculum development, see R. J. Campbell, *Developing the Primary School Curriculum* (London: Cassell, 1983) and J. Nias, G. Southworth, and R. Yeomans, *Whole School Curriculum Development* (London: Falmer Press, 1992); on support and growth, see J. Nias, G. Southworth, and R. Yeomans, *Staff Relationships in the Primary School* (London: Cassell, 1989) and Ann Lieberman, and Lynne Miller, 'Teacher Development in Professional Practice and School', *Teachers College Record* 92 (1990): 105–22; on teacher leadership, see M. Fullan, with S. Stiegelbauer, *The New Meaning of Educational Change* (New York: Teachers College Press and Toronto: OISE Press, 1991); on commitment to improvement, see S. Rosenholtz, *Teachers' Workplace: The Social Organization of Schools* (New York: Longman, 1989); on schoolwide change, see Ann Lieberman, Linda Darling-Hammond, and David Zuckerman, *Early Lessons in Restructuring Schools* (New York: National Center for Restructuring Education, Schools, and Teaching, 1991).

2. E. Hoyle, 'The Study of Schools as Organizations,' in *Management in Education, Reader 1*, ed. R. McHugh and C. Morgan (London: Ward Lock, 1975); Nias, South-worth, and Yeomans, *Staff Relationships*; and R. Barth, *Improving Schools from Within: Teachers, Parents and Principals Can Make a Difference* (San Francisco: Jossey-Bass, 1990).

3. See Michael Apple, *Teachers & Texts: A Political Economy of Class & General Relationship* (New York: Routledge & Kegan Paul, 1989); idem and S. Jungck, 'You Don't Have to Be a Teacher to Teach This Unit: Teaching, Technology and Control in the Classroom,' in *Understanding Teacher Development*, ed. A. Hargreaves and M. Fullan (London: Cassell, and New York: Teachers College Press, 1992); and K. Dens-more, 'Professionalism, Proletarianization and Teachers' Work,' in *Critical Studies in Teacher Education*, ed. T. Popkewitz (Lewes: Falmer Press, 1987).

4. T. Popkewitz and K. Lind, 'Teacher Incentives as Reforms: Teachers' Work and the Changing Control Mechanisms in Education,' *Teachers College Record* 90 (1989): 575–94.

5. S. M. Larson, 'Proletarianization and Educated Labour,' *Theory and Society* 9 (1980): 131–75, quotations are from pp. 165 and 166.

6. See, for instance, Apple, *Teachers & Text*; and idem and Jungck, 'You Don't Have to Be a Teacher to Teach This Unit'.

7. Apple and Jungck, 'You Don't Have to Be a Teacher to Teach This Unit'.

8. Ibid., p. 54.

9. Apple, *Teachers & Texts*, p. 45; see also Popkewitz and Lind, 'Teacher Incentives as Reforms'.

10. Densmore, 'Professionalism, Proletarianization and Teachers' Work,' pp. 148–49.

11. A. Hargreaves and R. Wignall, *Time for the Teacher: A Study of Collegial Relations and Preparation Time Use among Elementary School Teachers* (Final report of a project funded under Transfer Grant 51/1070, Toronto: Ontario Institute for Studies in Education, 1989).

12. P. Broadfoot and M. Osborn, 'What Professional Responsibility Means to Teachers: National Contexts and Classroom Constraints,' *British Journal of Sociology of Education* 9 (1988): 265–87.

13. D. J. Flinders, 'Teacher Isolation and the New Reform,' *Journal of Curriculum and Supervision* 14 (Fall 1988): 23.

14. For a more extended account of teachers' and administrators' subjective and micropolitical perspectives of time, see A. Hargreaves, 'Teachers' Work and the Politics of Time and Space,' *Qualitative Studies in Education* 3 (1990): 303–20.

15. P. Woods, *Sociology and the School* (London: Routledge & Kegan Paul, 1985); and J. Nias, *Primary Teachers Talking* (London: Routledge & Kegan Paul, 1989).

16. Quoted in *The Toronto Star*, September 24, 1987.

17. Quoted in *The Toronto Star*, September 27, 1987.

18. A. Hargreaves, 'Individualism and Individuality: Reinterpreting the Culture of Teaching,' *International Journal of Educational Research* (forthcoming; idem, *Changing Teachers, Changing Times* (New York: Teachers College Press, forthcoming).

19. Flinders, 'Teacher Isolation and the New Reforms', p. 25.

20. See Hargreaves, 'Individualism and Individuality'; and J. Neufeld, 'Curriculum Reform and the Time of Care,' *Curriculum Journal* 3 (forthcoming).

21. These and similar data are discussed more extensively in Hargreaves, 'Individualism and individuality'.

22. Apple, *Teachers & Texts*.

23. For readers unfamiliar with the Canadian educational system, in French-immersion schools, many or all subjects are taught in French, the chosen language of instruction but not the first language of the students. In many such schools, the program may be divided into two groups of subjects, one set of which will be taught in English, and the other set in French.

24. See A. Hargreaves, 'Contrived Collegiality: The Micropolitics of Teacher Collaboration,' in *The Politics of Life in Schools*, ed. J. Blase (New York: Sage, 1991).

25. See Hargreaves, 'Teachers' Work and the Politics of Time and Space.'

26. See, for example, B. Curtis, *Building the Educational State: Canada West* (Philadelphia: Falmer Press, 1989); G. Tomkins, *A Common Countenance: Stability and Change in the Canadian Curriculum* (Scarborough, Ontario: Prentice-Hall, Canada, 1986); and A. Prentice, 'From Household to School House: The Emergence of the Teacher as Servant of the State,' *Material History Bulletin* 20 (1984): 19–29.

27. Densmore, 'Professionalism, Proletarianism and Teachers' Work.'

28. On such career cycle issues, see M. Huberman, 'Teacher Development and Instructional Mastery,' in *Understanding Teacher Development*, ed. Hargreaves and Fullan.

29. See P. Poppleton and G. Riseborough, 'Teaching in the Mid-1980s: The Centrality of Work in Secondary Teachers' Lives,' *British Educational Research Journal* 16 (1990): 105–24.

30. See also S. Acker, 'Teachers' Culture in an English Primary School: Continuity and Change,' *British Journal of Sociology of Education* 11 (1990): 270.

PART 2:

Quantitative examples

5

PUBLISH AND BE DAMNED? THE PROBLEMS OF COMPARING EXAM RESULTS IN TWO INNER LONDON SCHOOLS

J. Gray

By the autumn of 1982 schools up and down the country will have had the experience of exposing their examination results to public scrutiny in order to satisfy the requirements of the 1980 Education Act. If the fears, widely expressed during the earlier debates about this proposal, prove right 'league tables' of schools' results will follow shortly afterwards and ambitious parents, making full use of their newly available option to choose the school they wish their child to attend, will begin to respond by pressing for admission to the 'better' schools. Whilst such fears may well be exaggerated, there can be little doubt that the systematic publication of examination data in a summary and rather rudimentary form offers a new dimension to political demands for a greater measure of school accountability.

There is a danger that many will interpret such evidence as straightforward measures of schools' performance or effectiveness. In this article I shall seek to show that public evaluation of schools' examination results has usually been conducted at too simplistic a level; that such evaluations could be placed on a firmer footing; but also that there is an urgent need to improve the framework of public knowledge about schools' performance, if inappropriate conclusions about their effectiveness in relation to examination results are to be avoided.

For this purpose I have chosen to concentrate on a comparison of two Inner London secondary schools whose results have been the subject of recent public controversy. The detailed study of these two schools forcibly underlines the present 'state-of-the-art' as regards public evaluation of what to expect from schools by way of examination results. The case is instructive because, whilst it leaves much to be desired, it represents one of the most sophisticated debates to have taken place publicly on this topic to date.

SCHOOLS AND PERSONALITIES

Highbury Grove Comprehensive in Islington was formed from an amalgama-
tion of three schools in 1967. One of these three had had a grammar school
tradition. With some 1300 boys on roll it had rarely been out of the public eye
during the seventies because of the claims made on its behalf by its former
headmaster, Dr Rhodes Boyson, Minister of State for Education (Boyson,
1974). In the late seventies it was being threatened with closure as a result of
the need to 'rationalize' provision brought about by falling rolls within Inner
London generally and Islington in particular. Not surprisingly in these circumstances, and given its previous record of publishing its results, the present head,
Lawrence Norcross, rose to his school's defence and released its 1979 examination results. He would scarcely have done so, one imagines, if he had not
believed them to be 'good' but, of course, quality in this context is relative; it
depends which other schools are brought into the comparison.

   The school with which the Fleet Street press compared Highbury Grove's
results was nearby Islington Green, a smaller mixed comprehensive of some
800 pupils, which had previously acquired something of a reputation as a
'sink' school. Its headteacher, Margaret Maden, had also received a good deal
of media attention, partly because of the work she was doing and her personality but also because, one suspects, she was, as the *Daily Telegraph* put it, 'a
well-known young member of the Communist party in the 1960's [who] be-
lieves in progressive teaching methods'. Intriguingly, as the *Telegraph* had
earlier revealed, although not on this occasion, Norcross too had confessed to
a 'misspent youth' in the party. Whilst the backgrounds of the two heads add
political colour to the media's presentation of the controversy, however, they
add little to the evaluation of the two schools' examination results with which
this article is concerned.

ROUND ONE: QUOTING 'RAW' RESULTS

The first shot in this debate was fired in the *Daily Telegraph* by Anthony
Doran, its Education Correspondent, who was following up a story which had
just broken in London's *Evening Standard*. Doran wrote:

> At O-level, 800 pupil Islington Green had 22 passes in grades A to C last
> summer whilst Highbury Grove, which has 1500 pupils, gained 10 times
> as many with 220.
>   At A-level Islington Green pupils achieved two passes, both at 'E'
> grade, while Highbury Grove gained 40. (*Daily Telegraph*, 6 November
> 1979, p. 2)

The comparisons, at this point, have considerable impact. Highbury Grove, it
is suggested, is doing ten times better at O-level and 20 times better at A-level.
This impression is indirectly reinforced by the comments Margaret Maden,

Islington Green's head, is reported as having made about her own school's performance:

> We are getting better results all the time. Last year some fourth-formers got good results in Maths, Music and French in the GCE O-levels. I think there were four passes in Maths, three in Music and five in French.
> Our CSE results are six per cent higher than the London norm.
> (*Daily Telegraph*, 6 November 1979)

Although these may well have been 'better results' they are unlikely to have carried much weight with readers in the context of the figures already presented; if there were four passes in maths and this was 'good', the sceptical reader might ask how many were there previously? The small numbers of passes in the individual subjects seem to underline the apparent paucity of 'success' of O-levels.

ROUND TWO: TAKING ACCOUNT OF INTAKES

The counter-blast to the *Telegraph*'s interpretation came about a fortnight later from the editor of the *New Statesman*, Bruce Page. 'Declaring an interest' as husband of the chairman of governors at Islington Green, he argued that it didn't make sense to compare the schools' results without relating them to the stage at which the examinations were taken (fifth-year or lower-sixth resits) and, more importantly, the quite considerable differences in intakes to the two schools. One should, in other words, be concentrating on the *progress* children had made whilst at secondary school rather than the standards they had eventually achieved. He wrote:

> Gleeful (Telegraph) comparisons were made between fifth-year results for Highbury Grove and Islington Green: allegedly 220 O-levels against 22. This was dud reporting indeed, for it compared Highbury's total for O-level and CSE-1 (equivalents) to Islington Green's simple O-level total. And it included second-try passes in the Highbury total against Islington's strict fifth-year passes.
> Highbury Grove's true fifth-year score for combined O/CSE-1 was 189, a decent performance, for on ILEA's rule-of-thumb a school should score five O/CSE-1's for each Band 1 entrant. In the relevant year, Highbury had 31 Band 1's (in 240) so might have expected only 155 passes. But Islington Green in that year had only *two* Band 1 children, so on rule-of-thumb it would only have expected about 10 O/CSE-1 passes. *In fact, 62 passes were achieved.* (*New Statesman*, 16 November, 1979, p. 757)

As the italicized original demonstrates, the introduction of the so-called 'rule-of-thumb' brings about a dramatic reversal. Highbury Grove averages just over six passes per Band 1 pupil whilst Islington Green apparently manages a massive 31. The article failed to expand on the assumptions built into the production of this unlikely figure and, at this point anyway, the story had faded from Fleet Street's attention.

ROUND THREE: MORE FIGURES

It was revived some 15 months later in *The Times Educational Supplement* by Maurice Kogan in the context of a full-page article on the media's treatment of educational issues; the only case discussed, however, was Islington Green's not-too-distant experiences. Kogan also had an interest; he was vice-chairman of Islington Green's governors, Professor of Government at Brunel University and previously a senior civil servant at the Department of Education and Science. He quoted at some length an interpretation of the results provided by Peter Wilby, Education Correspondent of *The Sunday Times*, who had been working on the story around the time of the *New Statesman*'s article but whose report had missed his paper's edition owing to production difficulties. Kogan reported:

> In 1979 Highbury Grove had 31 children with Group 1 gradings and Islington Green had two in the fifth year. The top 31 children at High-bury Grove accounted for a total of 141 O-level passes. This is an average of a little under five. Islington Green's two top pupils accounted for 14 passes. This is an average of seven. 209 pupils assumed to be Bands 2 and 3 at Highbury Grove got 48 passes; 123 pupils at Islington Green got 48 passes. With both able and less able pupils Islington Green did better, although of course these figures are so small as to be statistically pretty meaningless. Yet reporters attacked the school as being academically poor. (*The Times Educational Supplement*, 30 January 1981, p. 4)

Kogan continued:

> Such journalists have been remarkably silent on the subject of standards at Islington Green lately. *In 1980 the O-level and CSE results improved to a level commensurate with the balance of the intake.* I am told that a reasonable rule of thumb is that each pupil with Group 1 gradings might be expected to get an average of five GCE O-level passes in grades A to C. The 20 pupils who had had Group 1 gradings scored 120 A to C's between them, an average of six. (*ibid.*; my emphasis)

If one is trying to achieve, as Kogan probably was, some public re-assessment of Islington Green's overall standards, then the information provided here is important. The school had nearly doubled its total from 62 O-level/CSE grade 1 equivalents to 120, but then it had also increased its intake of Band 1 pupils. Kogan's assessment that they had 'improved to a level commensurate with the balance of the intake' seems odd in terms of the 'rule-of-thumb' he offers. I shall return to the question of whether the 'rule-of-thumb' is itself appropriate at a later point but, purely in terms of the argument Kogan presents, Islington Green's results had, in fact, declined. In 1979 two Band 1 pupils averaged *seven* passes each; in 1980 twenty Band 1 pupils averaged *six*. These figures, along with those comparing Islington Green's 1979 results for Band 1 pupils with ostensibly similar pupils at Highbury Grove, are, contrary to what Kogan asserts, entirely *meaningful*, always assuming that they are correct, something that Norcross subsequently questioned, and that like was being compared with like as regards pupils given the 'Band 1' label. The figures are small because the numbers of pupils in Band 1 in each school were small; they were, in other words, the populations of pupils in each of the two schools for that year. They do not, of course, provide a *statistically* sound basis for generalizing about the overall superiority of one school's results when compared with the other's for Band 1 pupils in general nor, given that they made up such relatively small proportions of the cohorts in each school, of the overall efforts of the two schools on behalf of *all* their pupils.

ROUND FOUR: ARGUING ABOUT FIGURES AND INTERPRETATIONS

Kogan's complaints brought a reply from Norcross to correct the 'misrepresentation of [his] school and its intake':

> Our total of O-level and CSE grade 1 passes for June 1979 was 248 (220 O-level plus 28 CSE). Of these, 193 (167 O-level plus 26 CSE) were awarded to fifth year pupils. With a band one (i.e. top 25 per cent of the ability range) intake of 31 pupils for that year – some of whom had emigrated by June 1979 – that would seem to make an average of over six for each band one pupil (with the true figure nearer to seven, not 'a little under five' as Professor Kogan claims). Not all of these passes were obtained by band one pupils, of course; neither were all of the 572 CSE passes obtained by band two pupils. Furthermore, we did not have 240 (Professor Kogan's 31 plus 209) fifth year pupils here by June 1979. (*The Times Educational Supplement*, 13 February, 1981)

Norcross, like Kogan, went on to provide the 1980 results for his school:

> In 1980, we obtained a total of 296 O-levels and CSE grade one passes (260 plus 36) of which 233 (197 plus 36) were awarded to fifth year pupils. Our band one 'quota' for that year was 25, some of whom again had left by June 1980, giving us an average of over nine . . . Our CSE results improved too. (*ibid.*)

Norcross, in his reply to Kogan was, in fact, employing the same basis for his calculations as Page had earlier done on Islington Green's behalf, namely, to take the total number of O-level or CSE grade 1 equivalent passes obtained by *all* pupils in the school and divide them by the number of Band 1 pupils. This procedure, it will be remembered, had produced an average of 31 passes for each of Islington Green's two Band 1 pupils. Kogan's figure, in contrast, was produced by a procedure which Peter Wilby of *The Sunday Times* was subsequently to explain:

My figures were: 193 O-level and equivalent passes for Highbury Grove's fifth form, 62 for Islington Green's. In 1974, when these year groups entered the schools, Highbury Grove recruited 31 band one pupils and Islington Green just two.

It was not likely, of course, that all these same pupils were still at the schools in 1979. But nor was it likely that the ability profiles had changed significantly. So, assuming them to be band one children, I looked at the 31 who did *best* in Highbury Grove's 1979 exams. They accounted for 141 passes, an average of just under five. The best two at Islington Green got 14 passes, an average of seven.

I assumed that the remaining fifth year pupils (123 at Islington Green and 209 at Highbury Grove, *including Easter leavers*) were bands two and three and that the remaining passes (48 and 52) were obtained by them, giving averages of 0.4 and 0.25.

Thus, say I triumphantly . . . Islington Green did better than Highbury Grove on all counts. (*The Times Educational Supplement*, 20 February 1981)

Norcross made one further rejoinder, commenting:

I am conscious of misleading Mr Wilby in one particular only – and then inadvertently. I failed to check whether all the 31 boys classified as band one at intake actually sat examinations in June 1979. In fact, they did not. As a result of movement in and out of the school, only 24 boys who could be regarded as band one sat the examinations. (*The Times Educational Supplement*, 27 February 1981)

Obviously, although Norcross does not labour the point, the effect of this reduction in the numbers of Band 1 pupils is to boost the apparent numbers of passes per Band 1 pupil. It also prompts a question about whether something similar was happening at Islington Green where only two Band 1 pupils sat the fifth-year exams. There is a hint in Kogan's piece (*op. cit.*) that this may be so. He referred, in the context of the 1979 results, to the fact that 'only six years ago [Islington Green] had an unbalanced entry when only about six per cent of the cohort had Group 1 gradings'. About 6 per cent of the cohort would, of course, be about seven or eight pupils. In brief, both schools seem likely to have had fewer Band 1 pupils actually sitting public examinations than they had had in their intakes.

Wilby concluded his contribution by observing that it 'might be fairer to say that statistics can be made to prove anything' (*op. cit.*). Norcross adopted a somewhat similar approach, commenting: 'Have I said enough to suggest that I am very well aware of the hazards involved in presenting and interpreting a school's examination results? Nevertheless, I believe it to be not only a necessary exercise but also a worthwhile one'.

THE CASE FOR MORE SYSTEMATIC COMPARISONS

In terms of the way public debates about examination results have typically been conducted this one developed to quite a sophisticated level.

Indeed, amongst the claims and counter-claims there are even some signs of both sides beginning to agree on a suitable basis for their comparisons by virtue of adopting the so-called 'rule-of-thumb' of five O-level or equivalent passes per Band 1 pupil. Whilst taking account of intakes is clearly a move in the right direction, the rule-of-thumb adopted was, of necessity, somewhat rough and ready. It was also, I suspect, somewhat on the optimistic side; the ILEA's reports on examination results reveal that in both 1979 and 1980 only about 10 per cent of pupils in the 15–16 (that is, fifth-year) age group obtained five or more O-level passes at grades A–C or CSE grade 1s (Table 7, Byford and Mortimore, 1981). Since the Band 1 group makes up 25 per cent of the cohort the shape of the distribution within this group would have to be heavily skewed to the upper end to produce an average of five apiece.

The new legislation will overcome one of the problems encountered in this debate. Because each school will have to publish the number of its pupils obtaining each level of 'higher grades' (at O-level and CSE grade 1), along with the number of pupils in its fifth-year cohort, this should deal with the initial problem encountered of establishing what percentages of pupils achieved specific levels of examination performance. At the same time, given the ready availability of such figures, it will have the welcome side-effect of making the habit of some headteachers and journalists of concentrating on the *total numbers of passes*, regardless of the numbers of pupils on whom they are based, seem like very selective pleading.

But the information required by law will tell us nothing about the other side of the present argument concerning the nature of the intakes to the two schools, which is essential if appropriate comparisons are to be made. Here we shall have to rely on school and local authority initiatives. Essentially, one needs to develop the 'rule-of-thumb' approach somewhat further by drawing upon the techniques employed in studies of school effectiveness to relate intakes to outcomes. Adoption of these techniques would enable one to establish whether schools were doing 'better' or 'worse' than one would have predicted and, if so, to begin to consider why this might be. There are signs that this sort of framework is beginning to emerge within the ILEA (cf. Mortimore and Byford, 1981) and one or two other local authorities (cf. Gray, 1981; Gray *et al.*, 1982) but there is a variety of questions that arise to which at present only tentative answers may be supplied. Whilst I believe the approach being proposed represents a considerable improvement upon present strategies for interpreting schools' results it still leaves much open to speculation and further research.

Bearing in mind these caveats, I shall now attempt to apply these techniques to the evaluation of the results in the two schools. Some constraints on the overall analysis must first be emphasized. In a situation where only just over one-third (37 per cent) of the age-group obtains *any* O-level passes at A–C (or CSE grade 1 equivalents), one is clearly failing to describe large parts of the activities of ILEA's schools if one focusses merely on the higher echelons of

O-level or equivalent achievement. For this reason, amongst others, the ILEA has developed an 'Examination Performance Scale' which seeks to relate O-level and CSE results in a single unified scale and it has used variants on this scale in all its more recent analyses of school performance. The last year in which it published information in terms of the specified level of O-level or CSE grade 1 performance used in the current controversy was 1976 (ILEA, 1978). Given that overall levels of performance within the ILEA seem to fluctuate very little indeed from year-to-year, there is no strong reason to suppose that the overall relationships produced in 1976 would have changed significantly by 1979, but obviously we cannot be fully confident of this fact from the evidence available.

The ILEA report presents information about the relationships between intakes and certain specified levels of examination performance for all ILEA secondary schools (ILEA, 1978, Appendix Table 2). Employing the probable values of Highbury Grove's Band 1 intake we would predict that just over 4 per cent of its pupils would obtain five or more O-level/CSE grade 1 passes. Since this represents just ten pupils and since we know that 31 pupils obtained 141 passes between them it seems very likely indeed that Highbury Grove was doing better than we would have predicted from knowledge of its intake.

At Islington Green, again taking the higher estimate of their Band 1 intake, the equation predicts that considerably less than 1 per cent of its pupils would obtain five or more passes, in other words less than one pupil. Since we know that two pupils obtained seven passes each, we may conclude that Islington Green was also doing better than we would have predicted from knowledge of its intake.

Before proceeding to interpret these results further it is important to underline some of the limitations of the analyses.

First and most obviously, by concentrating on the achievements of the most able (Band 1) pupils one is, in both schools, ignoring the larger parts of their efforts in relation to preparing pupils for public examinations; in Islington Green's case it might be more appropriate to say that one is ignoring virtually all their activities, if one employs the criterion of the percentage obtaining five or more passes.

Second, one is making the assumption that the 'Band 1' designation represents the same levels of attainments in both schools; obviously, since 25 per cent of pupils are included in this category one would expect pupils whose initial levels of performance placed them near the top of Band 1 to perform better than pupils who were around the borderline between Bands 1 and 2. We should require more information from both schools before we could be confident that they were similar.

Third, results from one or, at best, two years are not sufficient to infer a stable pattern of results favouring one school rather than the other.

Fourth, a model that is limited to information about pupils' Bands may well be ignoring other potentially important factors that could further differentiate between the intakes to the two schools and which might need to be taken account of. Some of these factors might be relevant to all schools – girls, for example, have tended to do better than boys in Inner London schools (Mortimore and Byford, 1981). Other factors might be known only to those who are familiar with the local circumstances of the two schools.

And fifth, whilst we may be able to say that a school is doing 'better' or 'worse' than we would have predicted from knowledge of its intake, this does not mean that we are necessarily in a position to say *why* it is doing so. Is it because of the school's policies and provision or because of additional factors associated with its intakes that we have, for whatever reason, ignored? These points must all raise doubts about the confidence with which assessments can be made and they constitute an agenda for further research.

Given the state-of-the-art the present analysis confirms the impression given by the rule-of-the-thumb approach that in 1979 *both* schools were doing at least as well as (and probably better than) other ILEA schools with equivalent intakes of Band 1 pupils. Whether one school was doing *significantly* better than the other, however, is more doubtful: my impression is that there was not much in it either way and that for the 1979 group both were probably schools of 'above average' effectiveness.

DISCUSSION

There is a tendency, given the ready availability of objective evidence such as examination results, for the evaluation of schools' performance to become rapidly and narrowly channelled into this area, even when such evidence is limited in its nature and not easily interpreted out of context. As the HMI reported in their recent survey of secondary education: 'schools were conscious of the degree to which [their] effectiveness [was] liable to be measured publicly by examination results' (DES, 1979, p. 262). And you might add, as a rider, that such interpretations are likely to be made solely in terms of schools' 'raw', unadjusted results.

There was little that was unusual about the 'opening shots' in the controversy addressed here. The attempts of those involved to place the discussion on a firmer footing must be seen as an important development. Furthermore, since both schools had results which would probably (in Highbury Grove's case) or definitely (in Islington Green's) place them well below the 'national average' it seems unfortunate that, in other circumstances, both might come out on the wrong side of a comparison.

Placing schools' examination results in the context of information about their intakes is a first, and necessary, step towards their proper evaluation; whether it is sufficient remains open to question and will be difficult to assess until more experience of this approach is available. The assessment that the two schools were probably of 'above average' effectiveness in 1979 may not merit Fleet Street's attention, of course, but that is another question.

REFERENCES

Boyson, R. (1974) *Oversubscribed: The Story of Highbury Grove*, London, Ward Lock.

Byford, D. and Mortimore, P. (1981) *School Examination Results in the ILEA: 1979 and 1980* (RS 787/81), Inner London Education Authority.

DES (1979) *Aspects of Secondary Education: A Survey by HM Inspectors of Schools*, London, HMSO.

Gray, J. (1981) 'Are examination results a suitable measure of school performance?' in Plewis I. (*op. cit.*).

Gray, J., McPherson, A. F. and Raffe, D. (1982) *Reconstructions of Secondary Education: Theory, Myth and Practice since the War*. London, Routledge and Kegan Paul.

ILEA (1978) *Examination Results in the ILEA* (RS 697/78), Inner London Education Authority.

Mortimore, P. and Byford, D. (1981) 'Monitoring examination results in a local education authority', in Plewis I. (*op. cit.*).

Plewis, I. (ed.) (1981) *Publishing Examination Results: A Discussion*. London, University of London Institute of Education (Bedford Way Papers No. 5).

6

BEYOND LEAGUE TABLES.
HOW MODERN STATISTICAL METHODS
CAN GIVE A TRUER PICTURE OF THE
EFFECTS OF SCHOOLS

I. Schagen

INTRODUCTION

In the present-day atmosphere of testing and reporting results for each school, many people are justifiably concerned that schools may be ranked in 'league tables' on the basis of some kind of crude average score.

This paper aims to show that, given suitable data and the use of appropriate statistical techniques, it is possible to use numerical outcomes (e.g. test results) to obtain useful, valid and helpful results about schools and their effects on children.

The two techniques we shall highlight in this paper are multilevel modelling and data envelopment analysis. Although each is quite different from the other in its assumptions, method of working and presentation of results, both share the common aim of moving beyond 'league tables' to derive more meaningful measures of schools' effects. They will help us to address the following types of question:

1. Are there apparent differences between schools, and if so, can they be explained by factors outside of the schools' direct control?
2. What are the effects of outside factors, and do these effects vary from school to school?
3. To what extent can schools be compared with each other, given their diverse priorities

MULTILEVEL MODELLING

Basic assumptions

The basic assumption of multilevel modelling is that individuals grouped together in some way (e.g. within the same school) experience a similar environment and are more likely to have things in common than children in different groups. To set up a multilevel model, we need to be able to define just a single outcome variable (e.g. a score on some kind of test), plus a number of other variables which could influence the outcome. These are known as 'background' variables and they can be measured either on individual pupils (e.g. age, sex, score on previous test) or at the school level (e.g. number of children in age group, type of school, school organization).

Whatever outcome variable we use, we can assume that there are differences in it at both the pupil and school levels. In other words, not only are individuals different from each other, but individuals within one school are collectively different from those in another school. These school differences are calculated in the multilevel model as 'school level residuals'. Their magnitudes tell us something about differences between schools, once we have allowed for everything else we can measure.

How it works

A very simple example will help to illustrate how multilevel models work. Suppose we have two schools, and we collect data on six pupils at each. In this simple example, we have just two levels: the child and the school. We measure attainment (with some kind of test) and another, background, variable (e.g. the score on a test taken at entry to the school) (Table 1).

If we were to set up a league table based on average attainment, then School 2 would be clearly ahead of School 1, with a value of 72.5 compared to 65. We could even compare the means for the two schools of the attainment and the background variable. From this we could estimate that a change of 43 units in average background variable yields a change of 7.5 units in attainment, a rate

Table 1

| | School 1 | | School 2 |
Background	Attainment	Background	Attainment
10	60	28	65
12	57	70	70
25	70	65	68
30	65	95	85
45	72	52	60
28	66	98	87
25 (Mean)	65 (Mean)	68 (Mean)	72.5 (Mean)

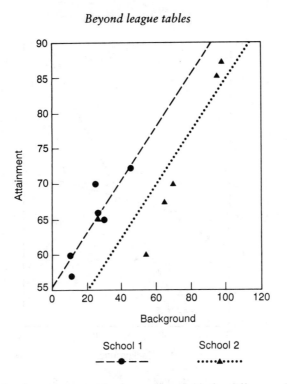

Figure 1 Example of attainment *vs.* background variable for different schools

of change of 0.17 attainment units per background unit. This type of analysis, known as 'means-on-means' analysis, is tempting but likely to give rise to fallacious results.

In practice, the effect of the background variable on attainment does not operate on the school as a whole, but for individual pupils within the school. If we plot a graph for each school of attainment vs background for its pupils, then we may see a rising trend. Fitting a straight line to the cluster of data points to represent this trend is known as 'regression analysis'.

In Figure 1 attainment is plotted against the background variable for the pupils at both schools in our example, and a separate line is fitted for each school. The lines, although parallel, do not coincide. For any value of the background variable, the School 1 line gives a higher value for attainment than School 2, suggesting that School 1 is in some sense the more effective.

In addition, Figure 1 gives us a better picture of the rate of change of attainment with the background variable, shown by the 'slope' of the two lines. This is approx. 0.4 attainment units per background unit, a much higher value than that given by the 'means-on-means' analysis.

Figure 1 illustrates a very simple multilevel model, with a common slope fitted to all schools. In fitting such a model by computer to a large data set, we would estimate not only the slope, but also 'residuals' at both pupil and school levels. The pupil level residuals are measures of the discrepancies between the data points and their individual lines; and the school level residuals measure

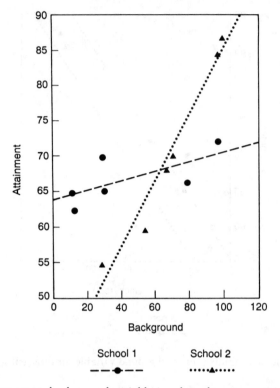

Figure 2 Attainment *vs.* background variable (random slopes)

the separation between the two lines. The simple multilevel model has brought us a great deal more insight than the misleading league table could, but there are further possibilities.

In the previous example, the lines were parallel for the two schools – we say that the background variable is a 'fixed' effect. It is possible for the slopes to vary from school to school, as in Figure 2, in which case we say it is a 'random' effect. In Figure 2 it is not possible to say that one school is uniformly 'better' than the other. School 2 is better for pupils with a high value of the background variable, and worse for the other end of the scale. Therefore finding random effects in our multilevel models will be an interesting discovery in its own right and will imply that the effects of schools are far more complex than can be accounted for in simple league tables.

Uses

The simple models we have been discussing have consisted of just two levels: school and pupil. More complex models can be used, incorporating more levels, such as pupil, class, school and local education authority (LEA), with associated variables at each level. Random residuals at each level measure the effect due to each school, class, LEA or whatever when the background vari-ables have been taken into account. So in principle a very sophisticated inves-tigation can be carried out using multilevel modelling techniques, provided that sufficient high-quality data is available.

So what do the results of such a sophisticated model tell us? First of all, we get the overall effects (slopes) of each of the background variables, plus an indication of whether or not each really influences whatever we are measuring. Secondly, we estimate residual effects at each level, so we can see not just how individual schools, etc. perform, but also tell how much of the overall variation in the data is at the pupil level, the school level or the LEA level (for example).

Thirdly, we can see which, if any, of the background variables have 'ran-dom' effects, which vary from school to school. If any such exist, we may be able to explain this variation using other variables at the school level. In this way, multilevel models not only describe what is happening, but also help us to explain why it should be so.

Advantages and disadvantages

The main advantage of multilevel modelling is its ability to unravel the com-plex interactions between variables in a hierarchical situation, and to model accurately what is really going on. Analyses of school results which ignore the multilevel aspect are likely to lead to fallacious conclusions.

The main drawback of this approach is the requirement that normally only one outcome can be modelled at a time – we therefore implicitly assume that this is the only output of interest for each pupil. This may not be desirable, as different schools, LEAs or even pupils will give different priorities to different outcomes, and a single outcome measure will not give a fair picture of this situation.

Example

Two examples of the use of multilevel modelling will be quoted here, both presented in a recently published paper (Schagen, 1990). The first involves the analysis of the 1982 Assessment of Performance Unit (APU) Maths survey of age 11 pupils at over 1000 schools. Twelve sub-categories of mathematics were tested, and each was analysed separately using a multilevel model which took account of school and pupil effects and a large number of background variables. The results obtained showed, for example, that hours of maths homework was positively related to the test percentage correct in all 12 sub-categories, while size of school (number in age group) only had a significant effect in one sub-category. Many other interesting results were derived, includ-ing the fact that about ten per cent of the total variation in the scores was due to school level effects.

The second example involved studying pupils' attitudes to their Technical Vocational Educational Initiative (TVEI) courses at three ages: 13+, 15+ and 17+. Scores relating to their positive or negative attitudes, expressed through a questionnaire, were used as outcome variables. Various background variables were fitted, and the model results were quite different at the different ages. Random effects were found, showing that the influence of some variables varied from school to school. For example, at age 13+ the effect of sex was generally negative (boys were more negative than girls), but this also had a random component which implies that some schools have a clearer difference in attitude between the sexes than others. A number of similar interesting discoveries were made by the multilevel analysis of this data.

DATA ENVELOPMENT ANALYSIS

Basic assumptions

This technique is quite different from the regression-based approach of multilevel modelling. It considers just one level of 'units' (e.g. schools) and treats each as a 'black box' which transforms a set of inputs into a set of outputs. Outputs from each school might include exam results, attendance figures, staying on rates, etc. Inputs consist of both variables which can be altered (e.g. financial commitment) and those which are basically unalterable measures of the school background (e.g. local unemployment rate, abilities of pupils entering the school, etc.).

How it works

The purpose of data envelopment analysis (DEA) is to position schools relative to each other in respect of inputs and outputs, and to look for schools which appear to fall short of what is being attained by comparable schools. A simple example will attempt to make this clear.

Suppose we just have two output measures, and three schools (A, B and C), which coincidentally all have the same values of the inputs. Figure 3 is a plot of the three schools relative to the two outputs. Schools A and B form a 'boundary', and a line can be drawn through them beyond which no other school lies. This line represents, in some sense, the 'trade-off' between the two outputs in the best-case schools. School C does not reach this line, and could be considered to be 'less efficient' than Schools A and B. A measure of its relative efficiency is the ratio of the distance O to C compared with O to D.

In Figure 3, Schools A and B have efficiencies of 100 per cent, which means that there is no other school with a better combination of outputs for the same inputs. School C, however, has an efficiency value of around 60 per cent and can be seen to suffer in comparison with Schools A and B. It is dangerous to

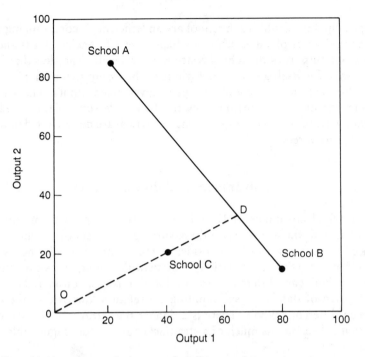

Figure 3 Data envelopment analysis example (all inputs the same)

conclude too much from this: saying that School C could improve its performance to the same level as A and B (i.e. reach position D on the diagram) is not
necessarily true. There may well be forces operating at School C which are not
taken account of in any of the input and output measures, and which reduce its
apparent performance relative to the other schools.

Uses

In brief, data envelopment analysis allows us to compare schools using multiple input and output measures. For example, some schools may regard as their
prime goal the achievement of good academic results for a minority of pupils;
others may give a higher priority to the attainment of some kind of qualifica-
tion by most pupils; and yet other objectives (behaviour, attendance) may also
be important. It would be unreasonable to rank all schools on a single criterion
when there is no consensus as to what it should be. Similarly, multiple inputs
allow us to include a number of background variables which may influence the
outputs we are studying. Each school is evaluated on its own terms, finding the
combination of inputs and outputs which show it in the best possible light
compared with other schools.

The results of data envelopment analysis tell us little about the overall
picture, but are concerned with the individual schools or other units of study.

The principal results for each school are an 'efficiency' score, ranging from 0.0 to 1.0, and a list of other schools which have efficiencies of 1.0 and similar inputs and outputs (if the school concerned has an efficiency less than 1.0). The efficiency value itself gives a rough guide to the extent to which improvements might be made to the school's outputs, given fixed inputs. The set of comparison schools is perhaps more useful; from it lessons might be learned, or alternatively, the existence of other factors which are not included in the model may be discovered.

Advantages and disadvantages

The principal advantage of DEA is its ability to cope with multiple output variables, with the emphasis on these varying from school to school. There is no need to be constrained to consider a single output for all schools, valid or not. However, DEA is not strictly a statistical technique, as no estimates of errors or significant differences are produced. It is best considered as a sophisticated form of data analysis, pointing up relationships within the data and between different schools. There is a danger that DEA will be used in such a way that it becomes as much of a straitjacket as a crude league table.

Example

The most accessible example in the literature involves not schools, but LEAs as the basic unit of DEA. Jesson, Mayston and Smith (1987) have analysed each English LEA on the basis of published DES statistics, using two output measures: percentage of pupils getting five or more O-levels, and percentage of pupils getting three or more CSE or O-levels. Four input measures were used: socio-economic status of the LEA's catchment area; percentage of children not from one-parent families; percentage of children from 'UK-born' families; and secondary school expenditure per pupil.

Applying DEA to this data gave efficiencies ranging from 0.88 up to 1.0. In a sense, this is good news for LEAs, for it shows that even the 'least efficient' is quite close to the apparent best case. The two different output measures allow one to distinguish between authorities whose main strength is the academic performance of the 'high fliers' (e.g. Harrow and Liverpool) and those which major on output 2, broad achievement at a lower level (e.g. ILEA).

CONCLUSIONS

League tables of schools based on a single output measure are statistically dubious, and educationally give us little information on the effectiveness of schools. Fortunately, it is possible to do a lot better. However, it is necessary to bear in mind three essential prerequisites before either of the techniques mentioned here can be used: access to appropriate software and computer power, expertise in fitting these models and good-quality data. The latter particularly is crucial. Data should be collected consistently and measure as closely as possible the real inputs and outputs that concern schools. Without this, any form of analysis of school level data, from league tables upwards, is going to be an example of the old computer adage: 'Garbage in, garbage out.'

For further reading on multilevel models, a good technical introduction is found in Goldstein (1987). The Jesson, Mayston and Smith (1987) paper, referred to above, gives a good introduction to the concepts of data envelopment analysis, and Smith (1990) includes it in his review of public sector performance indicators.

REFERENCES

Goldstein, H. (1987) *Multilevel Models in Educational and Social Research*. London: Charles Griffin/Oxford University Press.

Jesson, D., Mayston, D. and Smith, P. (1987) 'Performance assessment in the education sector: educational and economic perspectives', *Oxford Review of Education*, 13, 3, 249–65.

Schagen, I. (1990) 'Analysis of the effects of school variables using multilevel models', *Educational Studies*, 16, 1, 61–73.

Smith, P. (1990) 'The use of performance indicators in the public sector', *Journal of the Royal Statistical Society A*, Part 1, 53–72.

7

ESTIMATING DIFFERENCES IN THE EXAMINATION PERFORMANCES OF SECONDARY SCHOOLS IN SIX LEAS: A MULTI-LEVEL APPROACH TO SCHOOL EFFECTIVENESS

J. Gray, D. Jesson and N. Sime

Examination results for fifth-year pupils in six different local education authorities are analysed with a view to establishing what differences in their performance can be assigned to the schools they attend. Using multi-level models it is shown that, whilst in general the differences between schools are relatively small, the actual size in examination points is certainly not trivial. These differences are estimated for the schools in each LEA. Distinctions are drawn between explanatory models based on information about pupils' background as opposed to prior attainment; the latter are shown to be more appropriate for comparisons between schools. Amongst the 11 data sets analysed there was little evidence that schools were differentially effective with different groups of pupils.

INTRODUCTION

Interest in research on school effectiveness amongst policy-makers and practitioners can rarely have been higher. The reasons are not difficult to establish. The research has both substantive and methodological contributions to make to the identification of 'good practice' and to the development of frameworks for school evaluation. But, ironically, at a time when interest is so prominent, there is a danger that methodological (and notably statistical) advances will remove the opportunities for the practical application of the approaches adopted by school effectiveness researchers. This paper is designed, in part, to reduce the danger of such a gap developing still further. It demonstrates how local education authorities (LEAs) might make use of the most-up-to-date and sophisticated techniques to explore an issue which has become increasingly central to school evaluation over the past decade, namely the interpretation of schools' examination results. At the same time it aims to make a substantive contribution to research on the extent of differences between schools in their effectiveness.

The factors which have contributed to the development of interest in school effectiveness research are not difficult to identify. At the beginning of the decade, for example, the 1980s Education Act required secondary schools to publish their examination results amongst other items of information; there were understandable worries about the extent to which some schools (and especially those serving socially disadvantaged catchment areas) would be unfairly treated in any ensuing comparisons of their performance.

During the mid-1980s there was an extended debate about the effects of comprehensive reorganisation on pupils' performance; again concern that like was not being compared with like was central to the debate (see Gray & Jesson, 1989, for a review). There has also been considerable debate about the effectiveness of individual LEAs and the appropriateness of the underlying statistically-based models of evaluation that have been employed to establish their performance; in the process the limitations of existing data-bases and procedures have been exposed (see, for example, Gray & Jesson, 1987; Woodhouse & Goldstein, 1988).

The last couple of years have seen interest in comparing schools' results increase still further, partly as a result of the new roles for local education authorities prescribed in the 1988 Education Reform Act. The Task Group on Assessment and Testing, however, stepped back from recommending the full-blown 'contextualisation' of schools' performance in relation to the publication of pupils' results on the new national attainment tests (see DES, 1988; Cuttance & Goldstein, 1988). Most recently, in the latest policy statement from the Department of Education & Science (1989), some modest interest in 'value-added' approaches is hinted at but no whole-hearted endorsement, in practice, emerges. It is clear that there is still considerable unease about the application of the techniques of school effectiveness research to the everyday tasks of performance evaluation and review.

There have been a number of British studies of school effectiveness since Rutter's research into twelve Inner London secondary schools in the mid-to-late seventies (Rutter *et al.*, 1979). It is now generally recognised that the number of schools sampled in Rutter's study was on the low side for satisfactory estimates of differences in schools' effectiveness to be established. None the less, a decade later, there have still only been a handful of studies with sample sizes that have been larger. Amongst the studies which offer such estimates of schools' effects we would mention: the Inner London Education Authority's Junior School Project which looked at some 50 primary schools (Mortimore *et al.*, 1988); the studies of Scottish secondary schools conducted by members of the Centre for Educational Sociology at Edinburgh University (see Cuttance, 1988; and Willms, 1986); the study of 18 racially-mixed comprehensives conducted by the Policy Studies Institute and Lancaster University (Smith & Tomlinson, 1989); and a recent analysis of examination results over a period of three years in large numbers of secondary schools in the Inner London Education Authority (Nuttall *et al.*, 1989). To these we would add our own earlier and continuing work, conducted as part of the Contexts Project on school effectiveness and the interpretation of examination results (Gray *et al.*, 1986).

In addition to sharing overlapping substantive concerns each of these studies has incorporated (to a greater or lesser extent) the use of the most advanced statistical techniques currently available, known as multi-level modelling (also known as: Hierarchical Linear Models, see Raudenbush & Bryk, 1986; and Variance Components analysis, see Longford, 1986). The statistical problems posed by the underlying structure of educational systems (notably the clustering of pupils into schools and, crucially, the importance of collecting data on individual pupils), were first laid out in an accessible form for educational researchers during the early eighties (see, for example, Goldstein, 1984). Two or three years later, however, they were still largely unknown when Aitkin & Longford (1986) published their seminal paper, using a data-set we had provided on a single LEA as part of the Contexts Project. Since then the accessibility of the techniques has improved considerably (see Paterson, 1989 for an introductory account; and Goldstein, 1987 for a semi-introductory account) but much remains to be explored and understood about these new approaches and their implications. Crucially, each of the studies mentioned above has produced somewhat differing estimates of schools' effectiveness because each has, in practice, conceptualised the problems somewhat differently and pursued them using data collected from different localities incorporating different variables. An extended review of some of these issues, as well as some more general issues raised by studies of school and teacher effectiveness, has recently been completed by Preece (1989).

There has been some confusion about the extent to which these various studies have produced similar or conflicting results. The enduring questions of school effectiveness research remain the same, however, and we repeat them here by way of prefacing our own contribution. They are:

1. What information on pupils' backgrounds or prior attainments is required for appropriate comparisons to be undertaken?
2. What is the extent of differences in pupils' performance that may be attributable to differences in the effectiveness of the schools they have attended? What, in other words, are the overall consequences for pupils' progress of attending a more as opposed to less effective school?
3. Are schools differentially effective? Do they, in short, have more impact on the outcomes of some groups of pupils (the lower-attaining, ethnic minorities or females for example) than others?

The present analysis has something to add to existing research on all three of these issues. But such questions are, of course, preconditions for answering what is probably the most important question of all:

4. What factors (and especially factors under schools' own control) can be identified which contribute to schools' effectiveness?

SOURCES OF DATA

The present study uses data from six different local education authorities serving metropolitan, urban and rural communities in England. In four of these LEAs we have been able to obtain two (and in one case three) independent samples of pupils' performance. Eleven distinct data-sets were therefore available for subsequent analysis.

Under the terms of our agreement with participating LEAs we are not in a position to reveal the names of the authorities or their schools. The LEAs whose data we report in this study were situated in geographically distinct parts of the country; whilst they were not chosen to be 'representative' of anything other than themselves, it may nevertheless be observed that they serve a range of different types of communities. LEAs 1, 2, and 4 are situated in the north of England and serve metropolitan boroughs containing numbers of 'inner city' schools; they include significant areas of industrial decline. LEAs 3 and 6 serve urban and county populations in the south of England. LEA 5 comprises data from pupils attending schools in a Midland metropolitan borough; again some areas in this authority possessed 'inner city' characteristics.

Different strategies were employed to gather the data from each LEA. The (rounded) number of schools in each LEA and the average number of pupils per school for which we obtained data are shown in Table 1. In all we had data on some 14,000 individual pupils in some 290 schools (some of these schools were, of course, to be found in each of the data-sets covering a particular LEA; taking these into account, the data covered, in all, some 150 entirely different institutions). This table also reports the measures of pupil characteristics available in each data-set.

For each pupil the examination outcome is a scaled measure of their fifth form examination performance created by assigning a score to each level of pass obtained in GCSE/GCE or CSE examinations (see Table 1 for further details). We refer to this measure as their 'exam points score'. In addition, we had a number of items of information on pupils' characteristics available to us. These included:

1. measures of pupils' *background* characteristics in data-sets 1A, 1B, 1C, 2A, 2B, 3A, 3B and 4. In all cases these included parental social class, housing tenure (except for 1C and 4) and the number of siblings in the family;

2. measures of pupils' *prior attainment* at the point of transfer to secondary school in data-sets 5, 6A, 6B;
3. information on pupils' *gender* in all eleven data-sets.

The data available, therefore, provide a selection of the kinds of variables that might be obtained within an LEA that was prepared to invest some effort in data-collection. They represent the minimum that an LEA might try to assemble; clearly information on further variables would be valuable if the resources committed to data-collection enabled them to be collected. The variables described here have the distinct merit, in the present case, of being fairly readily available for the purpose of the analysis.

Table 1 Summary of the information on pupil characteristics available for each LEA and in each data-set in addition to examination results*

LEA data-set	Number of schools	Average no. of pupils per school	Prior attainment	Social class§	Variables available Gender	Housing tenure¶	Number of siblings
1A	40†	11	No	Yes	Yes	Yes	Yes
1B	40	12	No	Yes	Yes	Yes	Yes
1C	40	26	No	Yes	Yes	No	Yes
2A	30	11	No	Yes	Yes	Yes	Yes
2B	30	10	No	Yes	Yes	Yes	Yes
3A	10	38	No	Yes	Yes	Yes	Yes
3B	10	44	No	Yes	Yes	Yes	Yes
4	20	35	No	Yes	Yes	No	Yes
5	20	54	Yes‡	No	Yes	No	No
6A	30	181	Yes‡	No	Yes	No	No
6B	20	177	Yes	No	Yes	No	No

Notes

* For each LEA information about each pupil's examination results, subject by subject, was available. These were summed into an overall exam score using the following scoring system: grade A = 7, grade B = 6, grade C or CSE grade 1 = 5, grade D or 2 = 4, grade E or 3 = 3, grade 4 = 2, grade 5 = 1, failed or unclassified = 0.

† In order to preserve the confidentiality of the data on each LEA these figures have been rounded to the nearest ten in this column.

‡ In LEA 5 this was a measure of verbal reasoning at age 11; in LEA 6 this was a measure of reading attainment at the point of transfer.

§ In data-sets 1A, 1B, 2A, 2B, 3A and 3B social class was based on a measure of father's occupation coded into the Cambridge system; in data-sets 1C and 4, father's occupation was coded using the OPCS system.

¶ Housing tenure was coded into those in owner-occupied property/rented and others.

THE DISTRIBUTION OF EXAM RESULTS ACROSS PUPILS AND SCHOOLS

How far did pupils' fifth-year exam results differ across schools and LEAs? Figure 1 shows the distribution of pupil level achievement in each of the eleven LEA data-sets. We have used 'box' and 'whisker' plots to focus attention primarily on the interquartile ranges of pupils' scores (which are contained within the 'boxes'). The length of each box corresponds to the range of exam-

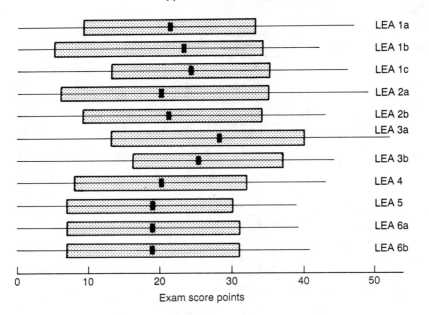

Figure 1 Distribution of individual pupils' achievement in six LEAs. The shaded area represents the interquartile range

ination score differences between pupils at the upper and lower quartiles. The interquartile range gives a fairly robust indication of the range of variation in each LEA. In all 11 data-sets these differences between individual pupils were fairly consistent at around 25 examination score points. Of course, the 'average' level of performance differed somewhat between data-sets and also between different LEAs; these differences reflected both the variation of pupils within the samples drawn from a given LEA and also between LEAs serving populations with different social characteristics.

The 'whiskers' of the plots (the lines stretching either side of the boxes) in Figure 1 represent the full range of variation between pupils in each data-set. A score of zero was assigned to those who: left school before examinations were taken, who did not take examinations, who took examination but achieved no credit for these attempts or who simply did not report on their achievement. All six LEAs had some pupils with the lowest scores although the precise percentages varied. The 'highest' scores were also subject to (sometimes considerable) variation. In LEA 3A, for example, the highest examination score was above 50 points whereas in LEA 5 it was below 40.

The pupils whose performance we report in Figure 1 were grouped by schools and the mean (or average) examination score for each school was also calculated. The resulting distribution of 'school mean' scores is displayed in Figure 2.

By contrast with Figure 1 we note that the interquartile range of 'school' performance was substantially less than that for pupil performance. Although this was an 'expected' result, it operated in different ways for different LEAs.

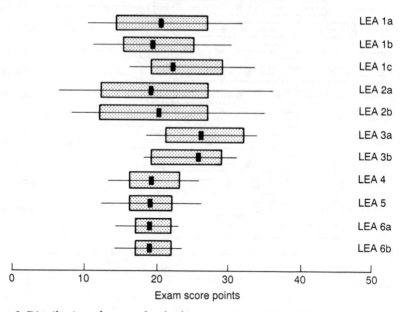

Figure 2 Distribution of mean school achievement in six LEAs. The shaded area represents the interquartile range

We observe that whilst the interquartile ranges were relatively consistent within LEAs they differed between LEAs. For example, in LEA 6 this range was only about five examination score points whereas in LEA 3 it was 15.

Such differences are not trivial; however, we can draw no conclusions about school performance from them, of course, in isolation since they may arise from a variety of different sources including: differences in pupils' prior attainment, in schools' effectiveness, in LEAs' policies for allocation of pupils to schools, or as a result of other informal 'selection' processes or, indeed, combinations of all or some of these factors.

The first stage of our analysis was to identify the variance lying between schools before any account was taken of differences in pupils' characteristics. This is basically just another way of exploring the extent of differences already presented in Figure 2. The results of this 'null' model (when no account is taken of differences in pupils' individual background or prior attainment characteristics) are presented in Column 1 of Table 2. They confirm the picture already revealed in Figure 2. The range of 'unadjusted' school differences was very marked ranging from a low value of just over 3% in LEA 6 to just over 30% in LEA 2.

Of course, none of the analyses to this point have taken any account of differences in the intakes to the schools in the six LEAs on the various measures we collected. Suffice it to say, at this stage, that these were also large and related, prima facie, to the schools' exam results. There was a general tendency in all six LEAs for the schools with more socially advantaged or higher attaining intakes to obtain the higher fifth-year results (tables not shown).

Table 2 Results of the model-fitting (Model 1)

LEA data-set	Column 1 Unadjusted school variance (%)	Column 2 Fixed effects (%)	Column 3 (Random) school effects (%)
1A	15.2	20.4	6.4
1B	10.8	11.4	5.2
1C	12.0	12.8	7.9
2A	30.8	12.6	25.0
2B	28.9	11.8	23.7
3A	5.4	14.3	3.7
3B	6.6	10.8	3.5
4	6.2	13.5	3.9
5	7.1	54.5	1.5
6A	3.5	56.3	5.0
6B	3.7	58.1	4.0

Notes

Model 1 fixed effects: pupil level variables, from those available, found to contribute significantly to the prediction of examination scores are included in the model. Random effects: school level (intercepts) and pupil level residuals are estimated.

Column 1: Variance attributed to (random) school effects prior to controlling for pupil-level characteristics (expressed as a percentage of the overall variance).

Column 2: Variance explained by fixed part of the model (expressed as a percentage of the overall variance).

Column 3: Variance attributed to (random) school effects (expressed as a percentage of the residual variance).

THE MAIN FINDINGS

We shall not dwell here on the statistical aspects of our methodology as these have already been explained elsewhere and by others in greater detail. Suffice it to say that the multi-level modelling procedures we have employed have become increasingly well understood amongst researchers of school effectiveness in the last two or three years. The results we report here, none the less, represent substantial additional evidence about the extent to which schools within particular LEAs differed in their effectiveness. In discussing our findings, therefore, we address four distinct issues raised by the analyses, namely:

1. estimates of the relative size of the variance attributable to schools after appropriate controls have been applied for differences in pupils' characteristics;
2. the consequent differences in expected examination scores obtained by pupils in different schools;
3. the nature of 'contextual effects' and the role of pupil-level measures aggregated to the level of the school; and
4. whether the schools were differentially effective, that is whether some schools 'did better' with more able pupils at the expense of less able and vice versa.

We then go on to consider the explanatory power (both substantive and statistical) of the procedures we have employed before addressing some of the practical issues arising for LEAs and others who might wish to use the framework and procedures we have outlined here.

The variance in pupil performance potentially attributable to schools

All the multi-level analyses reported here were conducted using a statistical package developed by researchers at the London Institute of Education (see Rasbash *et al.*, 1989). The extensive data sources which we have used gave consistently 'low' estimates of the extent to which schools contributed differentially to pupils' performance. In nine out of the 11 data-sets the variance attributed to schools was estimated to be 8% or less (see Table 2, Column 3); in six of the data-sets the estimate was 5% or less. These findings are broadly consistent with Aitkin & Longford's (1986) seminal study which reported that 'only around two per cent of the variation in outcomes was assigned to the schools.'

Aitkin & Longford's estimates have not passed without comment. Kilgore & Pendleton (1986), for example, claimed that this particular finding was 'not of special empirical importance, nor consistent with findings based on broader samples'. The present study, however, presents further evidence which casts doubt on the claims made by Kilgore & Pendleton. The results described here, representing extensive analysis of academic performance at age 16, come down clearly in favour of the lower levels reported earlier by Aitkin & Longford.

An important part of Kilgore & Pendleton's argument was based on the view that, because Aitkin & Longford's data were restricted to a single local education authority, the 'low' level of variation associated with schools was 'a consequence of the relative homogeneity of policies and practices within that LEA rather than (a general indication of) the relative importance of schools and pupil background'.

On closer examination, however, it appears that some other recent British studies of school effectiveness have reported similarly 'low' proportions of variance associated with schools. In the Scottish studies, for example, Willms estimated a figure of no more than 10% across the broad range of Scottish school types (Willms, 1987). From the tables in Nuttall's study of Inner London secondary schools it can be established that the equivalent figure was around 8% (Nuttall *et al.*, 1989) whilst in Smith & Tomlinson's (1989) study of racially-mixed schools the figures were also around these levels.

Each of these estimates is, of course, a little higher than the levels we report. These earlier studies have, however, employed different data-bases and definitions and, possibly, different estimation procedures. The particular significance of the work we report here is that the 11 data-sets we analysed had a largely common structure of variables and were all processed in much the same way. In at least three of them we also possessed better 'explanatory' variables, an issue we address in greater detail in a later section.

It may, of course, still be the case that the schools in each of our LEAs were 'relatively homogeneous in (terms of) policies and practices' but, since we are dealing with very diverse authorities, the nature of those policies is likely to have been different. Yet, despite this, the 'low' level of between school variation is a common finding. Our evidence suggests that rather than being a special feature of a single authority, the extent of school variation within an authority was, by and large, fairly 'low'. Our estimates cannot therefore be arbitrarily dismissed as 'not of special empirical importance'.

The unusual and exceptional case was LEA 2. This provides an interesting contrast to the other LEAs analysed. It may therefore provide some insight into the conditions under which any LEA might have larger than average differences between its schools. In Table 2 the unadjusted between school variances for LEA 2 were the highest recorded amongst the 11 data-sets, whilst the proportions of overall variance 'explained' by pupil-level characteristics through the modelling were amongst the lowest. This particular local authority had, at the time its pupils transferred to secondary schools, retained informal selection in some areas and with respect to some schools. Another form of 'selection' was also involved in recruitment to the relatively large voluntary sector. Both conditions seem likely to have increased the differences between schools. Added to this there were very marked social differences between some of the areas administered by the LEA and each area was served by relatively small schools. In sum, we have three sets of conditions which distinguish this authority from the others in our analyses.

Since the controls for pupil background in LEA 2 were relatively 'weak' it is likely that, in combination with the differentiating process described above, such conditions resulted in larger proportions of variance being attributed to 'school differences' than elsewhere.

The first, and most important, conclusion then to emerge from our analyses across a number of different LEAs was to confirm previous estimates of relatively low levels of between school variance.

Differences between similar pupils in different schools

Studies of school effectiveness are primarily concerned with establishing the effects schools have in improving (or diminishing) pupils' performance. We, therefore, translated the somewhat arcane concept of 'between school variation' into an expected examination points advantage (or disadvantage) for pupils attending different schools.

For this purpose we used estimates based on the interquartile range of school effectiveness scores. In general, we have found that these provide more 'robust' estimates of the differences between schools than those provided by comparisons between schools at one end of the range as opposed to the other (Gray, 1989). They may also represent more realistic 'targets' for policy-makers to keep in mind when discussing the impact of such differences on pupils' life-chances.

If LEA 2 is excluded, for the reasons already identified above, the results were remarkably consistent across the different LEAs (see Table 3). In all nine of the data-sets, relating to five distinct LEAs, the advantage for a pupil

Table 3 Average increments/decrements to pupils' exam scores for schools of differing effectiveness (Model 1)

LEA data-set	Most effective (Column 1)	Effectiveness of school attended				Range (Column 6)	Inter quartile range* (Column 7)	% of pupil SD† (Column 8)
		Upper quartile (Column 2)	Median (Column 3)	Lower quartile (Column 4)	Least effective (Column 5)			
1A	+5	+2	0	−2	−5	10	4	25
1B	+5	+1	0	−1	−5	10	2	13
1C	+9	+2	0	−2	−7	16	4	25
2A	+16	+4	+2	−5	−11	27	9	57
2B	+15	+4	+1	−6	−10	25	10	63
3A	+5	+2	0	−2	−4	9	4	25
3B	+3	+1	1	−1	−4	7	2	13
4	+6	+1	−1	−2	−3	9	3	19
5	+2	+1	0	−1	−1	3	2	13
6A	+4	+2	0	−2	−6	10	4	25
6B	+3	+1	0	−1	−5	8	2	13

Notes School effects were consistent across all groups.

* This column reports the range between the upper and lower quartiles reported in Columns 2 and 4. Thus a pupil who attended a school in LEA 1A that just fell into the upper quartile of effectiveness would have scored, on average, four exam points more than a pupil who attended a school in the same LEA that just fell into the lower quartile of effectiveness.

† This column expresses the interquartile range of school effects listed in the previous column as a percentage of an individual standard deviation on the exam points measure. From information available to us from the Youth Cohort Study we have established that this variable has a mean of approximately 21 points and a standard deviation of 16 points.

attending a school at the upper, rather than the lower, quartile of effectiveness was four examination points or somewhat less. The final column of Table 3 expresses those differences as a percentage of a standard deviation of an individual score on the outcome measure; in each case it was a quarter of a standard deviation or less. This was a consistent finding across all our data-sets in each LEA, and hence gives us some considerable confidence about its general order of magnitude. However, it should be noted that the results provided for particular schools are subject to errors of estimation which depend, in turn, on sample sizes within individual schools and the power of the model at the level of individual pupils.

Differences of this size are not, of course, trivial. Schools 'do make a difference'. On the other hand they suggest that pupils' performance depends much less on between school differences than some earlier (notably American) studies have implied (Gray, 1989). Putting the matter into the context of GCSE examinations, pupils attending more effective schools could be expected to obtain grade enhancements from say D to B in two subjects, or an enhancement of one grade (from D to C) in four subjects compared with their counterparts in less effective schools. A much earlier article referred to differences of this size as providing pupils with a 'competitive edge' (Gray, 1981a).

The range of differences in school effectiveness between the most and least effective schools was, of course, much wider; furthermore this range differed much more between LEAs (see Table 3 and Figure 3). We would, however, advise caution in accepting one year's results on their own as providing good

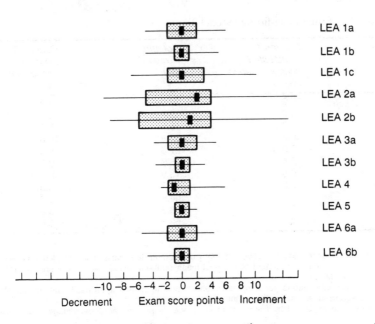

Figure 3 Average increments/decrements to pupil exam scores groups by school attended for Model 1 in six LEAs. The shaded area represents the interquartile range

estimates of the differences between schools at the extreme ends of the range since, as Goldstein (1987) has demonstrated, schools seem to vary almost as much between years as between themselves. The extremes of the range are, of course, the most likely to be affected. As one of us has commented, 'one year's results on their own are not, it would appear, a very good guide to a school's performance over time' (Gray, 1989). The general thrust of this conclusion has been confirmed in a recently-published analysis of the Scottish data which looked at changes in schools' performances over a four-year gap (Willms & Raudenbush, 1989).

[At this point, the original article includes a discussion of contextual or compositional effects: that is, the effects on achievement of different mixes of pupils within schools in terms of proportions from different social classes, ethnic groups, and prior achievement levels. The authors describe the results of incorporating contextual effects in their analysis as both 'dramatic and confusing':

' "Compositional" or "contextual" variables seem to be both massively important and trivial in their effects, depending on which LEA one is exploring.' However, they conclude that:

For reasons which we rehearse in greater detail in a later section we have both substantive and statistical grounds for believing that the estimates emerging from the data-sets on LEA 5, 6A and 6B may be more appropriate. In our view the evidence for strong 'compositional' or 'contextual' effects is relatively weak'.]

Table 4 Results of the model-fitting (Model 2)

LEA data-set	Column 1 Unadjusted school variance (%)	Column 2 Fixed effects (%)	Column 3 (Random) school effects (%)
1A	15.2	23.0	3.3
1B	10.8	13.6	3.5
1C	12.0	15.5	5.2
2A	30.8	22.8	15.6
2B	28.9	27.3	6.5
3A	5.4	15.3	2.7
3B	6.6	13.9	0.0
4	6.2	14.3	3.0
5	7.1	54.6	1.6
6A	3.5	56.3	5.0
6B	3.7	58.1	3.6

Notes

Model 2 fixed effects: as for Model 1 but with the entry of a composite variable. This provided a measure of school mean socio-economic background or a school mean on the available measure of prior attainment. Random effects as for Model 1.

Column 1: Variance attributed to (random) school effects prior to controlling for pupil-level and composite characteristics (expressed as a percentage of the overall variance).

Column 2: Variance explained by fixed part of the model (expressed as a percentage of the overall variance).

Column 3: Variance attributed to (random) school effects (expressed as a percentage of the residual variance).

The evidence for differential effectiveness

Multi-level modelling procedures open up the possibility of asking whether schools are 'differentially effective'. Do some schools, in other words, do better in assisting particular types of pupils (the above average, for example), to achieve examination success than they do with others, and vice versa? And, if they do, is this success apparently achieved at the expense of other types of pupils?

The approach adopted by researchers prior to the recent development of multi-level models has generally assumed that schools' effectiveness could be captured by a single figure and that this figure applied equally to all pupils, whatever their background characteristics. Since multi-level models have become available a great deal of emphasis has been placed on the possibility of relaxing this assumption and exploring the consequences for pupils of different characteristics within the same school. Both the Inner London study (Nuttall *et al.*, 1989) and Smith & Tomlinson (1989) report evidence of different effects for different pupils. In the former study the effects were most variable amongst the group of pupils whose prior attainment was highest (the Band One pupils). In some schools this group of pupils did quite a lot better than in others. Amongst the group of pupils whose prior attainment was lowest (the Band Three pupils) the effects were more homogeneous. In the latter study there was also some evidence of differential effectiveness amongst pupils of both above average and below average prior attainment; although the effects were statistically significant, however, they were also relatively small.

In one sense our own results were very straightforward: we found little substantive evidence for 'differential slopes' (see Table 5) in any of the data-sets

Table 5 Evidence of differential slopes and the major characteristics of each data-set

LEA data-set	Number of schools	Average number of pupils per school	Prior attainment	Social class	Evidence of differential slopes
1A	40	11	No	Yes	No
1B	40	12	No	Yes	No
1C	40	26	No	Yes	No
2A	30	11	No	Yes	No
2B	30	10	No	Yes	No
3A	10	38	No	Yes	No
3B	10	44	No	Yes	No
4	20	35	No	Yes	No
5	20	54	Yes	No	No
6A	30	181	Yes	No	Yes*
6B	20	177	Yes	No	Yes†

Notes
* This result was statistically significant (2.05 × s.e.).
† This result falls on the conventional boundary of statistical significance (1.87 × s.e.).

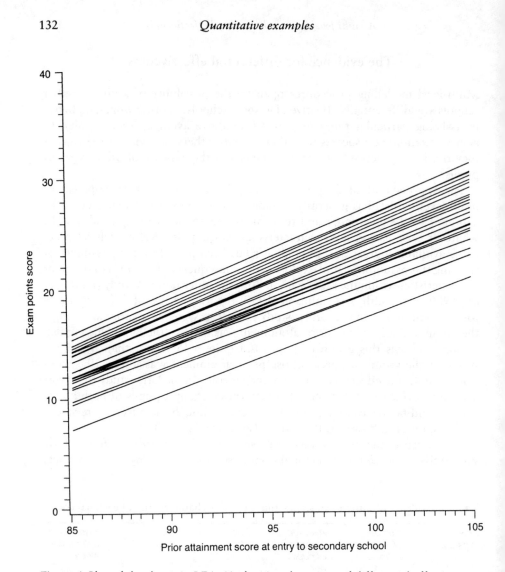

Figure 4 Plot of the slopes in LEA 6A showing the extent of differential effectiveness between schools. Each line represents the results of an individual school. For clarity the graph has been confined to those pupils whose scores fell in the middle 50% (from 85 to 105) in the LEA. The score obtained by a median pupil is represented by 95

we analysed. What is more surprising is the similarity of our findings across data-sets of very different characteristics. We found this to be the case for those with large numbers of pupils in a relatively large number of schools and with prior attainment as an explanatory measure. We also found similar results with small numbers of pupils in a smaller set of schools again using prior attainment. But even in those data-sets where we had relatively large, as well as relatively small, numbers of schools where we were using pupil background characteristics as explanatory measures, the overall findings were the same; there was little evidence of 'differential slopes'.

In only one case, LEA 6, was there marginal *statistical* evidence in favour of the 'differential slopes' hypothesis. Even here, however, when we sought a substantive interpretation of the finding we found it made practically no difference to the assessment of schools' effects on pupils' performance; the lines crossed a bit but not very much. Figure 4 shows that in LEA 6A the difference of four examination score points between schools at the upper and lower quartiles of effectiveness, which we earlier established for pupils at the median level of prior attainment, was maintained for pupils of both 'lower' and 'higher' intake characteristics. In this instance, where we had data on over 4,000 pupils (i.e. virtually all of them) in a relatively large number of schools within the LEA, it might be assumed that we were looking at the upper level of precision as far as estimates for a given LEA are concerned.

In brief, whilst the capacity of multi-level modelling procedures to test routinely for the existence of differential slopes is an essential feature of any attempt to analyse schools' effectiveness, it should not be assumed, equally routinely, that differential effectiveness is prevalent. Most of the schools in our study seem to have had similar effects on most of their pupils.

EXPLANATORY POWER: SUBSTANTIVE AND STATISTICAL ISSUES

Our analyses confirm many of the findings of earlier studies. None the less, there have clearly been some differences, both in terms of results and their interpretation, and it is worthwhile exploring some of the reasons why these may have occurred. The answers are probably both substantive and statistical.

School effectiveness studies are premised on a key assumption, namely that major differences in the intakes to different schools have been taken into account in the analysis. Although we have rarely seen it articulated in the precise way we outline below, researchers mostly agree about the relative importance and desirability of different kinds of 'explanatory' variables.

Assuming that they could arrange for the collection of the variables they wanted, rather than merely make the best use of those available, their rough order of hierarchy might go as follows:

(1) At the top would be *finely-differentiated measures of prior attainment* (say at age 11) of the same measures that were subsequently to be employed as outcome measures (say at age 16). If, for example, attainment in mathematics at 16 is of interest then the best 'intake' measure is a score on a test mathematics at age 11. In practice, researchers frequently have to settle for approximations such as a summary score of examination results at 16 and a summary score of attainment at 11 on a (related) cognitive test (or tests). To date, very few studies indeed have had satisfactory measures of this kind available to them.

(2) Next in line would come *grouped measures of prior attainment* for individual pupils. In the Inner London Education Authority, for example, pupils are assigned to one of three groups, based on cognitive tests, at the point of transfer to secondary schools. A complication, in this particular case, is that the three groups are not equal in size; 25 per cent are allocated to Band 1, 50% to Band 2 and the remaining 25% to Band 3, which means that the score eventually attributed to individual pupils is only a rough approximation of the actual score(s) that particular pupil achieved. This was a factor to be taken into account in Rutter's earlier study (see Gray, 1981b) and may well be important in interpreting the results from the latest ILEA study (see Nuttall *et al.*, 1989).

(3) Whilst there would probably be fairly general agreement about (1) and (2) above, there is not quite the same consensus amongst the researchers about the next-most-desirable strategies to adopt. One frequently adopted approach is to collect information on pupils' *social backgrounds*. Most, but not all, of the Scottish studies have used these kinds of measures and they have the advantage that they are independent of the effects of teaching provided by schools. Parental background may affect the kind of school a pupil attends but the school's effects are unlikely to influence the parents' background.

The main problem with social background measures is that they are not usually very finely-differentiated. Two pupils who are both recorded in the data as 'middle class' may, none the less, differ in various other important respects. One, for example, may have parents who take deliberate steps to get them into a particular kind of school with a strong orientation towards maximising exam achievement; another may not. The overwhelming desirability of employing prior attainment measures whenever possible, in preference to social background measures is underlined by one of the Scottish data-sets where both kinds of measures were available (see Willms & Raudenbush, 1989). The former variables dominate the modelling exercise.

Another strategy quite frequently adopted by researchers is to administer a so-called *'test of ability'* at or near the time when the outcome measures themselves are being collected (see, for example, Blakey & Heath, 1988). This approach, in contrast to measures of social background, has the disadvantage that it cannot be assumed to be independent of the schools' influence; the school which boosts pupils' exam achievements may also be boosting their performance on the tests of ability as well.

(4) Measures of the pupils' *social or cognitive characteristics aggregated to the level of the school* lag some way behind the above measures in terms of their desirability. An LEA might, for example, have calculated the percentage of pupils on free school meals or know what proportion of pupils entered a school with 'below average' reading scores as a result of some screening exercise. Obviously, such measures are the most worthwhile, the more they relate to the particular pupils whose outcome measures have been the focus of interest. Often the main function of the existence of such data is to signal the *possibility* of establishing individual-level records without actually providing it

at the time of analysis. A variety of such measures may be found in an earlier review by Gray (1981a).

(5) Finally, there are measures of the *characteristics of the neighbourhoods* in which particular schools are located, drawn from the 1981 Census and similar surveys. Measures of this kind have often been assembled by LEAs because they can be obtained without making demands on schools; they are the kinds of measures that the Task Group on Assessment and Testing (DES, 1988) recommended LEAs create to aid the interpretation of results from national attainment testing. However, these are generally the least useful for studying particular schools as they rarely relate to the actual pupils to be found in each school. Pupils attend schools outside their neighbourhoods; schools in particular areas draw pupils from (much) further afield; some pupils do not attend state schools at all; and the nature of whole areas can change between one census and the next.

In the present study we possessed information of types (1) and (3) above. As a direct consequence we were able to reconstruct our data in the form of (2) as well. In general, we found that our data behaved much as would have been predicted from knowledge of previous studies. The simple correlations between individual pupils' social background characteristics and their fifth-year examination results were around 0.35 (ranging from around 0.3 to around 0.4) and for measures of prior attainment and examination results around 0.7. These estimates are well within the range of earlier studies.

If the reasoning outlined in points (1) to (3) above is accepted, however, then there are good reasons for placing greater emphasis on the results emerging from the data-sets for LEAs 5, and 6A and 6B; in each case a finely-differentiated measure of prior attainment was available (see Table 2). There was a fair measure of consistency in the ways the data in these three data-sets behaved but they were also the data-sets which most strongly challenged some of the findings of earlier research. Amongst other things they yielded:

- estimates of the variation between schools that were at the lower end;
- weak (or non-existent) evidence for 'compositional' or 'contextual' effects; and
- little evidence of differential effectiveness across schools for sub-groups of pupils.

The substantive discussion outlined above indicates that, depending on the types of controls for intake that are employed, very different answers about the relative importance of between-school differences can be obtained. This view is reinforced by the statistical evidence. As Column 2 of Table 2 demonstrates, the amount of overall variation between pupils in results that can be 'explained' by social background factors varied between about 10% and 20%; the equivalent figures for models incorporating measures of prior attainment, in contrast, 'explained' getting on for 60%. The proportion of variance in the outcome measure which remains 'unexplained' is then apportioned (in the

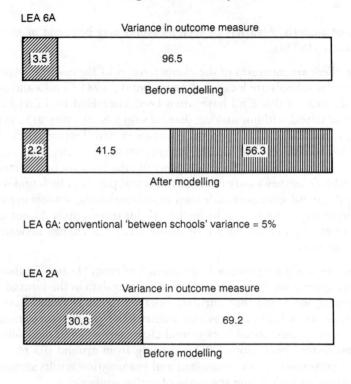

LEA 6A

Variance in outcome measure

| 3.5 | 96.5 |

Before modelling

| 2.2 | 41.5 | 56.3 |

After modelling

LEA 6A: conventional 'between schools' variance = 5%

LEA 2A

Variance in outcome measure

| 30.8 | 69.2 |

Before modelling

| 21.8 | 65.6 | 12.6 |

After modelling

LEA 2A: conventional 'between schools' variance = 25%

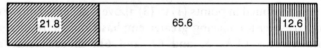

Key: variance assigned to schools;

         variance between pupils explained by the model

Figure 5 The percentages of total variance assigned to schools and pupils before and after modelling in two data-sets

two-level model) to variance which lies 'between pupils' and variance which lies 'between schools'. It is this latter estimate which has been presented in Column 3 of Table 2, where the 'between schools' variance ranges from about 1% to 5% in the models incorporating prior attainment measures, and from about 4% to 25% in those including just social background measures.

Focusing on the 'between schools' variance can be useful insofar as it has concentrated attention directly on the potential effects of schools on pupils' performance. However, there has been a tendency, in some recent multi-level analyses, to ignore to some extent the underlying 'goodness of fit' of the fixed part of the model and this can be misleading. As our discussion has already shown, the underlying explanatory power of the variables that are used to control for differences in schools' intakes can be crucial to the kinds of conclusions that are drawn. In brief, estimates of schools' effects need to be seen in the context of the *total* variance in the outcome measures as well.

We can best illustrate this issue by reference to some of our LEA data-sets. Take LEA 6A for example. The total variance in the exam outcome measure was scaled (as in all the data-sets) to 100%. Of this total 3.5% was assigned, in the null model, to variations between schools (see Column 1 of Table 2 earlier). For the purposes of explication this information is also presented in diagrammatic form in Figure 5.

When account was taken of differences in pupils' prior attainment 56.3% of this total variance was accounted for. The residual variance was therefore 43.7% (100 minus 56.3). Of this we reported (following the procedures hitherto employed) that 5.0% was estimated to lie 'between schools' (see column 3 of Table 2). To obtain this figure we concentrated just on the residual part of the model (the 43.7%) and expressed 2.2 (the proportion of the total variance attributed to schools) as a percentage of 43.7 (i.e. 5%). By way of contrast we have also presented in Figure 5 the estimates for another data-set (LEA 2A).

Table 6 Results of the model-fitting including estimates of variance between schools based on the residual and total variance

LEA data-set	Column 1 Unadjusted school variance (%)	Column 2 Fixed effects (%)	Column 3 School effects (residual) (%)	Column 4 School effects (overall) (%)
1A	15.2	20.4	6.4	5.1
1B	10.8	11.4	5.2	4.6
1C	12.0	12.8	7.9	6.9
2A	30.8	12.6	25.0	21.8
2B	28.9	11.8	23.7	20.9
3A	5.4	14.3	3.7	3.2
3B	6.6	10.8	3.5	3.1
4	6.2	13.5	3.9	3.4
5	7.1	54.5	1.5	0.7
6A	3.5	56.3	5.0	2.2
6B	3.7	58.1	4.0	1.7

Notes

Model 1 fixed effects: pupil level variables, from those available, found to contribute significantly to the prediction of examination scores are included in the model. Random effects: school level (intercepts) and pupil level residuals are estimated.

Column 1: Variance attributed to (random) school effects prior to controlling for pupil-level characteristics (expressed as a percentage of the overall variance).

Column 2: Variance explained by fixed part of the model (expressed as a percentage of the overall variance).

Column 3: Variance attributed to (random) school effects (expressed as a percentage of the residual variance).

Column 4: Variance attributed to (random) school effects (expressed as a percentage of the overall variance).

Here the extent of between school differences appears to be substantially larger, regardless of which estimate (the 21.8% or the 25%) we concentrate on.

In fact, both statistics (the proportion of the total variance and the proportion of the residual variance) are of interest but can usefully be seen alongside each other. In Table 6, therefore, we have repeated the estimates already presented in Table 2 but have, in addition, incorporated a fourth column providing evidence on the proportion of the total variance lying between schools, after incorporating differences in the schools' intakes.

The implications of the factors controlled for in the various models (social background as opposed to prior attainment) become clearer here. In the former cases, where social background factors alone were controlled for, the estimates of the between school variance are reduced a little but the substantive interpretations are not changed very much. In the latter cases, however, the estimates are roughly halved (from 1.5 to 0.7; from 5.0 to 2.2; and from 4.0 to 1.7). In other words, estimates which we had already described as 'low' have become lower still. Again the importance of taking into account the explanatory power of the model being employed is emphasised. Models which incorporate information about pupils' prior attainment produce different answers from those which are confined to social background factors alone.

IMPLICATIONS FOR POLICY AND PRACTICE

A number of lessons may be drawn from the research reported here, both for the development of policy and for the implementation of practice.

The first, and most important, relates to the creation of strategies for maintaining records on individual pupils. Without such procedures any attempts to foster more appropriate frameworks for the evaluation of school performance will founder.

The second concerns the data that are gathered to describe (and model) schools' intakes. The analyses reported here underline the value of obtaining data on the prior attainments of individual pupils; data on their social backgrounds can provide an important supplement, when prior attainment data are already available, but are unlikely to prove an adequate substitute.

The development of national attainment testing will potentially aid both these concerns, provided that LEAs take steps now to build suitable frameworks for the collection of the resultant data and their subsequent interpretation.

Third, we believe LEAs will need to give some attention to the ways in which they analyse and report their schools' results. The focus should be on the 'progress' made and the schools' contribution (the so-called 'value-added' approach). In particular, it will be necessary for them to test whether schools are differentially effective with pupils of different prior attainments. Only by providing firmly-based and realistic estimates of the extent of prevailing differences in schools' effectiveness (as well as their effects on particular subgroups of pupils) will they be able to counter the more extreme (and often 'raw') results that are frequently injected into public debates by the media and others. If schools are to be protected from inappropriate comparisons, then their LEAs need to be able not only to assert that 'schools make a difference' but to indicate by how much.

In our interactions with policy-makers and practitioners over the past few years we have frequently heard it asserted that sophisticated analyses of schools' performance are beyond the means and capabilities of most LEAs and their schools, even if they wanted to undertake them. We would merely remind them that the present paper stands as testimony to the future possibilities.

ACKNOWLEDGEMENTS

The authors would particularly like to thank Roel Bosker, Harvey Goldstein and Doug Willms for detailed comments on aspects of the analyses. Some of the data used here were collected during the course of two ESRC-funded research projects (C 0525 0012 and C 0023 0076). The remainder were assembled as part of the Performance Indicators Project at Sheffield University which is funded by several different LEAs at the present time. All the analyses reported here were conducted using a statistical package developed by the ESRC-funded Multi-level Models Project based at the London Institute of Education (see Rasbash *et al.*, 1989).

REFERENCES

Aitken, M. and Longford, N. (1986) Statistical modelling issues in school effectiveness studies, *Journal of Royal Statistical Society*, Series A, 149, pp. 1–43.

Blakey, L. and Heath, A. (1988) Differences between comprehensive schools: some preliminary findings for fifteen schools, paper presented to the International Conference on School Effectiveness, London University.

Coleman, J. S. *et al.* (1966) *Equality of Educational Opportunity* (US Office of Education, Washington, DC, US Govt Printing Office).

Cuttance, P. (1988) Intra-system variation in the effectiveness of schools, *Research Papers in Education*, 2(3), pp. 180–216.

Cuttance, P. and Goldstein, H. (1988) A note on national assessment and school comparisons, *Journal of Education Policy*, 3, pp. 197–202.

Department of Education & Science (1988) *Task Group on Assessment and Testing: a report* (the Black Report) (London, DES).

Department of Education & Science (1989) *School Indicators for Internal Management: an aide memoire*, 5 December (London, DES).

Gray, J. (1981a) A competitive edge: examination results and the probable limits of secondary school effectiveness, *Educational Review*, 33, pp. 25–35.

Gray, J. (1981b) Towards effective schools, *British Educational Research Journal*, pp. 59–69.

Gray, J. (1989) Multi-level models: issues and problems emerging from their recent application in British studies of school effectiveness, in: R. D. Bock (Ed.) *Multi-level Analysis of Educational Data*, pp. 127–145. (New York, Academic Press).

Gray, J. and Jesson, D. (1987) Exam results and local authority league tables, in: A. Harrison and J. Gretton (Eds) *Education and Training UK 1987*, pp. 33–41. (Newbury, Policy Journals).

Gray, J. and Jesson, D. (1989) The impact of comprehensive reforms, in: R. Lowe (Ed.) *The Changing Secondary School*, pp. 72–98 (Lewes, Falmer Press).

Gray, J., Jesson, D. and Jones, B. (1986) The search for a fairer way of comparing schools' examination results, *Research Papers in Education*, 1, pp. 91–122.

Goldstein, H. (1984) The methodology of school comparisons, *Oxford Review of Education*, 10, pp. 69–74.

Goldstein, H. (1987) *Multi-level Models in Educational and Social Research* (London, Griffin).

Heath, A. and Clifford P. (1980) The seventy thousand hours that Rutter left out, *Oxford Review of Education*, 6, pp. 1–19.

Heath, A. and Clifford, P. (1981) The measurement and explanation of school differences, *Oxford Review of Education*, 7, pp. 33–40.

Jencks, C. *et al.* (1972) *Inequality: a reassessment of the effects of family and schooling in America*, (New York, Basic Books).

Kilgore, S. and Pendleton, T. (1986) in: Aitkin and Longford, *op. cit.*

Longford, N. T. (1986) VARCL: interactive software for variance component analysis, *Professional Statistician*, 5, pp. 28–32.

McPherson, A. F. and Willms, J. D. (1986) Certification, class conflict, religion and community: a socio-historical explanation of the effectiveness of contemporary schools, in: A. C. Kerckhoff (Ed.) *Research in Sociology of Education and Socialisation*, vol. 6, pp. 227–302. (Greenwich, CT, JAI).

Mortimore, P., Sammons, P., Stoll, L., Lewis, D. and Ecob, R. (1988) *School Matters* (London, Paul Chapman).

Nuttall, D., Goldstein, H., Prosser, R. and Rasbash, J. (1989) Differential school effectiveness, *International Journal of Educational Research*, 13, pp. 769–776.

Paterson, L. (1989) An introduction to multi-level modelling, paper presented to the ESRC International Conference on Applications of Multi-level Methods of Educational Research, Edinburgh University.

Preece, P. (1989) Pitfalls in research on school and teacher effectiveness, *Research Papers in Education*, 4, (3), pp. 47–69.

Rasbash, J., Prosser, R. and Goldstein, H. (1989) *ML2 Users Guide: software for two-level analysis* (University of London Institute of Education).

Raudenbush, S. and Bryk, A. (1986) A hierarchical model for studying school effects, *Sociology of Education*, 59, pp. 1–17.

Rutter, M., Maughan, B., Mortimore, P. and Ouston, J. (1979) *Fifteen Thousand Hours: secondary schools and their effects on children* (London, Open Books).

Smith, D. and Tomlinson, S. (1989) *The School Effect: a study of multi-racial comprehensives* (London, Policy Studies Institute).

Smith, M. S. (1972) The basic findings reconsidered, in: F. Mosteller and D. P. Moynihan (Eds) *On Equality of Educational Opportunity* (New York, Random House).

Willms, J. D. (1985) The balance thesis: contextual effects of ability on pupils' O grade examination results, *Oxford Review of Education*, 11, pp. 33–41.

Willms, J. D. (1986) Social class segregation and its relationship to pupils' examination results in Scotland, *American Sociological Review*, 51, pp. 224–241.

Willms, J. D. (1987) Differences between Scottish education authorities in their examination attainment, *Oxford Review of Education*, 13, pp. 211–237.

Willms, D. and Raudenbush, S. (1989) A longitudinal hierarchical linear model for estimating school effects and their stability, *Journal of Educational Measurement*, 26, pp. 209–232.

Woodhouse, G. and Goldstein, H. (1988) Educational performance indicators and LEA league tables, *Oxford Review of Education*, 14, pp. 301–302.

8

THE QUALITY OF TEACHING IN PRIMARY SCHOOLS*

R. Alexander, J. Rose and C. Woodhead

[*Editors' note:* In December 1991, the Secretary of State for Education commissioned a report from Robin Alexander, Professor of Primary Education, Leeds University, Jim Rose, Chief Inspector, Her Majesty's Inspectorate, and Chris Woodhead, Chief Executive, National Curriculum Council. They were asked 'to review available evidence about the delivery of education in primary schools' and 'to make recommendations about curriculum organization, teaching methods and classroom practice appropriate for the successful implementation of the National Curriculum'. The Secretary of State emphasized his desire 'to initiate a discussion, not to impose solutions', and the authors declared this to be their aim. Their report was published in January 1992. After a brief introduction (paras 1–5) and a brief background to primary education in the 1990s (paras 6–23), the authors review 'standards of achievement in primary schools' (paras 24–50).

The section (IV) that follows this is the longest and most significant within the report, and is reproduced here in full, together with the list of 'the main sources consulted'. These were contained in an appendix, rather than being cited in the text, 'to maintain continuity in the discussion'. We have retained the original paragraph numbers.]

THE QUALITY OF TEACHING IN PRIMARY CLASSROOMS

The focus of classroom research and enquiry

51 This section of the report is based on a review of the available research evidence about teaching and learning in primary schools in England, as it has

---

* Section IV of *Curriculum Organisation and Classroom Practice in Primary Schools: A Discussion Paper*, Department of Education and Science, London.

accumulated over the past twenty years. The three main strands to this evidence are summarised below in order to define the context in which our discussion is set.

52 The first, and longest established, focus of enquiry is the empirical study of how primary pupils develop and learn. To teach well, teachers must take account of how children learn. We do not, however, believe that it is possible to construct a model of primary education from evidence about children's development alone: the nature of the curriculum followed by the pupil and the range of teaching strategies employed by the teacher are also of critical importance. Teaching is not applied child development. It is a weakness of the child-centred tradition that it has sometimes tended to treat it as such and, consequently, to neglect the study of classroom practice.

53 Recent research into children's learning does, however, emphasise young children's immense cognitive and linguistic competence. In the 60s and 70s, Piagetian theories about developmental ages and stages led to chronologically fixed notions of 'readiness', thus depressing expectations and discouraging teacher intervention. More recent studies demonstrate what children, given effective teaching, can achieve and, in particular, the young child's capacity to understand the structure of subjects. They show that learning is essentially a social and interactive process. They place proper emphasis on the teacher as teacher rather than 'facilitator'. Such insights are, in our view, critical to the raising of standards in primary classrooms, and we build upon them in later sections of the report.

54 The second research strand focuses on social factors in educational achievement. This research highlights both the destabilising impact on young children of adverse home circumstances and the potency of stability and support. While there was a time when home circumstances were offered as a convenient explanation for virtually any difficulty which a pupil might experience in the classroom, thus absolving teacher and school of any responsibility, there is now a much more balanced and realistic understanding of the relative impact of home and school.

Up to a point, the socially advantaged child can compensate for school inadequacy. The disadvantaged child is doubly disadvantaged by the weak school. Schools can and do make a difference, and, given the broad estimate that two thirds of pupils in inner city schools are disadvantaged, it is vitally important that all schools have the highest expectations of all their pupils.

56 The third strand of evidence, which includes both the work of HMI and research studies, shows how different professional practices affect the quality of pupil learning. HMI has reported extensively on issues of school management, curriculum planning, progression, and many aspects of classroom practice. Research studies have on the one hand helped clarify the ideas which shape classroom practice and, on the other, have generated a very considerable body of empirical data about the effectiveness of particular teaching methods. These data are highly significant in that the conclusions for differently-focused research studies are broadly complementary.

The changing task of the primary teacher

57   One obvious point which emerges from this material is that the task of the primary teacher has changed significantly with the advent of the National Curriculum. Year 1 and 2 teachers, in particular, have invested enormous time and energy in coming to terms with the new statutory requirements, and, as a consequence, a very great deal has been achieved in the last two years. As we write, primary schools are teaching the statutory Orders for six of the nine National Curriculum subjects, will shortly be planning for the introduction of the remaining three, and are preparing for the second full run of Key Stage 1 assessment. Inevitably, the initial effort has been to master the demands of the statutory Orders. The time is now right to examine the appropriateness of existing models of curriculum organisation, teaching methodology and staff deployment in the light of the National Curriculum requirements.

The importance of planning

58   Curriculum planning is one aspect of primary teaching which, traditionally problematic, is now improving significantly. HMI have, from the late 1970's onwards, identified weaknesses in planning at the level of both school and classroom. Much school planning in areas other than mathematics and reading (where published schemes provided a not always appropriate prop) amounted to little more than an attempt to list the content to be covered. As a result, continuity and progression in the arts and humanities were often suspect. HMI report that one of the first visible improvements in primary schools has been curriculum planning in relation to the National Curriculum core subjects. With the introduction of the National Curriculum and the School Development Plan initiative, there has been a recognition that teachers must plan together to ensure consistency and progression across classes and year groups and that formally structured short and long-term planning are essential to effective classroom teaching.

59   The National Curriculum has introduced a similar discipline into planning at classroom level. In the past, too many teachers have argued that rigorous and comprehensive planning militates against the need for spontaneity and flexibility. In fact, the two are perfectly compatible. With the introduction of the National Curriculum, this dichotomy is now simply untenable.

60   We wish to emphasise that planning is taking far more time than in the past. This may be a relatively short-term phenomenon as teachers become familiar with the demands of the Statutory Orders, but the situation must be monitored over the next few years as part of an overall drive to ensure that the National Curriculum provides a manageable framework for primary education. We also believe that schools need to monitor their use of non-contact time within the statutory 1,265 hours. There is evidence to suggest that head-teachers and senior staff can take a disproportionate amount of the limited

non-contact time available. All teachers need time to plan and prepare their work. There are strong arguments for a more equitable distribution of such non-contact time as exists.

61   We recognise, looking to the future, that further developments in the quality of curriculum planning depend upon the management of whole school planning across all National Curriculum subjects and both key stages. In some schools collective planning at Key Stage 2 has yet to move beyond the core subjects. It will also be necessary to consider how school and classroom planning can be effectively related, and, in particular, whether the new subject requirements can be reconciled with the established commitment to cross-curricular planning through such devices as 'topic webs'.

Curriculum structure and organisation: subjects or topics?

62   The vast majority of primary schools organise the curriculum in terms of subjects and topic work. A topic is generally understood to be a mode of curriculum organisation, frequently enquiry based, which brings elements of different subjects together under a common theme. A small minority of schools organise the whole of the curriculum in terms of separate subjects; virtually no primary school works solely through topics. HMI report that about 30 per cent of work in primary schools is taught as single subjects. Music, physical education, most mathematics and some English are usually taught as separate subjects. The other foundation subjects are very often taught, entirely or largely, as aspects of topic work.

63   Despite these demonstrable facts, the rhetoric of primary education has for a long time been hostile to the idea that young children should be exposed to subjects. Subject divisions, it is argued, are inconsistent with the child's view of the world. Children must be allowed to construct their own meanings and subject teaching involves the imposition of a received version of knowledge. And, moreover, it is the wholeness of the curriculum which is important rather than the distinct identity of the individual subjects.

64   Each of these familiar assertions needs to be contested. First, to resist subjects on the grounds that they are inconsistent with children's views of the world is to confine them within their existing modes of thought and deny them access to some of the most powerful tools for making sense of the world which human beings have ever devised. Second, while it is self evident that every individual, to an extent, constructs his/her own meanings, education is an encounter between these personal understandings and the public knowledge embodied in our cultural traditions. The teacher's key responsibility is to mediate such encounters so that the child's understanding is enriched. And, finally, the integrity of the curriculum as a whole is hardly likely to be achieved by sacrificing the integrity of its constituent parts.

65   In evaluating these arguments it is helpful to draw a distinction between integration, which entails bringing together subjects with distinct identities,

and non-differentiation, which does not concede that such distinctiveness is acceptable. Teachers (often of young pupils) who prefer to view the curriculum in terms of broad areas such as language, investigation and creative work are particularly committed to this second view.

66   We consider that a National Curriculum conceived in terms of distinct subjects makes it impossible to defend a non-differentiated curriculum. This does not mean that all the National Curriculum subjects must necessarily be taught separately: curriculum conception and modes of curriculum organisation must not be confused. But, whatever the mode of organisation, pupils must be able to grasp the particular principles and procedures of each subject, and, what is equally important, they must be able to progress from one level of knowledge, understanding and skill to another within the subject.

67   If it can be shown that the topic approach allows the pupil both to make acceptable progress within the different subjects of the National Curriculum and to explore the relationships between them, then the case for such an approach is strong on both pedagogic and logistical grounds. If, however, the result is that the differences between subjects are extinguished, then the strategy is indefensible.

68   There is no doubt that much topic work has been and still is very undemanding, particularly in history and geography. Too many topics amount to little more than aimless and superficial copying from books and offer pupils negligible opportunities for progression from one year to the next. Art is too often limited to the level of picture making to illustrate topic writing. Much pupil time can be wasted on so-called 'collaborative' projects. These are serious weaknesses in classroom practice.

69   Many schools have yet, moreover, to make full use of the National Curriculum programmes of study in planning topics. Some do not have clear, well documented schemes of work covering both key stages and detailing the subject content, knowledge and skills. Others do not provide appropriately differentiated work which caters for a full range of ability. The intrinsic complexity of topic work means that problems will remain until rigorous planning becomes the norm. Subject coherence can be lost in the attempt to subsume too much into the grand theme; key attainment targets may be given only cursory attention; monitoring and assessment can remain weak.

70   This is not to deny that the topic approach can, in skilled hands, produce work of high quality. There is evidence to suggest that some schools, recognising the problems outlined above, are planning carefully structured topic frameworks for Years 1 to 6 which map the attainment targets and programmes of study of the subjects involved. In particular, there are signs of a move away from 'divergent' topics (where pupils have considerable freedom to follow their own interests in response to a common starting point such as a visit or a book read to the class) to either 'broad-based' topics (where a theme like 'transport' is used to bring together content and skills from several subjects) or 'subject-focused' topics (where pupils concentrate upon a limited number of attainment targets from one particular subject but may also study

relevant material from other subjects). In that it can be planned more easily in relation to the Statutory Orders and can provide more appropriately for the sequential development of pupils' knowledge, understanding and skills, the subject-focused topic, in particular, offers an efficient way forward.

71   These are positive developments. The introduction of the National Curriculum means, however, that a substantial amount of separate subject teaching will be necessary if every aspect of each programme of study is to be covered effectively. This is particularly the case at Key Stage 2, but some Key Stage 1 teachers will need to move towards a greater amount of subject teaching than usually exists.

72   Such a move need not necessarily result in the highly fragmented, incoherent curriculum which is feared by exponents of the topic approach. Topic work, when planned and executed poorly, can be even more fragmentary. We must emphasise, however, that good subject teaching depends upon the teachers' knowledge, skills and understanding in the subject concerned. Mathematics, for example, has been consistently taught as a separate subject, has been, for the most part, supported by commercially produced teaching materials, and has received generous funding and INSET support. Yet criticisms of primary mathematics voiced in the 1970s persist into the 1990s. Standards will be raised only when the requirements of each subject are dealt with clearly and systematically.

Curriculum breadth, balance and consistency

73   Whatever the mode of curriculum organisation, the breadth, balance and consistency of the curriculum experienced by pupils must be of central concern.

74   There is considerable evidence that prior to the introduction of the National Curriculum there were significant and unacceptable variations in the curriculum provided between and even within schools. While all schools devoted considerable amounts of time to English and mathematics, some neglected important aspects of these subjects such as reading extension, oral work and mathematical problem solving. Others failed, moreover, to devote adequate attention to history, geography, art and music. The National Curriculum was introduced, in part, to ensure that all children have access to a broad and balanced curriculum that is consistent country-wide.

75   Concerns are now being expressed over the pressure which the core subjects are perceived to be exerting on the time available to teach other curriculum areas. And some aspects of the core subjects themselves, notably reading, appear to be squeezed as teachers concentrate their attention on hitherto less familiar attainment targets. These may be transitional problems inevitable in a period of radical curriculum change. But the structure of the National Curriculum as a whole and the weight of detail in individual subjects will need to be kept under careful review so that we can be confident that the

curriculum experienced by pupils is appropriately broad and balanced, but, nonetheless, rigorous.

76   It is also important to learn lessons from empirical research which predates the National Curriculum. This research tells us that:

i   Curriculum balance is not merely a matter of time. More fundamentally, it is about quality. The principle of curriculum entitlement means that subjects must be taught equally well whatever the amount of time devoted to them. Too often in the past those subjects most at risk in an overcrowded curriculum (the non-core foundation subjects and those not required by law) may also have been the very subjects which received least attention from national initiatives, LEA support and INSET, and from school curriculum review, development and resourcing. This imbalance in support needs to be addressed.

ii   Some teachers are much less efficient than others in their use of the time which is allocated to the core subjects. Pupils are more likely, that is, to spend a higher proportion of time off task in the reading and writing tasks which dominate mathematics and English than when engaged in other activities. In short, the time devoted to these subjects by such teachers is not well used.

iii To think about curriculum balance solely in terms of subject time allocations, however, is to neglect another and possibly more fundamental way in which the curriculum impacts upon the child. Classroom research, for example, has identified 'generic activities' (such as reading, writing, using apparatus, talking with the teacher and collaborating with other children) which pupils encounter daily regardless of subject labels. The balance which is struck amongst such activities is arguably as important as the balance which is struck amongst subjects.

The problem of curricular expertise

77   We use the phrase 'curricular expertise' to mean the subject knowledge, the understanding of how children learn, and the skills needed to teach subjects successfully. Effective teaching depends upon the successful combination of these understandings and skills. Opinion is divided about the relative importance of the teacher's subject knowledge, but few now dispute that it is important. Our own view is that subject knowledge is a critical factor at every point in the teaching process: in planning, assessing and diagnosing, task setting, questioning, explaining and giving feedback. The key question to be answered is whether the class teacher system makes impossible demands on the subject knowledge of the generalist primary teacher. We believe that it does.

78   The introduction of the National Curriculum with its statutory demands has brought the question sharply into focus, but HMI reports since the

seventies point to the close relationship which exists between the knowledge of the subject which the teacher possesses and the quality of his/her teaching. The idea of the curriculum coordinator was developed to try to ensure that a school could make maximum use of the collective subject strength of its staff. The idea was subsequently built into initial training courses through the Secretary of State's 1984 and 1989 accreditation criteria.

79 In principle, the curriculum coordinator ought, in the larger school at least, to be able to sustain the work of the generalist teacher. In practice, while coordinators have often had a significant impact upon both whole school curriculum planning and the management of resources, in many schools they have had little real influence on the competence of individual teachers and the quality of classroom teaching and learning. There is, moreover, the problem of the small school, where it is unreasonable to expect that two or three teachers can be expert in ten subjects to the depth now required.

80 While, therefore, recognising that the curriculum coordinator is a partial solution to the problem we believe that other strategies must be considered. [. . .]

Mixed and single age-group classes

81 The proportion of schools with mixed age-group classes has increased from 50 to 70 per cent in the past decade. For some schools this form of grouping is a matter of choice. For most it is not, and in all schools of less than one form entry how to organise the pupils for teaching purposes is a perennial problem.

82 Teachers adopt a variety of strategies for coping in such circumstances. Some seek to individualise the tasks they set. Some use whole class teaching but try to provide open-ended activities which ostensibly allow pupils to find their own level. Some group by age, others by ability.

83 There are schools where vertical grouping has been adopted on educational grounds, but most teachers confess to finding teaching in such classes harder than in classes where pupils are relatively close in age and ability. HMI evidence suggests, too, that the considerable ability spread inevitable in the mixed age class leads to poor match of task to pupil in a third of the classes and a general failure to challenge the most able pupils. Planning, monitoring and assessment are particularly demanding in these circumstances. These constraints must, we believe, be acknowledged as a factor to be considered whenever the viability of small schools is discussed.

Streaming

84 Streamed classes were common in the upper end of the primary age range during the era of the 11+. Since then, they have more or less been phased out.

85   Research into the effect of streaming on pupils undertaken in the 1960's showed that streaming could benefit the achievement of some pupils, notably the most able, but that there could be a significant and negative impact on the self-image of those pupils who, placed in lower streams, came to see themselves as failures. But the fundamental problem with streaming is that it is a crude device which cannot do justice to the different abilities a pupil may show in different subjects and contexts. For this reason, grouping according to ability is a more flexible device in that it allows the teacher to place a pupil in a particular ability group for a particular purpose. We believe that this is a sensible strategy. The mounting evidence about teacher under-expectation and pupil under-achievement means, however, that teachers must avoid the pitfall of assuming that pupils' ability is fixed. Assumptions about pupils' ability should be no more than working hypotheses to be modified as and when new evidence emerges.

Organisational strategies and teaching techniques

86   The substantial body of research which now exists about primary school teaching methods endorses what commonsense would expect: that the debate about the relative effectiveness of traditional and progressive methods ignores the fact that different organisational strategies and teaching techniques are needed for different purposes. Teachers need to evaluate the strengths and weaknesses of different approaches in order to make informed choices and, when necessary, should be prepared to learn new skills in the interests of effective teaching and learning.

87   We use the term 'organisational strategies' to describe the different ways in which the teacher can structure his/her class. There are three basic possibilities. Each pupil can be taught as an individual. The class can be taught as a whole. The class can be organised into groups. These strategies are, in practice, not mutually exclusive. Many teachers use all three.

Individual teaching

88   Given the self-evident fact that every child is different, individual teaching is an understandable aspiration. Indeed there are times when individual pupils will need particular help from one teacher. Pupils, for example, with learning difficulties will need one-to-one teaching for some of the time. However, it must also be said that children have much in common, and that, in practice, the effort to teach every pupil in the class as an individual is fraught with difficulties. In such circumstances, the evidence shows that however skilled and energetic the teacher, each individual pupil receives a minute proportion of the teacher's attention. The interaction between teacher and pupil is likely to be as superficial as it is brief and infrequent. Pupils, deprived of the attention from

either the teacher or other pupils which will maintain their motivation and challenge their thinking, work only intermittently. Not surprisingly, research studies show relatively low gains in pupil understanding in classrooms where teachers structure the day largely in terms of individual teaching. Teachers should not be tempted by approaches to teaching, which, when taken to extremes, can result in low level individual tasks and fleeting and superficial teacher/pupil interaction.

Whole class teaching

89 Whole class teaching appears to provide the order, control, purpose and concentration which many critics believe are lacking in modern primary classrooms.

90 To a significant extent, the evidence supports this view of whole class teaching. Whole class teaching is associated with higher-order questioning, explanations and statements, and these in turn correlate with higher levels of pupil performance. Teachers with a substantial commitment to whole class teaching appear, moreover, to be particularly effective in teaching the basic subjects.

91 The potential weaknesses of whole class teaching need, however, to be acknowledged. There is a tendency for the teaching to be pitched too much towards the middle of the ability range, and thus to risk losing the less able and boring the brightest. Observational studies show that pupils pay attention and remain on task when being taught as a class, but may, in fact, slow down their rate of working to meet the teacher's norm, thus narrowing the challenge of what is taught to an extent which advocates of whole class teaching might well find uncomfortable.

92 Despite these potential weaknesses whole class teaching is an essential teaching skill, which all primary school teachers should be able to deploy as appropriate. Provided that the teacher has a firm grasp of the subject matter to be taught and the skills to involve the class, pupils' thinking can be advanced very effectively.

Group work

93 The practice of organising the class into groups is common in all schools and inevitable in small ones. Teachers group pupils in various ways – by comparable ability, by mixed ability, by friendship, by gender, and randomly. Some use groups for some of the time; others for all of the time. Some maintain the same groupings; others vary the group according to the task or subject.

94 There will be times when grouping pupils by ability is the most appropriate way of teaching a particular aspect or subject. To be effective, such grouping depends on organisational skills which we discuss later, and,

critically, on efficient and flexible assessment procedures. The question then arises of whether ability groups should be formed irrespective of the pupil's age. We see no reason for rejecting this strategy, providing teachers are sensitive to the fact that the self esteem of lower ability pupils could be affected adversely. It is also important to recognise that wide differences in levels of maturity might pose problems.

95   Grouping pupils within the class enables resources to be shared; fosters the social development which primary schools rightly believe to be an essential part of their task; and, above all, provides for pupils to interact with each other and their teacher.

96   The fact, however, that pupils are seated in groups does not necessarily mean that they are working as a group. All too often there may be a mismatch between the collaborative setting of the group and the individual learning tasks which are given to pupils. The result is that the setting may distract pupils from their work. Since, moreover, pupils need to learn the skills and develop the attitudes upon which successful collaborative work depends, it can never be assumed that it is enough to divide the class up, announce the activity, and leave individuals within the group to interact purposefully. Effective group work depends upon careful preparation and meticulous management.

97   Group work may quickly become counterproductive if teachers try to manage too many groups of pupils within the same class and/or have pupils working on too many different activities or subjects simultaneously. This practice places considerable demands on the teacher's skills of organisation and assessment and often results in a mode of working which contributes little to pupil learning but much to teacher exhaustion. If group work is to be employed each teaching session should, therefore, focus on a manageable number of groups and learning activities.

98   Teachers also need to be very careful in their investment of time between groups. Proper planning and careful monitoring of what actually happens in the classroom can ensure that the teacher works purposefully with each group, and, over a period of time, that a balance is struck between different areas of the curriculum. If time is not monitored in this way subjects deemed to be of low priority and pupils who seem capable of working with little teacher intervention may both be neglected.

Striking the balance

99   The conclusion we draw from the above analysis is that teachers need the skills and judgement to be able to select and apply whichever organisational strategy – class, group and individual – is appropriate to the task in hand. The judgement, it must be stressed, should be educational and organisational, rather than, as it so often is, doctrinal.

100   There are, of course, many primary teachers who use just such a mix of modes and there is some evidence to suggest that the proportion of whole

class teaching has increased since the arrival of the National Curriculum. One recent research study shows teachers spending about a third of their time on whole class teaching, and another, which incorporates a national classroom sample, shows an almost exact three way balance between individual, group and whole class teaching. Bearing in mind that both studies relate to the infant stage, within which the tradition of individual and group work is strongest, it may well be that the proportion of whole class teaching is already, without any external pressure, higher at Key Stage 2.

101   But the issue is not one of mathematical proportion. The critical notion is that of fitness for purpose. The teacher must be clear about the goals of learning before deciding on methods of organisation. Whole class teaching, group work and one-to-one teaching are each particularly suited to certain conditions and objectives. Equally, they can be used in singularly inappropriate ways.

Teaching techniques

102   By 'teaching techniques' we mean the different methods a teacher can use to work with his/her pupils to promote their learning.

103   We endorse the common-sense view that teachers need to be competent in a range of techniques in order to achieve different learning outcomes. They need, for example, to be able to give precise instructions, to explain ideas clearly, to demonstrate practical activities, to pose different kinds of questions, and to help pupils understand how well they have done.

104   The importance of this range of techniques needs emphasising for three reasons. First, there is a persistent and damaging belief that pupils should never be told things, only asked questions. We believe that there are many circumstances in which it is more appropriate to tell than to ask, and we want, therefore, to underline how important it is for teachers to be able to explain ideas to their pupils. Pupils, for obvious reasons, value coherent and sensitive explanations very highly. Second, there is also a belief that teachers must never point out when a pupil is wrong. Proffer anything but unqualified praise, the argument goes, and the child's confidence will be undermined forever. There is no reason, in fact, why constructive critical feedback and encouragement should be regarded as incompatible. Finally, we think that these basic teaching techniques have been underrated in many schools and neglected in some primary initial training courses. The tendency has been to promote indirect teaching methods where, for example, pupils work on their own with books and work cards. The balance between direct and indirect teaching needs to be reviewed.

105   We say this because the research evidence demonstrates very clearly that the level of cognitive challenge provided by the teacher is a significant factor in performance. One way of providing challenge is to set pupils demanding tasks. But, equally, it is important for teachers to organise their classrooms so that they have the opportunity to interact with their pupils: to offer explanations which develop thinking, to encourage speculation and hypothesis

through sensitive questioning, to create, above all, a climate of interest and purpose.

106   Working in these ways allows the teacher to understand how the pupil is thinking and to influence that thinking. These are powerful techniques for promoting progress in learning. The problem is, of course, to find sufficient time, given the number of pupils typically to be found in a primary classroom. But teachers need to reject the essentially unrealistic belief that pupils' individual differences provide the central clue as to how the simultaneous teaching of many individuals can be organised. The goals of primary education are common to all pupils. It is with this reality that planning for teaching should start.

Matching the task to the pupil

107   Standards of education in primary schools will not rise until teachers expect more of their pupils, and, in particualr, more of able and disadvantaged children.

108   The problem is partly ideological. In some schools and local education authorities the legitimate drive to create equal opportunities for all pupils has resulted in an obsessive fear of anything which, in the jargon, might be deemed 'elitist'. As a consequence, the needs of some of our most able children have quite simply not been met. There has also been a tendency to stereotype, and, in particular, to assume that social disadvantage leads inevitably to educational failure. This waste of potential must not continue.

109   A second explanation lies in the classroom itself where a number of factors have combined to create a situation in which pupils may be set tasks which fail to challenge their level of understanding. The problem may be that the teacher's knowledge of the subject is inadequate. It may stem from a view of 'match', which, in emphasising a child's 'readiness' and requiring teachers to operate within some theoretical notion of what children of a given age or stage are capable of, positively invites low expectations. But research has shown that over-complex patterns of classroom organisation can also contribute to the problem. If teachers are submerged by low-level routine activities, they do not have the time needed for proper diagnosis and task matching. A reduction in class sizes and the use of non-teaching assistants would obviously remove some of the pressure, but teachers can and should, in our view, review how they currently organise their classrooms in order to ensure that they are making the most efficient use possible of one of the most valuable resources schools possess: teaching time.

110   Given that significant progress could be made through a more efficient use of teaching time, we must add that the idea that at any one time learning tasks in nine subjects can be exactly matched to the needs and abilities of all the pupils in a class is hopelessly unrealistic. Match and differentiation are critical to effective learning, but they are aspirations rather than absolutes. In current circumstances, the best the teacher can do (and it is a great deal) is to devise the classroom settings and pupil tasks which give the best chance of success.

Assessing and recording progress

111   HMI surveys since the 70's show that pupil assessment has often been a largely intuitive process. Records have been similarly idiosyncratic and have tended to be limited to the basics and to focus on tasks encountered rather than learning achieved. Until recently, parents often received generalised, laconic statements which offered little real insight into the progress their children had made.

112   Many schools and LEAs had attempted to address these problems before the introduction of the National Curriculum. There is no doubt, however, that, whatever the difficulties experienced in managing the first round of standard assessment tasks, National Curriculum assessment procedures have accelerated the development process. Assessment is now becoming more open, systematic and comprehensive.

113   It is clear from evidence gathered since the introduction of the National Curriculum that effective assessment and record-keeping are more likely to occur in schools which recognise that pupils' progress depends upon assessing their strengths and weaknesses and that records are needed to ensure the transmission of information from one teacher to another, from school to home and from school to school.

114   Classroom management and organisation are particularly critical to the quality of assessment. Teachers need to observe pupils systematically, to structure their learning, and to monitor their progress. If they are to do this, then the classroom must be organised in a way which makes best use of the time they can devote to such activities. Classrooms where too many activities are going on at once risk forcing the teacher into time-wasting crisis management, rather than purposeful assessment.

115   One obvious aspect of assessment which needs emphasis is that pupils need genuine feedback about the success or otherwise of their learning. The evidence suggests that while pupils are generally clear about what they have to do, they often do not receive enough information about the purposes of their learning and, what is even more important, how well they are doing. Marking pupils' work is one valuable means of feedback, provided that it offers specific, diagnostic comment and not only encouragement. Although it is logistically difficult, the act of marking work in the pupil's presence is an even more effective approach. Pupils should as far as is feasible be involved in the assessment of their own work.

116   Assessment and record-keeping are not synonymous, though they are frequently treated as such. There is little point in developing an elaborate record-keeping system if the evidence upon which the records are based is inadequate. The pre-condition for good records is, therefore, good assessment. Indeed, there is some evidence that record-keeping may become an end in itself: cumbersome, time consuming and of little value to either teacher or pupil. The purposes and recipients of records need to be clearly identified and the records constructed accordingly.

Conclusion: key issues in classroom practice

117 We wish, first, to acknowledge the professional commitment and skill shown by primary teachers over the last two years. It is primary teachers in general (and Year 1 and 2 teachers in particular) who have faced the most daunting challenge in implementing the National Curriculum. We have no doubt whatsoever that very significant progress has been made.

118 We believe, however, that a new professional climate is needed. In recent decades much teaching in primary schools has suffered from highly questionable dogmas which have generated excessively complex classroom practice and have devalued the role of subjects in the curriculum. The new climate must encourage teachers to review their teaching techniques in the light of evidence about effective classroom practice and how well the pupils are making progress.

119 The introduction of the National Curriculum has meant that previously neglected subjects (such as science) are now receiving appropriate attention. It will, however, be important to review the overall structure and weight of detail of the National Curriculum Orders in order to ensure that there is sufficient time in the teaching day to provide a properly balanced curriculum.

120 Teachers must possess the subject knowledge which the Statutory Orders require. Without such knowledge, planning will be restricted in scope, the teaching techniques and organisational strategies employed by the teacher will lack purpose, and there will be little progression in pupils' learning.

121 The subject knowledge required by the National Curriculum makes it unlikely that the generalist primary teacher will be able to teach all subjects in the depth required. This is particularly the case in Key Stage 2, but is true also in Key Stage 1.

122 Successful teaching depends upon thorough planning. Progress has been made in recent years, but much remains to be done in order to ensure that all National Curriculum subjects are planned effectively across both key stages.

123 Subject teaching has an essential place in modern primary education. When topic work focuses on a clearly defined and limited number of attainment targets it, too, can make an important contribution to the development of pupil learning.

124 The organisational strategies of whole class teaching, group work and individual teaching need to be used selectively to achieve different educational outcomes. The criterion of choice must always be fitness for purpose. In many schools the benefits of whole class teaching have been insufficiently exploited.

125 Effective teaching, regardless of the organisational strategy used, requires the teacher to be able to deploy a range of techniques. These include: explaining, instructing, questioning, observing, assessing, diagnosing and providing feedback.

126 Standards will not rise until teachers demand more of their pupils. Over-complex patterns of classroom organisation frustrate assessment, diag-

nosis and task matching, and preoccupy teachers with management matters rather than learning tasks.

127   It is particularly important that schools undertake regular assessment of pupil progress in the fundamentally important areas of literacy and numeracy.

128   The achievement of progress in learning is the touchstone for all decisions about teaching. Good teaching does not merely keep step with the pupils but challenges and stretches their thinking.

MAIN SOURCES CONSULTED

Publications

Alexander, R. J. (1984) *Primary Teaching*. Cassell.

Alexander, R. J. (1991) *Primary Education in Leeds*. University of Leeds.

Alexander, R. J. (1992) *Policy and Practice in Primary Education*. Routledge.

Bennett, S. N. (1976) *Teaching Styles and Pupil Progress*. Open Books.

Bennett, S. N. (1991) *Group Work*. Routledge.

Bennett, S. N. (1992) *Managing Learning in the Primary School*. Association for the Study of Primary Education.

Bennett, S. N., Desforges, C., Cockburn, A., Wilkinson, B. (1984) *The Quality of Pupil Learning Experiences*. Lawrence Erlbaum.

Bennett, S. N., Dunne, E. (1992) *Managing Classroom Groups*. Simon and Schuster.

Bennett, S. N., Turner-Bissett, R. (1991) 'Subject matter knowledge and teaching performance'. University of Exeter.

Bennett, S. N., Wragg, E. C., Carré, C. G., Carter, D. S. G. (1992) 'A longitudinal study of primary teachers' perceived competence in, and concerns about, National Curriculum implementation'. *Research Papers in Education*, February 1992.

Blyth, W. A. L. (1990) *Making the Grade for Primary Humanities*. Open University Press.

Board of Education (1931) *The Primary School* (Hadow Report). HMSO.

Campbell, R. J. (1985) *Developing the Primary School Curriculum*. Cassell.

Campbell, R. J., David, T. (1990) *Depth and Quality in Children's Learning*. University of Warwick.

Campbell, R. J., Evans, S. St J., Packwood, A. (1991) *Workloads, Achievement and Stress: Two Follow-Up Studies of Teacher Time in Key Stage 1 Commissioned by the Assistant Masters and Mistresses Association*. University of Warwick.

Campbell, R. J., Neill, S. St J. (1990) *Thirteen Hundred and Thirty Days: Final Report of a Pilot Study of Teacher Time in Key Stage 1 Commissioned by the Assistant Masters and Mistresses Association*. University of Warwick.

Carré, C. (1991) 'Understanding of subject matter knowledge during a one year initial training course for primary teachers'. University of Exeter.

Cato, V., Whetton, C. (1990) *An Enquiry into LEA Evidence on Standards of Reading of Seven Year Old Children: a Report by the National Foundation for Education Research*. NFER.

Central Advisory Council for Education (England) (1967) *Children and their Primary Schools* (Plowden Report). HMSO.

Council for the Accreditation of Teacher Education (1992) *Report on the Review of the Training of Teachers to Teach Reading*. DES.

Cresswell, M., Grubb, J. (1987) *The Second International Mathematics Study in England and Wales*. NFER.

Croll, P., Moses, D. (1985) *One in Five*. Routledge.

Croll, P., Moses, D. (1988) 'Teaching methods and time on task in junior classrooms'. *Educational Research* 30:2.

Department of Education and Science (1975) *A Language for Life* (Bullock Report). HMSO.

Department of Education and Science (1978) *Primary Education in England: a Survey by HM Inspectors of Schools.* HMSO.

Department of Education and Science (1982a) *Education 5–9: an Illustrative Survey of 80 First Schools in England.* HMSO.

Department of Education and Science (1982b) *The New Teacher in School: a Report by HM Inspectors.* HMSO.

Department of Education and Science (1982c) *Mathematics Counts* (Cockcroft Report). HMSO.

Department of Education and Science (1983) *9–13 Middle Schools: an Illustrative Survey.* HMSO.

Department of Education and Science (1987) *Primary Schools: Some Aspects of Good Practice.* HMSO.

Department of Education and Science (1988) *The New Teacher in School: a Survey by HM Inspectors in England and Wales 1987.* HMSO.

Department of Education and Science (1989a) *Aspects of Primary Education: the Teaching and Learning of Science.* HMSO.

Department of Education and Science (1989b) *Aspects of Primary Education: the Teaching and Learning of Mathematics.* HMSO.

Department of Education and Science (1989c) *Aspects of Primary Education: the Teaching and Learning of History and Geography.* HMSO.

Department of Education and Science (1989d) *Standards in Education 1987: the Annual Report of HM Senior Chief Inspector of Schools.* DES.

Department of Education and Science (1990a) *The Teaching and Learning of Language and Literacy.* HMSO.

Department of Education and Science (1990b) *Standards in Education 1988–9: the Annual Report of HM Senior Chief Inspector of Schools.* DES.

Department of Education and Science (1991a) *Standards in Education 1989–90: the Annual Report of HM Senior Chief Inspector of Schools.* DES.

Department of Education and Science (1991b) *The Implementation of the Curricular Requirements of ERA: an Overview by HM Inspectorate on the First Year, 1989–90.* HMSO.

Department of Education and Science (1991c) *Assessment, Recording and Reporting: a Report by HM Inspectorate on the First Year, 1989–90.* HMSO.

Department of Education and Science (1991d) *In-Service Training for the Introduction of the National Curriculum: a Report by HM Inspectorate, 1989–90.* HMSO.

Department of Education and Science (1991e) *English, Key Stage 1: a Report by HM Inspectorate on the First Year, 1989–90.* HMSO.

Department of Education and Science (1991f) *Science, Key Stages 1 and 3: a report by HM Inspectorate on the First Year, 1989–90.* HMSO.

Department of Education and Science (1991g) *Mathematics, Key Stages 1 and 3: a Report by HM Inspectorate on the First Year, 1989–90.* HMSO.

Department of Education and Science (1991h) *National Curriculum and Special Needs: Preparations to Implement the National Curriculum for Pupils with Statements in Special and Ordinary Schools, 1989–90.* HMSO.

Department of Education and Science (1991i) *Testing 7 Year Olds in 1991: Results of the National Curriculum Assessments in England.* HMSO.

Department of Education and Science (1991j) *Aspects of Primary Education in France: a Report by HMI.* DES.

Department of Education and Science, Assessment of Performance Unit (1981) *Mathematical Development: Primary Survey No 2* HMSO.

Department of Education and Science, Assessment of Performance Unit (1982) *Language Performance in Schools: Primary Survey Report No 2*. HMSO.

Department of Education and Science, Assessment of Performance Unit (1983) *Science Report for Teachers 1: Science at Age 11*. HMSO.

Department of Education and Science, Assessment of Performance Unit (1988a) *Science at Age 11: a Review of APU Survey Findings, 1980–84*. HMSO.

Department of Education and Science, Assessment of Performance Unit (1988b) *Language Performance in Schools: a Review of APU Language Monitoring, 1979–83*. HMSO.

Department of Education and Science, Assessment of Performance Unit (1989) *Science at Age 13: a Review of APU Survey Findings, 1980–84*. HMSO.

Desforges, C. (1986) *Understanding the Mathematics Teacher: a Study of First School Practice*. Falmer.

Elliott, J. (1980) 'The implications of classroom research for professional development' in Hoyle, E. (ed) *World Yearbook of Education*. Kogan Page.

Foxman, D., Keys, W. (1989) *A World of Difference*. NFER.

Galton, M. (1989) *Teaching in the Primary School*. David Fulton.

Galton, M., Fogelman, K., Hargreaves, L., Cavendish, S. (1991) *The Rural Schools Curriculum Enhancement National Evaluation (SCENE) Project: Final Report*. HMSO.

Galton, M., Patrick, H. (eds) (1990) *Curriculum Provision in the Small Primary School*. Routledge.

Galton, M., Simon, B., Croll, P. (1980) *Inside the Primary Classroom*. Routledge.

Galton, M., Simon, B. (eds) (1980) *Progress and Performance in the Primary Classroom*. Routledge.

Galton, M., Williamson, J. (1992) *Groupwork in the Primary School*. Routledge.

House of Commons (1986) *Achievement in Primary Schools: Third Report from the Education, Science and Arts Select Committee*. HMSO.

Inner London Education Authority (1985) *Improving Primary Schools: Report of the Committee on Primary Education*. ILEA.

Keys, W. (1987) *Aspects of Science Education in England and Wales*. NFER.

Lake, M. (1991) 'Surveying all the factors: reading research' *Language and Learning*, 6.

Lapointe, A. (1989) *A World of Difference*. ETS/LAEP.

McNamara, D. (1991) 'Subject knowledge and its applications: problems and possibilities for teacher educators'. *Journal of Education for Teaching*. 17:2.

Mortimore, P., Sammons, P., Stoll, L., Lewis, D., Ecob, R. (1988) *School Matters: the Junior Years*. Paul Chapman.

National Curriculum Council (1991) *Report on Monitoring the Implementation of the National Curriculum*. NCC.

Nias, J. (1989) *Primary Teachers Talking: a Study of Teaching as Work*. Routledge.

Nias, J., Southworth, G., Yeomans, R. (1989) *Staff Relationships in the Primary School: a Study of Organisational Cultures*. Cassell.

Pollard, A. (1985) *The Social World of the Primary School*. Cassell.

Postlethwaite, N. (1985) 'The bottom half in lower secondary schooling' in Worswick, G. (ed) *Education and Economic Performance*. Gower.

Postlethwaite, N. (1988) *Science Achievement in 17 Countries: a Preliminary Report*. Pergamon.

Robitaille, D., Garden, R. (eds) (1989) *The IEA Study in Mathematics II: Contexts and Outcomes of School Mathematics*. Pergamon.

School Examinations and Assessment Council (1989) *APU Mathematics Monitoring 1984–88 (Phase 2)*. SEAC.

School Examinations and Assessment Council (1991a) *Language for Learning: a summary report on the 1988 APU surveys of language performance*. SEAC.

School Examinations and Assessment Council (1991b) *The APU Experience*. SEAC.

School Examinations and Assessment Council (1991c) *APU Mathematics Monitoring, Phase 2*. SEAC.

Shulman, L. S. (1986) 'Those who understand: knowledge growth in teaching'. *Education Researcher* 15:2.

Shulman, L. S. (1987) 'Knowledge and teaching: foundations of the new reforms'. *Harvard Educational Review, 57*.

Simon, B., Willcocks, J. (eds) *Research and Practice in the Primary Classroom*. Routledge.

Smith, P. J., Tomlinson, S. (1989) *The School Effect: a Study of Multi-Racial Comprehensives*. Policy Studies Institute.

Taylor, P. H. (1986) *Expertise and the Primary School Teacher*. NFER-Nelson.

Tizard, B., Blatchford, P., Burke, J., Farquahar, C., Plewis, I. (1988) *Young Children at School in the Inner City*. Lawrence Erlbaum.

Turner, M. (1990) *Sponsored Reading Failure*. Education Unit, Warlingham.

Wittrock, M. (ed) (1986) *Third Handbook of Research on Teaching*. Macmillan.

Woods, P. (1990) *Teacher Skills and Strategies*. Falmer.

Wragg, E. C. (1989) *Classroom Teaching Skills*. Routledge.

Wragg, E. C. (1992) *Primary Teaching Skills*. Routledge.

Wragg, E. C. (1992) *Class Management*. Routledge.

Wragg, E. C. (1992) *Explaining*. Routledge.

Wragg, E. C. (1992) *Questioning*. Routledge.

Wragg, E. C. (1992) *Effective Teaching*. Routledge.

Wragg, E. C., Bennett, S. N. (1990) *Leverhulme Primary Project Occasional Paper, Spring 1990*. University of Exeter.

Unpublished research material

We have also had access to as yet unpublished material from the following sources:.

Evaluation of National Curriculum Assessment at Key Stage 1 (ENCA 1): final Report to the School Examinations and Assessment Council. University of Leeds.

Leverhulme Primary Project. University of Exeter.

National Foundation for Educational Research (NFER).

Primary Assessment, Curriculum and Experience Project (PACE). Bristol Polytechnic/ University of Bristol.

Other sources

We worked within an exceptionally tight timescale (one month). Our main data source was the published and unpublished material listed above. Apart from requesting updated material from leading researchers in the field of primary education time did not permit us to invite new submissions and evidence. Despite this, we received unsolicited statements from a large number of individuals and organisations. We have attempted to take full account of all this material and are grateful to those who submitted it.

PART 3:

Critiques

9

FAILING TO REASON OR FAILING TO UNDERSTAND?

M. Donaldson

The term 'deductive inference' is apt to suggest something daunting. But basically, deductive inference is very simple indeed. It is the drawing of the conclusion that if something is true, something else must also be true.

Here is an example. If the number of sweets in a red box is greater than the number in a green box; and if the number in the green box is greater than the number in a blue box; then the number in the red box is greater than the number in the blue box. This conclusion is self-evident to any normal adult.

We can state the essence of the thing in a number of ways. The truth of the first two statements – the premises – makes the truth of the third statement – the conclusion – *necessary*. If the first two are true, then nothing else is *possible* than that the third is true also. The truth of the first two statements is not *compatible* with the falsehood of the third.

The key notions are compatibility, possibility and necessity. No one who totally lacked a sense of these could make deductive inferences. (It is not of course at all necessary to know these words or to have reflected upon these ideas.)

The notions of compatibility, possibility and necessity are very closely connected with one another but perhaps there is a case for saying that compatibility is the most fundamental. Having a sense of compatibility and incompatibility amounts to understanding that we live in a world where the existence of one state of affairs may sometimes rule out the existence of another. This is so fundamental that it is impossible to imagine a 'real world' where it would not be true. If an object is a tree it cannot also be an aeroplane; if it is a circle it cannot also be a square; if it is bigger than another object it cannot at the same time be smaller than that same object.

As soon as language is used to describe the world, even in a rudimentary fashion, then questions of compatibility arise. The use of any form of language to make descriptive statements must rest on some recognition that certain states of affairs cannot exist together. As soon as a child identifies an object as a dog by saying 'That bow-wow' his statement is incompatible with an infinite number of others that could be made. To assert is also to deny. And if the child did not in some sense recognize this he could not make meaningful utterances at all, or understand what other people mean when they speak to him. On the other hand the statement, 'That bow-wow' is evidently *compatible* with many others – e.g. 'That's brown'; 'That's big'; 'That's a spaniel'. The child needs to learn which statements are compatible with one another and which are not.

It seems likely that the earliest recognition of what an utterance *excludes* may be very dim indeed. And it may be some time before the fundamental sense that certain things cannot occur together is used as a way of extending knowledge. For that, in practice, is the usefulness of deductive inference. It means that there are some things which we can know without checking upon them directly. Given certain information, we can be sure of other things about which we have no direct evidence – things perhaps which we are in no position to verify, but on which we can nevertheless rely. For a creature that has to cope with a complex world, this is obviously a very valuable skill. And the growth of this skill is of very great interest to anyone who is concerned to understand the growth of the mind.

To say that some sense of compatibility and incompatibility is essential for deductive inference is not, of course, to say that this is all that is required. Piaget considers that the growth of the ability to decentre is crucial. His argument is that the making of inferences demands skill in the flexible shifting of point of view.

To illustrate what he means, let us take a task which he has devised and which bears on a matter with which logicians have traditionally been much concerned: the relation of a class of objects to its sub-classes. Any class can in principle be divided up into sub-classes in a variety of ways. For instance, the class of toys can be divided into those which represent animals, like teddy bears, and those which do not. Given such sub-divisions, various simple inferences are possible, such as that all toy animals are toys, that some (but not all) toys are toy animals and so on. The fundamental inference, however, is that, if there are two or more sub-classes each of which contains at least one member, then the number of objects in the total class has to be greater than the number in any sub-class: the number of toys must be greater than the number of toy animals.

All of this seems self-evident, as is the way with certain elementary inferences. Is it so to a child? Piaget claims that before the age of six or seven it is not self-evident at all, and he supports his claim in the following way.

The child is shown a number of objects of some familiar kind – say, a bunch of flowers, or a number of beads. Whatever the objects chosen, they must divide into two sub-classes in some fairly obvious manner: some of the flowers must be red, some white, some of the beads must be wooden, some plastic, and so on. Also the numbers in the two sub-classes should, for the normal version of the task, be unequal. (See *The Child's Conception of Number* (by Piaget) and *The Early Growth of Logic in the Child* (by Inhelder and Piaget).)

Suppose that there are in fact four red flowers and two white flowers. The question for the child to answer is then: Are there more red flowers or more flowers? And the usual answer from a child of, say, five is that there are more red flowers.

This finding has provoked a great deal of controversy, and much research beyond that which initially produced it. The first thing to look at, however, is Piaget's own explanation.

He points out that if you ask a child who has given this answer what would be left if you took away the red flowers, he will promptly tell you 'the white flowers'; and if you ask him what would be left if you took away all the flowers he will tell you 'nothing'. So it looks as if he knows what these terms mean, and as if he knows in some sense that the total set is more numerous than the sub-set. But this second form of question allows him to think successively of the whole class (the flowers) and the sub-classes (the red and the white). The other form of questioning (Are there more flowers or more red flowers?) requires him to think of them simultaneously. Now Piaget's claim is that, if the child *centres* on the whole class, he cannot at the same time think of the parts which compose it. Thus the seemingly simple comparison of whole with part is impossible. He lacks the particular sort of mental flexibility which this de-mands. His thinking is still a succession of separate views of things, poorly co-ordinated with one another [. . .]. So he cannot reason as to the relations between them.

The deficiency is held to be general. The young child's response to the 'class-inclusion' task is seen as just one manifestation of an extremely important and widespread limitation which is usually overcome around the age of seven when, in Piagetian terminology, the thinking of the child becomes 'oper-ational'. [. . .]

We have already seen that there is good reason to doubt whether the child's difficulty with decentring is as severe and widespread as Piaget claims. However, none of the research we have so far discussed deals explicitly with any task which Piaget takes to be criterial for the appearance of operational thought. It would be entirely possible for difficulties with decentration to occur when the child is presented with a task like class inclusion, even if they do not arise in certain other contexts. So, direct study of these tasks is necessary. A very enlightening set of experiments was designed and carried out by James McGarrigle a few years ago, to see if the Piagetian explanation would really stand up to rigorous scrutiny.

There is not much doubt about what a child *does* when he makes the standard type of error and says there are more red flowers than flowers: he compares one sub-class with the other sub-class. His spontaneous remarks often make this quite clear. He will say: 'More red flowers because there are only two white ones' and so on. The question is why does he compare sub-class with sub-class? Is it because he *cannot* compare sub-class with class, as Piaget maintains? Or is it because he thinks this is what he is meant to do?* Is there [. . .] *a failure of communication?*

If the latter explanation is correct it ought to be possible to find different ways of presenting the problem which will make it easier or harder, and one should be able to discover just what it is that makes the child misinterpret the question that is asked of him.

Notice that even an adult may well misinterpret this question initially; but repetition of the question, perhaps with added stress on the word *flowers*, will quickly enable him to get it right. This is not normally enough to make a young child change his mind, but it does suggest the idea that the giving of some greater emphasis to the total class might be effective; and so might the reduction of emphasis on the contrast between the sub-classes.

McGarrigle tried ways of achieving both of these effects. In relation to the first he used four toy cows, three of them black, one of them white. He laid all the cows on their sides and he explained that they were 'sleeping'. The experiment then rested on comparison of the difficulty of two different forms of question:

1. Are there more black cows or more cows? (the standard Piagetian form); and
2. Are there more black cows or more sleeping cows?

For both of these questions the cows were in fact laid on their sides: the situations were identical except for the wording of the question. McGarrigle's argument was that the introduction of the adjective 'sleeping' would increase the emphasis on the total class.

The average age of the children was six years. Question 1 was answered correctly by 25 per cent of the group (12 children); question 2 was answered correctly by 48 per cent (23 children). The difference was statistically significant – there was only one chance in a hundred of having obtained this result by chance alone. And a very similar finding was obtained in another study. So manipulation of the wording of the question in such a way as to vary the emphasis placed on the total class did affect difficulty.

To look at the effect of varying emphasis on the contrast between sub-classes McGarrigle used different material. This time he had a small teddy bear, a toy table and a toy chair, laid out in a line. Four discs, referred to as 'steps', separated the teddy bear from the chair; a further two discs lay between the chair and the table [Figure 1].

This material gave McGarrigle a number of advantages. The main one was that he could vary the perceptual contrast between the sub-classes (all the steps could be the same colour, or alternatively the steps from Teddy to the chair could be one colour while the steps from the chair to the table could be

---

* There is also the possibility that he knows what he is meant to do, is capable of doing it, but chooses not to, because he is unwilling to play the experimenter's game. This might happen occasionally. But few children give any sign of being perverse in this way. The amazing thing is how willing they usually are to try to do anything that is asked of them.

Figure 1

another) and at the same time he could vary the way of referring to the steps, either mentioning colour or leaving it out. So he could compare the effects of perceptual variables with those of linguistic ones.

In the first experiment which McGarrigle carried out with this material, the four steps to the chair were red, the two others were white. The child was told that Teddy always walked on these steps to go to his chair or to his table. Two forms of question were then used:

1. Are there more red steps to go to the chair or more steps to go to the table?
2. Are there more steps to go to the chair or more steps to go to the table?

Of a group of 32 children, 38 per cent (12 children) answered question 1 correctly while 66 per cent (21 children) answered question 2 correctly. This difference was statistically significant, there being about two chances in a hundred that it might arise by chance alone.

In this experiment *perceptual* contrast was always present; but one form of question referred to this contrast, while the other did not.

Let us look now at what happens when there is no perceptual contrast. If all the steps are white, it is still possible to include the colour adjective in one case and exclude it in the other. McGarrigle did this in a second study, using a different group of children, but now the variation in question form was found to make a much smaller difference. When the adjective 'white' was included ('Are there more white steps to go to the chair or more steps to go to the table?') 56 per cent of the children answered correctly. When it was omitted ('Are there more steps to go to the chair or more steps to go to the table?') 69 per cent of them answered correctly. This difference was not statistically significant, that is, we are not justified in concluding that one of the questions was genuinely more difficult for the children than the other.

Even though there was no difference between the question forms it might have proved to be the case that the absence of *perceptual* contrast would make this task easier overall than the earlier task where some of the steps were red. Notice that no such effect was found. The basic question: *Are there more steps to go to the chair or more steps to go to the table?* was answered correctly by almost the same proportion of children (drawn from a different group of subjects) whether the steps were all the same colour or whether they were sharply contrasted.

This is an important set of findings. Neither perceptual contrast nor change of wording alone made a difference. The two together made a considerable one. Also it is interesting to notice that the change of wording which made such a difference when perceptual contrast was present was a very slight one: the insertion or omission of a single adjective.

The 'steps' task may seem to be rather different from the standard Piagetian class-inclusion one, but it is closely analogous to a variant used by Piaget himself. Sometimes he took as material a set of beads – all of them wooden, most of them brown, a few of them white – and in this case he would sometimes ask which would make a longer necklace: the brown beads or the wooden beads. And the young child would typically answer: 'The brown beads because there are only two white ones.' But this material, unlike McGarrigle's, did not make it possible to manipulate the relevant linguistic and perceptual variables so as to lessen contrast between the sub-classes. Perceptual contrast was necessarily present: the beads could not be all of one colour or there would be no way of referring to the sub-classes. And by the same token the perceptual contrast always had to be marked in the language of the question. Thus the situation was the one which McGarrigle has shown to be maximally difficult for the child.

McGarrigle, on the other hand, was able to find a form of wording even easier than any of those we have discussed so far. He asked the question: 'Is it further for Teddy to go to the chair, or further to go to the table?' Now at this point one may not properly speak of *class* inclusion, but rather of the inclusion of one distance within another. However, what is particularly interesting is that not only was this question form easier (72 per cent success in one study, 84 per cent in another), but when the other questions were repeated after this one they were considerably facilitated. The question 'Are there more steps to go to the chair or more steps to go to the table?' was now answered correctly by 88 per cent of the children and even the 'red steps' version led to 53 per cent success.

It seems as if the question that asks *which is further?* helps the children to grasp what it is that the experimenter intends them to consider; and once they have grasped this they may be able to hang on to it even in the face of wordings which would otherwise tend to lead them astray.

However, a fair number of children continue to find the 'red steps' wording intractable: in the experiment we have been considering 47 per cent persisted in answering in terms of sub-class comparison when 'red steps' were mentioned. This makes one begin to wonder whether their mode of interpretation has anything to do with their grasp of the inclusion situation *per se* or whether it stems from something much more general.

To decide this, it is necessary to look at similar question forms in contexts where inclusion does not arise. McGarrigle did so, both with the toy cows and horses and with Teddy and his steps.

He arranged black and white toy cows and horses on either side of a wall facing one another [Figure 2].

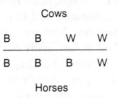

Figure 2

The children were then asked a number of questions of which the following is an example:

Are there more cows or more black horses?

Of 36 children only 5 (14 per cent) answered this correctly. Why were the others wrong?

It is evident that Piaget's explanation will not serve. There is no question here of inclusion or of having to hold on simultaneously to a whole and to the parts that compose the whole. What the children are doing is, however, clear. For the most part they are comparing the black horses with the black cows, for they make remarks like: 'There's more black horses 'cos there's only two black cows.'

A version of the 'steps' experiment which did not involve inclusion led to a similar finding. This time Teddy, the chair and the table did not lie along a straight line, but were arranged as in the diagram [Figure 3]. So the 'steps to the chair' did not constitute a sub-set of the 'steps to the table'. The questions were exactly as in the original 'inclusion' version, namely:

1. Are there more red steps to go to the chair or more steps to go to the table?
2. Are there more steps to go to the chair or more steps to go to the table?

Figure 3

And, just as before, question 1 was significantly harder. The children's remarks showed that sometimes they compared 'red steps to the chair' with the sub-set of red steps to the table. Sometimes, however, the comparison made was with the sub-set of white steps. And occasionally it seemed that the children were answering a rather different question, for they would say things like: 'There's red all along there [to the chair] but there's white there,' or 'They're all red there.' It was as if they were answering a question which ran something like this: 'Are more of the steps to the table red – or are more of the steps to the chair red?' – a question, that is, which asked for some sort of comparison of proportions.

In any event, the questions the children were answering were frequently not the questions the experimenter had asked. The children's interpretations did not correspond to the experimenter's intention; nor could they be regarded as normal, given the rules of the language. The children did not know what the experimenter meant; and one is tempted to say they did not strictly appear to know what the language meant. Or, if that seems too strong, one must at least say that something other than 'the rules of the language' was shaping their interpretation – something perhaps like an expectation about the question that would be asked, an expectation that could be influenced by the nature of the experimental material. However, it is essential to notice that we may not conclude that the children were, in some general way, not *bothering* to attend to the language – for we must recall the dramatic effect, in some of the studies, of the inclusion or omission of a single adjective.

REFERENCES

Inhelder, B. and Piaget, J. (1964) *The Early Growth of Logic in the Child: Classification and Seriation*, Routledge & Kegan Paul, London.

McGarrigle, J. and Donaldson, M. (1974) Conservation accidents, *Cognition*, Vol. 3, pp. 341–50.

Piaget, J. (1952) *The Child's Conception of Number*, Routledge & Kegan Paul, London.

10

AN APPRAISAL OF 'LABOURING TO LEARN'

M. Hammersley

This article provides a methodological assessment of a study of an industrial training unit for 'slow learners' in South Wales, the research for which was carried out in the late 1970s (Atkinson, Shone and Rees, 1981).[1] While much has changed since that time, the study retains relevance given the persistence of high levels of unemployment and the continued existence of government-sponsored training initiatives of this kind. The appraisal was written as one of several attempts to explore what is involved in assessing the validity of qualitative research (see Hammersley, 1991). Out of this work came a framework around which the description of studies can be organized as a basis for methodological assessment. This specifies the need for information about the focus of the research and its rationale, the case(s) studied, the methods of data collection and analysis employed, the main claims made and the evidence offered for them, and the conclusions drawn. The discussion that follows is structured along these lines.

THE FOCUS

The main focus of this study is government-sponsored projects designed to facilitate the transition of 'slow learners' from school to work; though the results may also be intended to be applicable to similar projects not restricted to slow learners. The goal of the account is presented as descriptive, being concerned to identify some of the assumptions implicit in the socialization of young people for work by such units. However, the origins of the research lie in a programme of work concerned with the *evaluation* of projects tackling the transition from school to work (p. 21)[2]. The character of the account is somewhat ambiguous, then, between description and evaluation.

The rationale presented for the focus is that, at the time, training units of this kind were on the increase as part of State intervention designed to deal with the social problems resulting from growing unemployment. The authors note that in the years preceding the study the Manpower Services Commission had shown increasing concern with work socialization rather than just with work experience; and in response to complaints from employers about the attitudes of young job seekers they had mounted a variety of schemes designed to mould young people to the needs of industry (p. 5). The authors also comment on the special difficulties of 'slow learners' in competing effectively in the labour market (p. 3). In short, the rationale presented for the study is that these industrial units are part of a growing trend in government policy, and can be seen as particularly important in attempting to improve the success rate of those with learning difficulties in getting jobs.

If we examine this rationale, it appears to be entirely factual. That there has been an increase in the number of industrial units for slow learners (and for young people in general) designed to prepare them for work, and that slow learners experience special difficulties in obtaining jobs, are taken to imply that this research focus is important. There is no reason to doubt the validity of these factual claims, even though the authors provide no evidence for them. We can take their truth to be common knowledge, I think. However, the rationale for a focus can never be solely factual. We must ask: in terms of what values is a study of this phenomenon justified? While the authors do not make the values involved explicit, it is not difficult to identify them. They relate to a common theme in discussions about education and training in modern industrial societies: how far should education/training be geared simply to prepare young people for work, in the sense of fitting them to the requirements of employers, as opposed to being designed to prepare them for work in a more general sense (for example, by informing them of their rights, maximizing their career prospects, etc.) and/or to enhance their personal development? Some of the values implicated in this theme are: ensuring that the economy has a labour force with the right skills and attitudes for smooth, effective and efficient operation; ensuring that young people (and especially those who are disadvantaged in some way) can compete as successfully as possible in the labour market; and ensuring that young adults experience the maximum personal development possible[3]. It seems to me that few people would question any of these values in principle. What *is* a source of discord is their priority in particular cases. But this is not an issue that arises when judging the validity of the rationale for a descriptive study like this one. For this purpose it is enough that these values are legitimate, and are widely regarded as legitimate, for the focus to be established as relevant. So, in my judgement, the rationale for the focus is valid, if partly inexplicit.

THE CASE STUDIED

The research consisted of an in-depth study of a single case, over a limited (though unspecified) time period. The authors provide some background information about this case. It was a training unit in industrial South Wales that formed part of a college of further education (though it was located in a manufacturing industrial site not on campus). It consisted of a woodwork/ metalwork workshop, and an industrial sewing room. It catered for 21 male and female students, and was staffed by four male woodwork/metalwork lecturers, one of whom was the manager, plus a sewing teacher, a part-time machinist/nurse and a part-time literacy/numeracy tutor (all of whom were women).

There is no reason to doubt that this background information is accurate, since it is of a kind where serious error is unlikely. Whether this background information is sufficient is an issue that can only be decided in the light of what would be required for conclusions about the focus to be drawn on the basis of information derived from this case, an issue I consider later.

METHODS OF DATA COLLECTION AND ANALYSIS

The authors tell us very little about the methods used to collect data about this case. We can glean from what they write that some form of participant observation was used, both in the workshop and in staff meetings, plus some interviews with the staff. However, when and over what period the data collection took place, how intensive it was, how many observers were involved and what roles they adopted, how many of the staff were interviewed and in what way, etc., we do not know. This makes it difficult to judge the appropriateness of the methods adopted in relation to the focus of the research and the nature of the case, and therefore difficult to judge what threats to validity might be involved. There is also no information about the methods of analysis employed, though these seem to have been of a conventional ethnographic kind.

MAIN CLAIMS

As I indicated earlier, the explicit goal of the research was descriptive, and in this section I shall begin by discussing the authors' account of the main features of the unit and its operation.

The descriptive claims

Two aspects of the operation of the unit are highlighted by the authors:

1. The staff's attempts to socialize students for work.
2. Their assessments of students and the consequences of these assessments.

The unit's day-to-day work was organized around production in the workshop and sewing room which was directed towards meeting outside contracts. Most of the machine tasks were simple and repetitive, but some made more demands on the students than others. The fact that production work was central to the unit reflected the staff's commitment to work preparation:

> The project is overtly attempting to increase the students' life-chances by preparing them for working life: this involves not only the inculcation of certain industrial skills designed to make them more marketable, but also the instilling of a range of social skills seen to be appropriate in a 'good worker'.

(p. 3)

However, they argue that 'There is also little to suggest that the actual skills and tasks mastered in the workshop correspond to those most appropriate for the available sectors of the labour market. Training in carpentry may be unlikely to produce directly marketable skills (p. 21).

Over and above participation in work tasks, the students were given lectures, both scheduled and impromptu, designed to achieve the same goal of work preparation. The authors identify four broad types of lecture, varying according to topic. These were concerned with

1. workshop practice, dealing with safety;
2. training for working life, aimed at inculcating the attitudes and habits of the 'good worker';
3. training for adult life, concerned with interpersonal relationships; and
4. social training, pertaining to more general and diverse issues such as democracy, advertising and classical music.

However, despite this variety of topic, the authors argue that the primary emphasis in the lectures was on inculcating attitudes and motivations in the students that employers were believed to require:

> A common strategy is for the lecturer to suggest that some supposedly undesirable characteristic is liable to give employers, or potential employers, a poor or false impression of the student. They therefore attempt to point out the undesirablility of such behaviour and exhort the students to adopt more acceptable characteristics.

(p. 9)

This extract relates to lectures classified as concerned with 'training for working life'; but the authors also quote what they call 'the capitalism lecture', dealing with training for adult life, which praised self-help and the virtue of work, themes which the authors claim were central to the staff's attempts to socialize students.

Subsidiary to this description of the *content* of the lectures, Atkinson, Shone and Rees also give some attention to the pedagogical strategies that the staff employed. They report that the use of 'dramatic and vivid demonstrations of matters of danger and safety precautions' was a common ploy in the lectures (p. 7). More generally, they note that students are 'allowed, even encouraged, to "answer back", and agree or disagree with the points being made' (p. 10);

and that the staff use colloquial speech to produce 'an informal, relaxed atmosphere' (p. 12).

As regards assessment, the authors claim that this takes place informally on the basis of the staff's judgements of the ability and 'attitude' of students, mediated by global appraisals of their personalities. The authors report that these assessments were 'based on (the staff's) observation of the students rather than the use of standardized tests', and they comment that 'it seems that the staff feel themselves qualified to make such assessments of students' skill, character and personality' (p. 15).

As might be expected the main basis on which the staff assess students is the extent to which they match the image of the 'good worker', and this was by no means solely a matter of ability. The authors report that 'appearance, demeanour and a willingness to accept subordinate roles and discipline have a far greater influence on staff impressions . . . (p. 17). And they elaborate this theme as follows (p. 16):

> In practice, a major criterion of 'good work' is a student's willingness to conduct tasks for relatively long periods of time, on his or her own, without disruptive contact with other students. A good worker, then, can be left to get on with his or her work, without needing constant supervision, and without upsetting the work of other students.

These staff assessments of students were not merely independent judgements on the part of particular staff members, staff discussed students among themselves and reached more or less consensual views about the capabilities and characters of particular students. However, the authors also argue that staff assessments of students have a contingent character: 'Although the staff may operate an implicit conception of work readiness this is subject to shifting criteria in response to day-to-day contingencies. Thus, the age of students, the imminence of their course termination, their length of stay at the unit, are all aspects that may be taken into account . . . (p. 19).

Staff assessments had two related types of consequence, it is claimed

1. they were the basis for the allocation of students to tasks within the unit.
2. they also determined the staff's recommendations of students to employers for jobs. The students tended to get jobs through the unit manager's contacts with local employers, and the authors suggest that there was a 'bias' against students looking for jobs themselves.

The process of assessment and allocation of students to tasks within the unit cannot be entirely separated from socialization. Atkinson, Shone and Rees suggest that

> Since 'good-workers' are given 'good' jobs, and may be left to get on with it, there is an inbuilt bias against any systematic attempts to introduce students to progressively more demanding tasks, or to rotate students through a large range of available jobs. Rather, there is a tendency for students to be allocated to their perceived level of competence, and then

to stop there[;] . . . and hence to work constantly at the same level, in terms of the demands made on them, intellectually and manually.

(p. 16)

And they claim that this has serious consequences for student learning: 'For the most part, it is not at all clear that the students' skills are significantly changed, in terms of their competence with industrial machinery. There is little or no sense of their progressing through graded tasks, and, of measurable improvement in performance' (p. 21).

The authors also note the sexual division of labour operating in the unit. Girls are allocated to sewing machines (whereas boys are presumably not), except for those judged to be unsuited on the basis of ability and/or attitude. The latter are allocated to the simple and boring tasks in the workshop; and all girls are given these tasks when the sewing room is not operating.

The authors are claiming, then, that the way in which the allocation of tasks took place minimized the extent to which students learned new skills, and was based on assumptions about gender-specific abilities. They also argue that students are given a passive role by the unit, both in relation to their assessment and allocation to tasks within it and in terms of obtaining jobs outside. It is suggested that they are expected to be (and perhaps encouraged to be?) dependent on the staff (p. 20):

> There may be something of a paradox in the way in which most of the students are found jobs. That is, jobs are often found by the manager of the unit, using the network of informal relationships he has built up in local firms. As we have suggested, students are selected for vacancies which arise in line with the staff's evaluations as to their 'readiness' and suitability . . . The resulting overall impression is that jobs are 'rewards', allocated by the manager, on the basis of compliance, good behaviour and hard work. This is not necessarily a matter for criticism in itself. The process may well be a reasonable approximation of how such youngsters might find work anyway: through the intervention of a parent, relative or elder brother or sister, rather than through formal agencies. Nevertheless, there does seem to be a tension between the way jobs are found and allocated, and the professed aim of the unit's training, in fostering a degree of self-reliance and competence in the students when it comes to the world of work. Our strong impression as a result of the fieldwork so far is that the students are very *passive* in the process whereby they are channelled towards jobs. They rarely object to jobs which are found for them and are generally acquiescent.

Assessing the descriptive claims

Here we need to consider both the relevance of the claims made and their validity.

Assessing the *relevance* of the claims is not straightforward since, because the values providing the rationale for the study were not explicit, all we have is my reconstruction of them. We can assess the consistency of the descriptions with those reconstructed relevances, but any incoherence is as likely to reflect the inadequacies of the reconstruction as inconsistency on the part of the authors.

Given my reconstruction of the rationale for the study, we would expect the unit's operation to be described in terms of a framework of concepts that map the various features we would expect to find in the unit if each of the values identified had been pursued exclusively and effectively as a goal. So, we might expect information about such things as:

- whether there are attempts to socialize students into the sorts of skills and attitudes required by employers (this would be relevant both where the unit is geared to smooth integration of students into industry and/or to maximizing students' chances of getting and retaining jobs);
- whether students are introduced to new skills and in a way that allows them to acquire these effectively (this might be expected if the unit were geared to maximizing students' career prospects and/or their personal development); and
- whether students are encouraged to play an active role in the organization of the unit and in decisions about their future (this might be expected if the unit were committed to some notion of industrial democracy and/or to the personal development of the students).[4]

If we look at Atkinson, Shone and Rees's account of the staff's attempts to socialize students, it does seem that much of it conforms to these relevances. The organization of the work in the unit and the content of the lectures are described in terms that suggest their closeness to the goals of integrating the students into the workplace and/or maximizing their chances of getting a job (and their distance from forms of socialization designed to facilitate industrial democracy or personal development).

The relevance of the descriptions of pedagogical strategies is not so obvious. In the case of the use of 'dramatic and vivid demonstrations', this can only be relevant background information, since we might expect to find it whichever of the goals was being pursued. The same may be true of the other two descriptions of pedagogical strategies, though these could be relevant to the values of industrial democracy and personal development.

The relevance of the descriptions of assessment also seems assured; and once again the import is that the predominant concern of the staff is with economic integration and with the students getting jobs. By contrast, the authors indicate that there is a relative neglect of improving students' skills and of developing their capacity for autonomous decision-making. There are, however, one or two aspects of the description of assessment procedures whose relevance is not immediately obvious. Notable here are the report that assessments are based on observations by staff rather than on standardized tests, and the description of the assessment process as affected by contingencies of various kinds. The relevant value here is perhaps the rationality of the assessment process, but it is difficult to unpack the interpretations of this value assumed here and such claims do not seem to be central to the article.

The argument that the students are allotted a passive role within the unit is obviously relevant to the value of personal development, conceived in terms of taking control of one's own circumstances, or at least participating in decisions about one's life and future. The authors are also pointing here to a discrepancy between the 'professed aim' of the unit and its practice. Of course, apparent discrepancies between aims and actions are not automatically relevant and worthy of discussion, but this one is clearly central to the relevances that seem to underly the account.

Besides assessing whether all of what is presented is relevant, we must also consider whether there is anything that would have been relevant that is omitted. There are two areas that might be mentioned here. First, one wonders about the nature of the contacts between the staff and individual students in the workshops. Did these have the same character as the public lectures? And what about informal contacts between staff and students, for instance in the canteen? Was there much of this, and how did it relate to the relevances identified? Second, the account focuses primarily on the socialization *attempts* of staff, rather than on socialization *effects*. But, of course, effects are at least as important from the point of view of the rationale for the study, and the authors do make claims about effects in at least one place (as regards students' skills not improving). Relevant here would be students' perspectives towards the unit, and accounts of changes in attitude over time.

Turning to the *validity* of the descriptive claims made, the account of the industrial tasks on which students were employed and of the lectures designed to socialize students in preparation for work seem convincing at face value. It does seem clear that the staff were very much concerned with work preparation, conceived in terms of a fairly traditional and employer-centred conception of work. Even their more general concerns with safety and preparation for adult life are apparently framed within a political philosophy that accords a central place to the notion that students must be trained to be 'good workers' who conform to work requirements.

Many of the claims about the lectures are supported by evidence, usually in the form of quotations from the researchers' observations (including transcriptions of what the staff said in key incidents). The four types of lecture are illustrated with examples. However, we are not told how frequent the impromptu lectures were, or how frequent examples of each type of lecture were. This wold have been useful information, particularly in allowing us to judge the degree to which the 'good worker' formed the core theme of the socialization. It would also have been useful to know whether the lectures were the same irrespective of which staff members gave them, and whether there was any change in their content over time. (Here, of course, we are concerned with the accuracy of the authors' generalizations within the case they studied.)

The account of the pedagogy is also supported by evidence. However, in the case of one claim the evidence seems less than conclusive. The authors argue that the students are encouraged to answer back, but in the example cited the lecturer's response to a student's refusal to accept what he says does not seem calculated to encourage this (it seems concerned above all with getting the students to accept his point of view – see p. 10).

There is generally rather less documentation about assessment, its basis and its consequences. Thus, there is little information about the process by which students are allocated and reallocated to tasks. The authors imply that this was based on judgements of students in terms of the criteria of the 'good worker'. This is plausible given the previously described content of the socialization, and a case study of one student (Tina) is provided. But more detail about the formation and use of the staff's assessments would have strengthened the basis for judging the validity of this aspect of the account.

There is no evidence about the extent to which assessments of students were a matter of staff consensus (indeed, at one point some dissensus is noted, see pp. 19–20). Nor are we given information about the relative power of the manager in relation to other staff in making assessments. Furthermore, the contingent character of the assessment process is not explored or documented. There is an implied contrast here, perhaps with a more universallistic allocation procedure, but certainly with one that is geared to the development of student attitudes and skills rather than simply matching tasks to existing capacities. Clearly this focus would have been illuminated considerably by information about particular allocation decisions.

Similarly, the argument about the relative immobility of students between tasks and its effects is not established, though there seems no reason to doubt the authors' claims about the sexual division of labour among students in the unit. No support is offered for the claim that students' competence in dealing with industrial machinery is not significantly changed by the work of the unit, and this is a claim whose significance and character requires considerable evidence for it to be accepted, it seems to me. Nor are the claims about the passivity of students in relation to their assessment and their recruitment to jobs supported with evidence; and once again this is necessary, in my judgement, especially given the claim that this passivity is discrepant with the expressed aim of the unit.

Information about the recommendation of particular students, or the failure to recommend students, for jobs would also have enabled us to get a clearer idea of the criteria underlying assessment. The authors do use the case of Tina to illustrate this, but more detailed information about more students might have helped to clarify the criteria and the contingencies involved.

Evaluative claims

I noted earlier that while presented as a descriptive account, the research on which this article is based had its origins in an evaluation. Not surprisingly then, there are places in the account where explicit evaluations occur, and others where evaluations seem strongly to be implied. For example, at a mundane level, Atkinson, Shone and Rees commend the staff's concern with safety precautions. They note that 'given the nature of the workshop, the machinery in it and the nature of the youngsters who work there, safety must be a major preoccupation for the staff' (p. 7). Similarly, they comment that 'staff supervising the workshop must . . . be on the lookout for [students taking dangerous short cuts]' (p. 8). However, evaluations are not restricted to positive evaluations of the staff's concern with safety. Here is another evaluation (p. 17):

> Guidelines for student assessment are explicitly included in a *Readiness for Work Chart*, which forms part of the student's record, but staff rarely articulate their assessments in terms of these explicit criteria, but rather in terms of students' personal idiosyncracies and characteristics. Thus those students who seem unable to conform to the standards expected, or who appear to possess less favourable or likeable attributes are often those who benefit least from their stay at the unit, in that they will not be considered for placement if a work vacancy arises.

Here we have an explicit evaluation of which students benefit most from the unit, though it should be noted that there is no explicit evaluation of the fact that some benefit more than others, or of which ones benefit.

In addition, implicit evaluation seems to be contained in the use of qualifiers, and of scare quotes, which are presumably intended to distance the authors from what they are describing. For example:

> A common strategy is for the lecturer to suggest that some *supposedly* undesirable characteristic is liable to give employers, or potential employers, a poor or false impression of the student.
>
> (p. 9, my emphasis)

> There were, for instance, two boys who were regarded as exceptionally *'bright'*. They were routinely given relatively skilled carpentry jobs to perform, and were eventually channelled into relatively skilled employment of this sort. After *'proving'* their ability in routine work they were rarely allocated to repetitive tasks.
>
> (p. 16, my emphasis)

It is also possible that some of what I have treated as descriptions were intended to be read as evaluations in the sense that the authors assume a particular evaluation of what they describe to be automatic on the part of their audience.

In the case of evaluations about safety, the value involved and its justification is obvious, and in no need of explicit treatment. However, the other evaluations are more questionable, and therefore suffer from the fact that the basis on which they are made is not explicit or provided with justification. It also seems to be necessary to consider how far the staff would have been able to rectify the defects the authors claim to identify, given the circumstances in which they had to work. Little attention is given in the account to the constraints under which the staff worked, and yet these must be of considerable relevance to any assessment of the unit's operation.

CONCLUSIONS DRAWN

While the authors investigate a single case, their focus seems to be the wider population of industrial training units. However, they seem ambivalent about the generalizability of their findings. They state that they '. . . make no claims as to the "typicality" of this one institution: indeed, we have reason to believe that in some respects it is rather unusual. On the other hand, we do wish to claim that the issues *raised* by this "case study" are of more general relevance' (p. 5). The same point is repeated towards the end of the article: '. . . we advance no claims as to the "typicality" of the unit we describe. It does, however, exemplify a number of themes which are generic to contemporary programmes to ease the transition from education to working life' (p. 20). The authors seem to believe that the findings of their study have general relevance even though the unit may not be typical.

Given this argument, we must ask about the grounds for the authors' claim that the issues/themes that they discuss are of general relevance. It is true that the issue that underlies the authors' account (concerning the balance between work preparation – narrowly defined – and personal development) is undoubtedly of general relevance. But, presumably, the information that this study is intended to provide does not consist of this issue itself, but rather of information about industrial training units relevant to it. If this is so, and given that events in this unit at the time it was studied have little intrinsic relevance for a wide audience, we must conclude that the value of the information will depend not only on whether it is true for the unit studied but also on whether it is generalizable to other units. Indeed, the authors make this quite explicit at the end of their article in claiming that they have 'attempted to draw out into the open some of the implicit assumptions that *projects set up to ease the transitional process for slow learners* appear to make' (p. 21, my emphasis). Here it is quite clear that what is being claimed is that some of the features of the unit studied, namely some of the assumptions made by the staff, are typical of many such units.

The information about the wider population of units necessary to make an assessment of the generalizability of the findings of this study is not provided, however.[5] Given this, I think we must reserve judgement on this issue.

CONCLUDING COMMENTS

In this discussion of Atkinson, Shone and Rees's article I have outlined the focus of the research, the case studied, the methods used, the main findings reported and the conclusions drawn. I have also assessed the rationale for the focus, as well as the relevance and validity of the findings and conclusions. It is worth emphasizing that this is not intended as an assessment of the competence of these researchers. I have given no attention to the constraints under which the research was carried out or to those on the length and character of the article that they have been involved in its publication. The aim, rather, has been to assess the value of the knowledge that the study provides. However, there are features of the account which make it difficult to judge the relevance and validity of the claims. Notable here is the absence of information about the methods of inquiry used and the lack of explicitness about the relevances and values that structured the account. The former is important because it makes it more difficult to assess the threats to validity that may have distorted the account. The latter is an important weakness in a descriptive study because it makes the assessment of the relevance of the findings problematic; and it is even more serious to the extent that what is intended is an evaluation.

In general, the article seems to offer valid and useful information about the unit studied, though some parts of the account are questionable. Whether the authors' claims are generalizable to other similar units is much more doubtful in the absence of more information about the target population. In these terms the value of the account is limited, but could be increased substantially if it were possible to derive such information from other sources.[6]

NOTES

1.   The appraisal relies solely on the cited account of the research.
2.   Page references are to this volume.
3.   See Bowles and Gintis's (1976) discussion of the conflict within Dewey's writings (and in US culture generally) between economic integration and other values like personal development. Much the same conflict is to be found in Britain. Wringe (1991) provides a useful general discussion of the values involved.
4.   It is impossible to specify all the relevances that might be applicable. Relevances are not derived in strict logical fashion from values: they depend on what are and are not accepted as constraints and on how values are interpreted in particular situations.
5.   For discussions of the problem of generalizability in relation to case studies, see Schofield (1990) and Hammersley (1992, Chs. 5 and 11).
6.   Since the publication of this study at least one other study of a unit concerned with the preparation of unemployed youth for work has been carried out (see Corbett, 1990). The staff of this unit had a rather different ideological orientation, though Corbett's conclusions about the staff's treatment of students and its effects are consistent with those of Atkinson, Shone and Rees.

REFERENCES

Atkinson, P., Shone, D. and Rees, T. (1981) Labouring to learn: industrial training for slow learners, in L. Barton and S. Tomlinson (eds.) *Special Education: Policy, Practices and Social Issues*, Harper & Row, London.
Bowles, S. and Gintis, H. (1976) *Schooling in Capitalist America*, Routledge & Kegan Paul, London.

Corbett, J. (1990) It's almost like work: a study of a YTS workshop, in J. Corbett (ed.) *Uneasy Transitions: Disaffection in Post-Compulsory Education and Training*, Falmer Press, Lewes.

Hammersley, M. (1991) *Reading Ethnographic Research: A Critical Guide*, Longman, London.

Hammersley, M. (1992) *What's Wrong with Ethnography?*, Routledge, London.

Schofield, J. W. (1990) Increasing the generalizability of qualitative research, in E. Eisner and A. Peshkin (eds.) *Qualitative Inquiry in Education: The Continuing Debate*, Teachers College Press, New York, NY.

Wringe, C. (1991) Education, schooling and the world of work, in D. Corson (ed.) *Education for Work*, Multilingual Matters, Clevedon.

11

QUESTIONING ORACLE: AN ASSESSMENT OF ORACLE'S ANALYSIS OF TEACHERS' QUESTIONS

J. Scarth and M. Hammersley

The ORACLE project – Observation Research and Classroom Learning Evaluation – based at the University of Leicester is the most extensive piece of classroom observation research in Britain to date. It is a longitudinal study following a sample of pupils through from primary to secondary schools. Besides repeatedly observing the classroom behaviour of pupils and subjecting them to a variety of tests the researchers also observed the classroom practice of a large number of teachers. One of the aims of the project was to describe 'some of the richness and variety of what goes on in a modern primary classroom' and 'to search for patterns from among those events in order to help explain why certain teachers do one thing while others do something else' (Galton, Simon and Croll, 1980, p. 4). At the same time the researchers also sought to provide evidence about the distribution of 'progressive' teaching methods, and to discover whether variations in the behaviour of teachers affected pupils' progress, as measured by tests of basic skills (reading, mathematics, language) and 'study skills', and by teachers' own judgements.

This is a huge project. Our focus in this paper is much narrower. We examine the way in which ORACLE analyse teachers' questions. However, while this topic may seem trivial against the background of the project as a whole, there are two reasons why we think it is very important. First, the frequency of various types of question is one of the main bases upon which ORACLE distinguish styles of teaching before going on to assess the effects of these styles on pupils' orientations and achievement. Second, many of the problems which we identify in the treatment of questions also arise with other aspects of the analysis: for example, in the treatment of teachers' statements and the estimation of pupils' levels of involvement (see Barrow, 1984). Given our focus on teachers' questions, we shall concentrate primarily upon the initial stage of the ORACLE research reported in the book *Inside the Primary Classroom* (Galton, Simon and Croll, 1980).

Before break (am)

Day 1												
Day 2	T			E	F	G	H	A	B	C	D	
Day 3												

After break (am)

Day 1	A	B	C	D	T		E	F	G	H
Day 2										
Day 3	E	F	G	H	A	B	C	D	T	

Afternoon

Day 1	T		C	D	E	F	G	H	A	B
Day 2	G	H	A	B	T		C	D	E	F
Day 3	C	D	E	F	G	H	A	B	T	

Figure 1 Daily observation timetable for observers*

Key: T: Teacher; A–H: Target pupils; Each pupil column: 4½ min; Teacher block: 19 min; Total observation time per session: 55 min

* The observer using this timetable would be free before break on day 1. After break he would start his first observation session and observe target pupils A, B, C and D (in that order) for 4½ minutes each using the Pupil Record. He would then switch to observing the teacher, using the Teacher Record for 19 minutes. He would then finally return to the Pupil Record and observe target pupils E, F, G and H (in that order) for 4½ minutes each. In the afternoon the observer would complete his second session of the day observing the teacher with the Teacher Record at the beginning of the lesson and then moving on to the Pupil Record for the remainder of the lesson. On days 2 and 3, he would follow the timetable shown in a similar manner.

Source: Galton, Simon and Croll (1980, p. 20)

In its first phase the ORACLE project was based on a sample of 58 teachers and 464 pupils in 19 schools located in three different LEAs. A team of nine observers recorded teachers' and pupils' classroom behaviour during the course of one academic year.[1] Each observer went to six or seven classrooms, observing the teacher and eight pupils in each class. The pupils were selected to represent a cross section of the ability range of all pupils in the class. The observers visited the classrooms for three days each term, carrying out six observation sessions during each visit. An observation session was approximately 55 minutes, of which 19 minutes was spent observing the teacher and 36 minutes observing pupils. The six observation sessions for each visit were divided equally between morning and afternoon. Moreover, observers had a detailed timetable for the sequence of observing the teacher and pupils to ensure that teachers and pupils were observed at the beginning, in the middle and at the end of each visit (see Figure 1).

Observers recorded teacher or pupil behaviour every 25 seconds as indicated by pre-recorded time-signals from a cassette recorder. Naturally each observer made a large number of such observations during the academic year. In fact Croll reports in a methodological appendix (Galton, Simon and Croll, 1980, pp. 172–80) that the data base for the first year of the project was 47,000 observations of teachers and 84,000 observations of pupils. In other words each teacher was observed for about 5.5 hours (338 mins) and each pupil for around 1.25 hours (75 mins).

Observation of teachers and pupils was carried out on the basis of two structured observation schedules, the Teacher Record and the Pupil Record, developed from the earlier work of Boydell (1974, 1975). The data produced were subjected to a form of cluster analysis, a technique designed to identify groupings of objects on the basis of their similarities and differences (see Everitt, 1974; Egan, 1984). The ORACLE team used a relocation procedure whereby teachers and pupils were randomly allocated to groups and then reallocated in order to minimize the variation within these groups. The number of groups was reduced until a further reduction in groups would lead to a disproportionate increase in intra-group variation compared to inter-group variation. Using this form of clustering the project team identified four distinct teaching styles (called 'individual monitors', 'class enquirers', 'group instructors' and 'style changers') and four pupil strategies ('attention seekers', 'intermittent workers', 'solitary workers' and 'quiet collaborators'). In the second year of the project the researchers carried out classroom observation of the same pupils with, in the majority of cases, different teachers. However, since some children had transferred schools, the second-year teacher and pupil samples were smaller than the first: 334 pupils were observed in 40 classrooms (of the 40 teachers, 14 had been in the initial sample). By adopting a longitudinal approach ORACLE were able to attempt a replication exercise. ORACLE argue that replication is unusual in educational research and that its neglect is regrettable. In particular, they warn of the dangers of 'one-off' research projects:

> Problems of sampling and the generalization of results are common in social science research and the potential danger that the 'one-off' use of powerful multi-variate techniques, such as factor analysis and cluster analysis, will turn chance fluctuations into apparently meaningful patterns is well known (Galton and Simon, 1980, p. 223).

ORACLE used the same observation schedules for teachers and pupils in the replication as in the first year's data collection.

CODING OF TEACHERS' BEHAVIOUR

One important difference between 'systematic classroom observation' of the kind used by ORACLE and more 'unstructured' kinds of observation used by qualitative and ethnographic researchers is that observation is carried out on the basis of clearly specified categories and coding rules. These facilitate replicability and high reliability. Moreover, ORACLE's coding manual (Boydell and Jasman, 1983) is one of the most explicit and thorough observational instruments for studying classroom interaction currently available. As already noted, it consists of two schedules: the Teacher Record and the Pupil Record. We shall discuss only the former.

The Teacher Record contains two main categories, namely *conversation* and *silence*, each divided into two major sub-categories, with a number of elements (see ibid., p. 104):

Conversation	*Silence*
QUESTIONS	SILENT INTERACTION

Task

Q1	recalling facts	Gesturing
Q2	offering ideas, solutions (closed)	Showing
Q3	offering ideas, solutions (open)	Marking
		Waiting

Task supervision

Q4	referring to supervision	Story Reading

Routine

Q5	referring to routine matters	Not observed
		Not coded

STATEMENTS	NO INTERACTION

Task

S1	of facts	Adult interaction
S2	of ideas, problems	Visiting pupil
		Not interested

Task supervision

S3	telling child what to do
S4	praising work or effort
S5	feedback on work or effort

Routine

S6	providing information, directions
S7	providing feedback
S8	of critical control
S9	of small talk

At each 25 second time-signal the observer records the teacher's behaviour by indicating which *one* of these categories is operating.[2]

While the distinction between the two main categories ('conversation' and 'silence') is relatively clear, the separation of conversation into 'questions' and 'statements' is rather more problematic as the ORACLE researchers recognize. Questions are distinguished as follows:

A question as defined here refers to any utterance which *seeks an answer*. In other words an utterance is coded as a question if there is any spoken response (other than reading aloud or acknowledging a request or command) or clear evidence, such as a long pause, to indicate that the teacher expects one. A *statement* refers to all other utterances (ibid., p. 56).

On this definition all teacher utterances which 'would carry a question-mark if written down are coded as questions if the teacher waits for a reply' (ibid.). As further clarification the ORACLE team identify three particular conditions under which an utterance should be coded as a statement rather than as a question. First, rhetorical or pseudo-questioning to which no pupil response is expected or given is coded as statement. An illustration of the distinction that is being made is provided in the coding manual (ibid.):

i) T – Have you finished?
    P – Yes, almost   Pupil reply
                                 Code as *question*

(ii) T – Have you finished?
      (crossly)   No pupil reply
      P – (stops talking and returns   Code as *statement*
      to his work)

A second qualifying condition for questions is that commands, even though not featuring a question-mark if written down, are treated as questions if 'the pupil responds by saying something rather than doing something (ibid., p. 57). However, if a pupil responds by *doing* something or by *saying something and doing something*, then the teacher utterance is coded as a statement and not a question. The coding manual again provides examples which demonstrate these differences in coding (ibid.):

i)   T – Describe this picture, Michael.   Pupil reply
     P – Well, it shows an old house . . . Code as *question*
ii) T – Describe this picture, Michael.   No pupil reply
     P – (gets out paper, starts writing) Code as *statement*
iii) T – Describe this picture, Michael.   Acknowledgement only
     P – Yes. (starts writing)   Code as *statement*

A final condition for the identification of teacher questions is that commands or requests to read aloud are treated as statements even though the pupil response is spoken.

In summary form, then, the ORACLE team identify the following six types of teacher utterance, of which only two are questions (ibid.):

	Utterance	*Code*
i)	Question-mark *and* reply or expectant pause	Question
ii)	Command *and* reply	Question
iii)	Question-mark *but* no reply or pause (rhetorical)	Statement
iv)	Command *and* acknowledgement only	Statement
v)	Command and reading aloud	Statement
vi)	Other	Statement

Besides distinguishing between questions and statements ORACLE also differentiate within these two categories between utterances directly concerned with academic tasks, those relaing to the supervision of such tasks and those involved in routine classroom management. Moreover, within some of these sub-categories further distinctions are made. For example, task questions are divided into those requiring the recall of facts, those demanding ideas or problem solutions where there is one right answer, and those demanding ideas or problem solutions where the teacher accepts more than one right answer:

> All questions were classified in terms of the answers that the pupil gave. There were three kinds of task questions, namely those answered by recalling facts (Q1), those answered by offering closed solutions (Q2) and those which resulted in open solutions (Q3). The distinction between closed and open is an important one and in order to differentiate between these two categories the observer had to listen and see how the teacher handled the pupil's high level imaginative or reasoned response. This then revealed if, despite outward appearances, the teacher was only interested in one particular answer (Q2 – closed), or whether she was prepared to accept a range of answers (Q3 – open) (Galton, Simon and Croll, 1980, p. 18).

The researchers give quite detailed specifications of task, task supervision and routine utterances and of sub-types of task utterances. As an example here are the rules for the identification of recall questions (see Boydell and Jasman, 1983, pp. 65–6):

Category Q1 *Recalling facts*
Included here are all types of task questions which result in factual answers rather than imaginative or reasoned responses or problem solving. However, the recall of task instructions which tell the child what to do or how to do it is coded as Q4 (. . .). Q1 covers task questions answered by the child:

a. recalling *information about task content* without giving reasons.
   This includes information in books or on work cards.
   e.g.   T – Do you remember how they built canoes?
         P – They scooped out the trunks of trees.
   e.g.   T – Which city is the capital of Scotland?
         P – Edinburgh.

b. recalling *procedures or answers already worked out* without giving reasons.
   e.g.   T – How did you dissolve the sugar?
         P – We shook it up with water and put it on the radiator.
   e.g.   T – What did the answer work out at?
         P – Two metres.

c. reporting *counts and simple measurements* like length or weight without interpretation.
   e.g.   T – How many red shapes can you find?
         P – . . . eight, nine, ten!
   e.g.   T – How long is the classroom?
         P – Ten metres.

d. reporting *low-inference observations* like colour without interpretation.
    e.g. T – What happened to the water?
            P – It went blue!
    e.g. T – What is happening?
            P – The sugar is going!

e. *labelling* equipment, animals, plants, natural materials, etc. (or their constituent parts).
    e.g. T – Does anyone know what this is?
            P – A fossil
    e.g. T – Who can remember the name of this?
            P – The windpipe.

f. *naming examples* of classes of animals, plants, objects, etc. where many answers are acceptable.
    e.g. T – Name some big cities.
            P – Nottingham, Birmingham . . .
    e.g. T – Suggest an odd number, Susan.
            P – Three.

g. *reading an odd word or phrase or spelling aloud.* If the child reads more than a sentence code as S3.
    e.g. T – What is that word?
            P – Hol . . . iday.
    e.g. T – Tell me how to spell 'Friday'.
            P – F-r-i-d-a-y.

ORACLE, then, pay considerable attention to the specification of coding rules in an attempt to ensure that different coders would code the same events in the same way. They also carried out a reliability exercise in which the reliability coefficients were as follows (see Galton, Simon and Croll, 1980, p. 174):

Reliability: Teacher Record

	Percentage agreement	Scott coefficient
Interaction category	81.0	0.79
Audience	95.5	0.93

As we noted earlier, the same schedule was used to observe 40 teachers in the second year of the project, though corresponding data on observer reliability are not provided.

AN ASSESSMENT OF ORACLE

Galton, Simon and Croll (1980) spend some time discussing alternative strategies for investigating teaching styles. They argue strongly that studies which rely primarily upon questionnaires, such as Bennett's *Teaching Styles and Pupil Progress* (Bennett, 1976), are unlikely to capture accurately differences in classroom behaviour. They also criticize unstructured observational research such as that of Sharp and Green (1976) for its failure rigorously to measure variability in teacher behaviour (Croll, 1981). And it is true that in some respects the systematic observation strategy adopted by ORACLE is superior to these other approaches. At the same time, though, there are some serious problems with this research strategy and these are exemplified in ORACLE's analysis of questions. We shall discuss these under three headings:

1. the reliability and validity of their measurements;
2. the implications of point sampling; and
3. the sampling of lesson time.

Reliability and validity

In his methodological appendix to *Inside the Primary Classroom* Croll stresses the importance of explicit coding rules as the basis for achieving high levels of reliability:

> In a successful systematic observation system the categories on the sche-
> dule and the criteria for determining their use should be sufficiently un-
> ambiguous and explicit to ensure that any observers using it will arrive at
> identical descriptions of a particular occurrence. Fundamental to sys-
> tematic observation is high inter-observer reliability – implying that dif-
> ferent observers make identical recordings at particular points in time
> (Galton, Simon and Croll, 1980, p. 172).

In reporting an inter-observer reliability figure of 81 per cent for the Teacher Record the ORACLE researchers comment that this was 'not quite so satisfac-tory' as reliability on the Pupil Record (see ibid., p. 174). However, it is difficult to assess the satisfactoriness of this figure since, unlike some previous studies (e.g. Eggleston, Galton and Jones, 1975), separate scores for each category and for each observer are not provided. All one can do is to confirm that 81 per cent may be a rather low level of reliability, especially given that with a few of the categories (e.g. some of those under the heading 'Silence') agreement is likely to be close to 100 per cent. This suggests that the reliability of other categories, perhaps including the different types of questions, was lower than the aggregate score of 81 per cent.

As we have seen, the ORACLE coding manual is quite detailed in its specifica-tion of the coding rules. However, these rules are not 'sufficiently unambiguous and explicit to ensure that any observers using it will arrive at identical descrip-tions of a particular occurrence'. We shall take the rules for distinguishing between types of question as an example. First, there is some ambiguity about what is being measured. Is it the pupils' behaviour (in the form of answers) which a question elicits? Or is it what the teacher expects/requires as an answer? The procedural rules for coding questions seem to draw on both these criteria at different points. However, a teacher's intentions or expectations may not match the production processes that generate pupils' answers. Since the differential frequency of types of question is used by ORACLE to distinguish between different teaching styles, it would seem that it is the teacher's expectations which should be the criterion.

The second question that arises is: 'how are we to know what the intended demands of a question are?' The ORACLE manual implies that it is relatively unproblematic for an observer to distinguish recall questions from those intended to produce imaginative or reasoned responses. Yet such a distinction requires inference about the mental processes of the teacher. Nor are the particular inferences required straightforward. For example, considerable scope for judgement remains in ORACLE's procedures for identifying recall questions, cited earlier. Even with the examples provided, it is possible to imagine how they might be interpreted differently. 'Which city is the capital of Scotland' could, under some circumstances, require a reasoned response. If, for example, pupils could not be expected to know the answer, but were examining a map of Scotland, they might be required to infer that Edinburgh was the capital from its size or location, or from some of the facilities to be found there. Similarly an observer, especially one who had been in a classroom only a relatively short time, would not necessarily know when a question was asking for recall of 'procedures or answers already worked out'. These will not always be as clearly marked as in the examples given. In the case of questions 'reporting counts and simple measurements', and 'low-inference observations', 'labelling' objects and 'naming examples', it is clear that the terms involved (e.g. 'reporting', 'simple', 'low-inference', etc.) will be found to be vague or ambiguous in some cases. And, in fact, in identifying 'low-inference' observations observers are being required to judge on a scale where there are no fixed points. In the case of 'reading an odd word or phrase or spelling aloud', of course, the problem arises as to how many words an 'odd word or phrase' amounts to. The ORACLE team define it as less than a sentence, but sentences can be of variable lengths, nor are they unambiguously identifiable in speech.[3]

Now it might be argued that there will always be some ambiguous cases in classification procedures of this sort, but that this does not matter if their number is low relative to the size of the differences in frequency among the categories which the study reports. This is a reasonable argument. However, ORACLE provide us with no information about the number of ambiguous cases. They report that only a small proportion of cases found their way into the 'not coded' category but, as Barrow (1984) points out, this may simply mean that ambiguous cases have been allocated to one or other of the relevant categories rather than placed in the 'not coded' category. This seems particularly likely under conditions of live coding.

Moreover, some of the differences that ORACLE report as findings *are* relatively small. As we have noted, ORACLE use the frequencies of different types of teachers' questions as an indicator of different teaching styles. The differences between three of the styles in this respect are so small that it seems

Table 1 Percentages of different types of question for the four teaching styles

Task questions	Teaching styles			
	Individual monitors	Class inquirers	Group instructors	Style changers
Q1 (recalling facts)	73.6 (3.9)*	48.8 (4.1)	45.3 (2.4)	53.1 (3.4)
Q2 (closed solution)	20.8 (1.1)	39.3 (3.3)	37.7 (2.0)	37.5 (2.4)
Q3 (open solution)	5.7 (0.3)	11.9 (1.0)	17.0 (0.9)	9.4 (0.6)
All task questions	100.1 (5.3)	100.0 (8.4)	100.0 (5.3)	100.0 (6.4)

* Figures in brackets give the percentage of all observations for teachers in each style.
Derived from: Galton, Simon and Croll (1980, Table 6.1, p. 121).

that they could easily be an artefact produced by variations among observers. Table 1 shows the differences between the four styles in the proportions of different types of question used. The number of ambiguous cases would not have to be large to throw doubt on the differences between class inquirers and group instructors and perhaps even between these and style changers. Of course the ORACLE team could respond to this line of argument by pointing to the replication exercise which, in their words,

> confirmed the analysis and conclusions from the first year alone. The over-all use of interaction, audience and curricular categories remains much the same. The relationship between the audience and content of interactions, in particular the striking difference between class and individual interactions, is confirmed and the cluster analyses give similar groupings of teachers in the two years (Galton and Simon, 1980, p. 232).

However, we are far more cautious in our interpretation of ORACLE's second phase of data collection. This is because the replication does not overcome the measurement problems that we have pointed to in our analysis. Even if the first phase findings were replicated perfectly, this would only show that random error was low – it would still not test the level of systematic error in the results obtained. While reliability is important, it is so only as one indicator of the validity of measurement (Hammersley, 1987). Surprisingly, in his methodological appendix Croll makes no reference at all to validity (Galton, Simon and Croll, 1980, pp. 172–80). What this amounts to is a neglect of sources of systematic error which might be operating upon observers. For example, it may be that observers tend to rely upon teachers' use of such words as 'remember' and 'think' – using the former as an indicator of recall questions, the latter as evidence that more than recall is required. Unfortunately such inferences are not always correct. Teachers do sometimes ask pupils to remember something as a basis for problem-solving and the word 'think' can be used to cover 'remember'. Systematic error of this kind is much more difficult to estimate than the random error identified by reliability checks or replications. It would require comparison of data produced by the Teacher Record with that generated by other indicators of teachers' requirements for pupils' answers to questions. One strategy, for example, would be to interview teachers after the period of observation and to ask them what they wanted as answers to particular questions. This would not provide a definitive criterion, but it would supply useful additional evidence. Without such checks we have no way of knowing the extent of such sources of error on the original data collection or the replication.

There is an even more important consequence of this neglect of the issue of validity, however. At no point in their work do the ORACLE researchers make it clear what the differentiation of types of question in the Teacher Record is intended to measure. As a result of this, ORACLE's coding rules often seem arbitrary. Why, for example, are all teacher utterances treated as either questions or statements when, as the authors themselves recognize, there are other functional categories relevant in classrooms, notably commands? Why should a teacher's utterance followed by a pupil's oral response be coded as a question whereas one followed by an oral response plus a non-verbal act on the part of a pupil be a statement? Why should the researchers seek to distinguish between task utterances, task supervision utterances and routine management utterances? Why should they distinguish between questions which require the recall of facts and those which require the production of ideas? While we can speculate about the reasons for these distinctions, the ORACLE researchers do not explicitly present these distinctions and their coding rules as designed to measure, say, the extent to which teaching is intended to encourage, or actually encourages, exploratory thinking on the part of pupils. As a result, one cannot begin to assess the validity of their measurements.

Point sampling

Like many studies employing systematic observation ORACLE did not record every instance of their categories of teacher behaviour within a specified time, but instead recorded the occurrence of activities at regular points in time. In ORACLE's case classroom process was sampled every 25 seconds. As a number of commentators have pointed out, one problem with this strategy is that it conflates frequency and duration of types of activity (Sackett, 1978). The scores which result are a product of *both* frequency and duration, but the relative contributions of these two factors are unknown. The same score for a particular question type could be produced by a high frequency of short questions or a low frequency of long questions. And this may have serious implications for the conclusions to be drawn from the results. For example, on these grounds we might well question ORACLE's claims that Style Two teachers (class inquirers) use a higher *proportion* of both open and closed questions than teachers in the other styles, or that Style Four teachers (style changers) ask the *highest number* of questions relating to task supervision (Galton, Simon and Croll, 1980, pp. 123–4). Unless the distinction between duration and frequency is of no significance for a study, and this does not seem to be the case for ORACLE, point sampling is an inappropriate research strategy. Activities such as statements and questions should be timed and counted if quantitative conclusions about their length and frequency are required.

Sampling of lesson time

Besides the sampling of activities within classroom process there is also the question of the sampling of lesson time itself. ORACLE use fairly large samples of time compared with many previous systematic observation studies. In addition, they sample across different school terms, presumably to avoid their samples being affected by cyclical patterns over the course of the school year. Even so, the size of their time samples is very small when compared with the total amount of classroom time in a year. Moreover, their samples are not random and the question of representativeness remains open. An additional problem here is the possibility of reactive effects. While this problem faces all classroom research, it seems likely that relatively short and announced visits of the kind employed by ORACLE may involve higher levels of reactivity than observation which occurs over longer periods of time.

There are no easy solutions to the problems of time sampling and reactivity, but they do require attention. ORACLE make no reference whatsoever to them. Moreover, they overlook the possibility of checking the extent of variation in teachers' activity over time. While they collected data in visits at different times of the year for each classroom, they give no indication of the scale of variation in scores between visits. If our own experience in studying secondary school lessons is generalizable, however, there is likely to be a high level of intra-classroom variation in such features as the number, duration and type of questions asked (Hammersley and Scarth, 1986). There are two important implications from this. First, that the behaviour of each teacher over time may vary as much as does the behaviour of different teachers, and this indicates that other major factors affect levels of questioning and type of questioning besides teaching style. This does not imply that teaching style is unimportant, only that if we are interested in explaining variation in teachers' questioning we may have to study these other factors. Second, if there is a high level of intra-classroom variation, then this suggests that even if our samples were random large samples of classroom time would be necessary to get a reasonably accurate sense of the occurrence of questioning of different types. This could be an important source of error in ORACLE's results. For example, ORACLE report that there is less questioning in open classrooms than in boxed classrooms but the difference is only 0.5 per cent of total observations. If there were variation for this category *within* each type of classroom, this small difference could easily have been produced by sampling fluctuations.

CONCLUSIONS

In this article we have examined one aspect of the work of ORACLE: the coding of questions. While this is a very small part of the focus of ORACLE, we believe that the problems we have identified apply to one degree or another to many other aspects of this research, and indeed to systematic observation research in general. We have noted the emphasis given by ORACLE to the issue of reliability, but argued that their coding rules involved a level of ambiguity and inference that could produce a degree of inconsistency between observers threatening some of the study's major findings. We also drew attention to the researchers' neglect of the question of validity. While we recognize that validity is more difficult to assess than reliability, this does not alter the fact that validity of measurement is the more fundamental issue. That ORACLE do not tackle this matter – and indeed are not even very clear about what is being measured – is, we feel, an important defect of the research. We have also pointed out the limitations of point sampling as a way of assessing the frequency of different types of activities. Finally, we drew attention to the relatively small samples of lesson time employed by ORACLE and their neglect of intra-teacher variations in the frequency of different types of question.

Systematic observation has been subjected to severe criticism over the past ten years or more, on the grounds, for instance, that it involves the imposition of crude, static categories upon a complex and processual reality (Coulthard, 1974; Walker and Adelman, 1975; Mehan, 1979; Delamont and Hamilton, 1984). Such criticisms have also been applied directly to ORACLE itself (notably by Barrow, 1984). It may seem that our article simply continues this tradition. However, in our view such attacks are seriously misleading. While they identify a number of important problems with, and likely sources of error in, systematic observational research, they are premised on the assumption that there is some radically different approach which avoids or solves these problems. Sometimes the recommended alternative is ethnography (Delamont and Hamilton, 1984), sometimes a reliance upon philosophy and/or the development of teachers' own professional experience and knowledge (Barrow, 1984). However, in neither case has the viability of the alternative been established convincingly.

In our view the problems faced by research on teaching are much the same whatever approach is adopted and whoever carries it out. There are the problems of sampling cases and of measuring features of those cases relevant to the theoretical ideas being developed and tested and, given consistency between theoretical predictions and empirical findings, there is the problem of showing that it was the factor(s) specified by the theory which produced the effects observed and not some other variable(s). There are of course different ways of tackling these problems but there are no simple solutions, nor does it seem likely that there will be any in the immediate future.

We have examined ORACLE, then, not from the point of view of some alternative paradigm, but simply as a piece of research exhibiting certain strategies designed to solve the problems which face research of any kind. And our aim has been to lay some of the groundwork for the development of more effective solutions to these problems. Above all, our concern is that these problems are currently either dismissed as the troubles of an obsolete paradigm or treated as minor irritations which can be safely ignored. Instead they must be recognized and systematically investigated. In our view, until they have been, judgement about the validity of the conclusions of ORACLE, and of much other classroom research, must be suspended.

ACKNOWLEDGEMENTS

We should like to acknowledge the comments of Paul Croll and Maurice Galton on an earlier version of this paper. They will still not agree with the conclusions we draw!

NOTES

1. A total of 334 pupils in two of the LEAs (40 classes) were observed for a second year as part of the longitudinal design of the project, which offered the possibility of a replication exercise: see Galton and Simon (1980).
2. The Record also makes provision for the observer to record the teacher's *audience* (class, group or private individual), the *composition* of the audience (with respect to the participation of the target pupils) and the curricular *activity* in which the teacher is engaged.
3. This kind of problem seems to be endemic in coding questions and tasks: see Scarth and Hammersley (1986).
4. Croll (personal communication) has argued that ORACLE's replication of its findings suggests that sampling error was low. The point is, though, that in all but 14 cases the replication involved different teachers not collection of further samples of the behaviour of the same teachers. Our argument is about the sampling of *each* teacher's behaviour, not the sampling of the population of teachers.

REFERENCES

Barrow, R. (1984) 'The logic of systematic classroom research: the case of ORACLE', *Durham and Newcastle Research Review*. X, 53, 182.

Bennett, N. (1976) *Teaching Styles and Pupil Progress*. London: Open Books.

Boydell, D. (1974) 'Teacher–pupil contact in junior classrooms', *British Journal of Educational Psychology*, 44, 313–18.

Boydell, D. (1975) 'Pupil behaviour in junior classrooms', *British Journal of Educational Psychology*, 45, 122–9.

Boydell, D. and Jasman, A. (1983) *The Pupil and Teacher Record: A Manual for Observers*. Leicester: University of Leicester.

Coulthard, M. (1974) 'Approaches to the analysis of classroom interaction', *Educational Review*, 26, 3, 229–40.

Croll, P. (1981) 'Social class, pupil achievement and classroom interaction.' In: Simon, B. and Willcocks, J. (Eds) *Research and Practice in the Primary School*. London: Routledge and Kegan Paul.

Delamont, S. and Hamilton, D. (1984) 'Revisiting classroom research: a continuing cautionary tale.' In: Delamont, S. (Ed.) *Readings on Interaction in the classroom*. London: Methuen.

Egan, O. (1984) 'Cluster analysis in educational research', *British Educational Research Journal*, 10, 2, 145–53.

Eggleston, J. F., Galton, M. and Jones, M. E. (1975) *A Science Teaching Observation Schedule*. London: Macmillan.

Everitt, B. (1974) *Cluster Analysis*. London: Heinemann.

Galton, M. and Simon, B. (1980) *Progress and Performance in the Primary Classroom*. London: Routledge and Kegan Paul.

Galton, M., Simon, B. and Croll, P. (1980) *Inside the Primary Classroom*. London: Routledge and Kegan Paul.

Hammersley, M. (1987) 'Some notes on the terms "reliability" and "validity" '. *British Educational Research Journal*, **13**, 1.

Hammersley, M. and Scarth, J. (1986) The impact of examinations on secondary school teaching. Unpublished report.

Mehan, H. (1979) *Learning Lessons*. Cambridge, Mass.: MIT Press.

Sackett, G. P. (Ed.) (1978) *Observing Behavior. Vol. II, Data Collection and Analysis Methods*. Baltimore, Md.: Baltimore University.

Scarth, J. and Hammersley, M. (1986) 'Some problems in measuring assessment and learning tasks for closedness'. In: Hammersley M., (Ed.) *Case Studies in Classroom Research*. Milton Keynes: Open University Press.

Sharp, R. and Green, A. (1976) *Education and Social Control*. London: Routledge and Kegan Paul.

Walker, R. and Adelman, C. (1975) 'Interaction analysis in informal classrooms: a critical comment on the Flanders system', *British Journal of Educational Psychology*, **45**, 1, 73–6.

12

FIGURING OUT ETHNIC EQUITY:
A RESPONSE TO TROYNA

R. Gomm

This paper is a commentary on Barry Troyna's paper 'Underachievers or Underrated? The experience of pupils of South Asian origin in a Secondary school' (1991), which claims to offer hard evidence of racially discriminatory practices by teachers against Asian pupils in a co-educational, comprehensive school called Jayleigh. In commenting on this paper I draw attention, in particular, to the need to specify standards of ethnic equity when claims of ethnic inequity are made.

Troyna's argument is relatively simple. At Jayleigh School, Asian pupils on entry are put into sets lower than their ability warrants. There is limited movement between sets and what there is downgrades more Asian pupils than it upgrades. This initial disadvantage is carried forward and exaggerated so that when it comes to entry for GCSE, Asian pupils achieve less than their white peers, and less than their ability should allow them to achieve. Troyna's conclusion is that:

> The data in this article provide clear cut evidence of the way Asian pupils, at the time of the study, were denied equality of opportunity in the school.

My conclusion, however, is that the data in the article do not provide clear evidence to substantiate this claim. Rather the data, which are patchy and often confusingly given, seem to be used by Troyna to make a claim which they do not warrant. For the sake of brevity I will only discuss Troyna's data on mathematics. These are the most adequate data in his article and his treatment of them also illustrates the shortcomings of his treatment of data on English, Social Studies and Craft subjects.

For Troyna the first stage of the process by which Asian pupils are disadvantaged starts with their allocation to mathematics sets on entry to the school. As

Table 1 Last year junior mathematics assessment by 1st year mathematics sets: percentages

	Outstanding		Good		Average		Weak		Very weak		Total
	White	Asian	White	Asian	White	Asian	White	Asian	White	Asian	
Number of pupils	3	—	35	13	48	18	25	10	9	3	164
Sets (%)											
A or AA	67	—	60	46	25	22	—	—	—	—	
B or BB	33	—	31	38	42	33	12	—	—	—	
C or CC	—	—	9	8	27	33	48	60	11	—	
D or DD	—	—	—	8	6	11	40	40	89	100	
Total	100	—	100	100	100	99	100	100	100	100	

Table 2 Last year junior mathematics assessment by 1st year mathematics sets: numbers

	Outstanding		Good		Average		Weak		Very weak		Total
	White	Asian	White	Asian	White	Asian	White	Asian	White	Asian	
Number in category	3	—	35	13	48	18	25	10	9	3	164
Sets											
A or AA	2	—	21	6	12	4	—	—	—	—	45
B or BB	1	—	11	5	20	6	3	—	—	—	46
C or CC	—	—	3	1	13	6	12	6	1	—	42
D or DD	—	—	—	1	3	2	10	4	8	3	31

data he presents the table included here as Table 1. His comments are as follows:

> [The] Table . . . shows the relationship of pupils' set placements to their junior school assessments. It demonstrates clearly that placement settings were not entirely in accordance with junior schools' mathematics assessment and that the ethnicity of the pupils played a mediating part in structuring their opportunities in the higher ability sets. Stated simply, Asian pupils were likely to be placed in lower ability sets than white pupils with comparable assessment profiles.

It can be fairly said that the table demonstrates that 'settings were not entirely in accordance with junior schools' mathematics assessment', but it certainly does not demonstrate that 'the ethnicity of the pupils played a mediating part in structuring their opportunities in the higher ability sets'. Firstly, since the figures are given in percentages, and 67% can mean two pupils, or 100% can mean 3, it is virtually impossible to read it 'at a glance'. Table 2 gives the same data in numbers. Secondly, to make such a demonstration it is necessary to set up some picture of what distribution should obtain were ethnicity to play no part in the allocation of pupils to sets, and compare the extant distribution with it. Troyna does not do this, so I will supply the missing models.

THE DECANTING PROBLEM

As evidence of mathematical ability Troyna takes as given the junior school ratings of pupils into five categories ranging from 'outstanding' to 'very weak'. There are eight maths sets, two equivalent sets each in four bands. We can guess from the tables also that the school attempts to keep the numbers in the top three bands roughly equal, each not exceeding (say) 46 and that it probably uses the bottom band as a variable size sink for the remainder.

Once the junior school gradings are put together with the school's set system the basis of a claim for one kind of inequity is established. This arises simply from the fact that there are five maths ability categories and four bands. However the school decanted the one into the other, some pupils of the same ability category would end up in different bands. In this particular year 72% of pupils are rated average or better, but the top half of the banding system contains places for only 56% of the pupils. At the very least there are going to be 26 'average' pupils allocated to the bottom half of the banding system while 40 'average' pupils will be allocated to the top half. Thus the system has the basis for inequity claims built in. Without changing the system of sets there will always be a residuum of inequity, claimable on the basis of a mismatch between junior school estimated ability and set placement.

Troyna is not primarily interested in equitable placement by ability, but in equitable placement by ethnic group, looking at deviations from the one as evidence of inequity in the other. Given that there is a claimable inequity built into the system already, we have to ask what would an equitable distribution by ethnicity look like, which is not necessarily an equitable distribution in terms of ability rating.

ETHNIC EQUITY: MODEL 1

Let us tackle this as if it were a practical problem and ask how we could divide the pupils in the ability categories into the extant system of sets and bands, as equitably as possible with regard to ability and without committing ethnic inequity. One way of solving this puzzle is something like this:

- There are 45 places in the top band. Those pupils who are rated 'outstanding' should have a place as of right in this band. There are three of them. They are all white. We give them top band places.
- We now have 42 places in the top band to fill. We will fill them from the category 'good' on the basis of ethnic equity, i.e. proportionately. This means that 31 more whites and 11 Asians will get top band positions: leaving four whites and two Asians unplaced from the 'good' category. These will take the first six places in the B band.

We proceed in this fashion until all places in the set system are filled as in Table 3. Table 3 is constructed to show the expected figures (E) had the distribution been as outlined above and the actual figures (O) extrapolated from Table 2.

The first thing to note is how close the school actually came to the ethnically equitable allocation I provided. The deviation between the actual figures and the ideal could be remedied by swapping just three Asian pupils from the bottom two bands with three white pupils demoted from the top two. All that could be claimed as an ethnic inequality is the equivalent of just under 7% of Asian pupils misplaced downwards, but 7% is only three pupils.

A second point to make is that the difference between the ideal distribution and the actual distribution is not just one obtained by subtracting 'O' figures from 'E' figures or vice versa. In terms of the placement of individual pupils, it could be claimed that at least 35 pairs of individuals should be swapped around. For example 15 pupils rated as 'outstanding' or 'good' but placed in

Table 3 Observed and expected figures for equitable distribution through maths sets by ability and ethnicity – model 1

| | Whites | | Asian | | |
	E	O	E	O	
A/AA	34	35	11	10	
B/BB	33	35	13	11	
C/CC	31	29	11	12	
D/DD	22	21	9	11	
TOT	120	120	44	44	164

sets B/BB and C/CC would have to be promoted, and 16 of the pupils rated as average but placed in sets A/AA would have to be demoted. This includes Asian pupils being demoted to the advantage of Asian pupils, and white pupils being demoted to the advantage of white pupils. Ethnic equity thus turns out to involve one Asian pupil's over-placement being compensated for by another's placement in a set lower than his/her ability seems to warrant. Ethnic equity does not match up to equity between individuals within groups, and this of course is often the case. Remember also that in terms of the logistical problem set for the school there can never be fewer than 25 pupils misplaced. The school managed a 79% match between junior school rated ability and placement, and the best it could have achieved was 85%.

While the school actually managed to come close to ethnic equity, they did not achieve it through following a strict policy of using junior school ratings. Troyna tells us:

> the sets . . . in year 1 were mainly based on a common test given to all pupils after they had been in the school for some six weeks. These tests provided attainment and effort grades . . . The school did, however, check pupils' test results with their primary school assesments. If there was a significant difference between a pupil's performance in the Jayleigh School tests compared to primary school assessments the latter could influence the sets in which a pupil was placed.

The pattern of set placement shown in Tables 1 and 2 must be viewed then in terms of a set of agreements and disagreements between secondary school teachers' interpretations of their own tests and the junior school ratings. If these set placements indicate racial discrimination then surely we would find this in deviations between secondary school test results and set placement, and not in the data in Troyna's Table 2. That is, unless Troyna were pursuing an argument that the experience of secondary schooling impacted so adversely on Asian pupils in the first six weeks that in secondary school tests they underperformed. He does not make this claim.

Troyna cites the secondary school staff as saying that:

> the reason they relied so heavily on their own tests for setting purposes was that in their experience it provided a better indication of pupils' ability in Mathematics . . . than primary school assessments.

The primary school tests were NFER tests. Their predictive validity has never been claimed to be 100%. Secondary school procedures were just as likely to remedy the junior school asessments in the direction of accuracy, as to represent distortion. 'Ability' after all is a much more ineffable quality than Troyna seems to treat it as, and it is not at all clear how we can ever come to a correct definition of it, let alone arbitrate between two definitions without access to the raw data on which they were based, and at the same time find good grounds to set up a third version as the arbiter. As it is, Troyna sets up junior school ratings as the truth about ability. He provides us with no reason why we should not instead locate the truth with the secondary school teachers and speculate on why junior school assessments were awry.

Logistically, junior school ratings had to be awry, insofar as they provided a distribution of pupils through a classification system which would not fit the setting pattern adopted by the school. Thus the secondary school tests had at the very least to divide 'average' pupils into 'high average' and 'low average'. Secondary school placements in fact depart from primary school judgements more than this, but if Table 2 is scrutinised it can be seen that 16 white pupils and four Asians might have a claim for saying that they had been 'over-placed', while 37 white pupils and 15 Asian pupils might have a claim for saying they had been under-placed: remembering always that if junior school assessments are the bench mark, the school can never get it exactly right. On this basis 13% of white pupils, and 9% of Asians were over-placed: a difference equivalent to a disadvantage of 1.7 Asian pupils: 31% of white pupils and 34% of Asian pupils were claimably under-placed: an additional disadvantage to Asian pupils of less than one and a half pupils. These considerations give us a measure of inequitable treatment of Asian pupils of much the same magnitude as that reached by the earlier method.

In addition, it would be unreasonable to expect test results necessarily to show a one to one correspondence with ability setting, even after the decanting problem is accommodated. The reason for this lies in setting systems themselves. In this school, excluding the sixth form, there were 44 maths sets. There were certainly not 44 maths teachers and, since teachers cannot be in more than one place at once, maths sets must have been organised in rotation with sets for other subjects. Most such systems easily facilitate a pupil being in the same level set for everything, but render impossible some hybrid combinations. Thus it is that placement in maths sets, say, can be determined by placement in another system of sets, resulting in departures from what ability measures might predict. If we knew what the secondary school test results were and the setting pattern for pupils, we might account for deviations between them and set placement in these terms. We do not know what they were, and cannot pursue this further, but it would be surprising if the vagaries of setting did not create some anomalies in the relationship between school estimates of ability and set placement.

ETHNIC EQUITY: MODEL 2

There are other ways in which we might model ethnic equity, and it might be argued that I have chosen one which serves to hide greater real inequities from view. Troyna has only given us junior school ratings to work with, which is not the best data for demonstrating racial discrimination. However it is the data he uses for his argument and I will continue to use it to show that even were we to allow its relevance his argument would continue to be weak.

To provide another picture of ethnic equity we might say that given that the system of allocation is bound to raise claims of inequity with regard to junior school rated ability, ethnic inequity is represented by a greater departure from ability placement for one ethnic group rather than another. To set up this comparison we proceed as follows. There are no 'outstanding' Asian pupils, so we allocate the three white outstanding pupils to the upper band. We then observe that of the white pupils in the 'good' category 21 (60%) were allocated to the top band, 11 (31%) to the second band and 3 (9%) to C/CC. Therefore we argue that Asian pupils should be distributed in the same inequitable way with regard to ability to create equity in ethnic distribution. This time we will allow the bands to expand or contract to accommodate this manoeuvre. Table 4 expresses the expected and observed figures for Asians only, since the figures for whites are as in Table 3.

Table 4 Observed and expected figures for distribution of Asian pupils in maths sets: ethnic model 2

	Asian	
	E	O
A/AA	12.5	10
B/BB	12.8	11
C/CC	10.9	12
D/DD	8.4	11
TOT	44	44

On this calculation there is a claimable ethnic inequity equivalent to about four Asian pupils being misplaced in the lower two bands, rather than in the upper two bands: a greater degree of inequity than in the earlier calculation, but not much. The reason why a greater degree of inequity shows is that this time we allowed set size in the expected figures to expand and contract enough to accommodate movements of Asian pupils, while in the observed figures the set sizes are fixed. (But of course we did not extend the benefits of this to white pupils!)

ETHNIC EQUITY: MODEL 3

Let us follow the logic of this and check whether further ethnically related inequity can be discovered in the rigidity of the setting system itself. To do this we will assume that the pupils ought to be setted such that all outstanding and good pupils should be in A/AA, all average in B/BB, all weak in C/CC and all very weak in D/DD. Table 5 expresses the expected and observed for this calculation.

To bring the actual figures into line with this ideal we would have to promote 16 white pupils and 10 Asian pupils. How you regard this depends on whether you opt to express matters in numbers or percentages. In terms of numbers, ethnic inequity now appears reversed with six more white pupils under-placed than Asian pupils. In terms of percentages, inequity to Asian pupils is restored: 13% of white pupils are under-placed and 23% of Asian

Table 5 Observed and expected figures for distribution through maths sets: ethnic equity model 3

| | Whites | | Asian | | |
	E	O	E	O	
A/AA	38	35	13	10	
B/BB	48	35	18	11	
C/CC	25	29	10	12	
D/DD	9	21	3	11	
TOT	120	120	44	44	164

pupils, a percentage difference of 10% (4.4 pupil equivalents) to the disadvantage of Asian pupils. We seem to have reached much the same conclusion that Asian pupils are very marginally disadvantaged, so long as we accept that junior school teachers are better judges of ability than secondary school teachers.

GENDER

It is very odd that Troyna, writing in the 1990s, gives no attention to the fact that the school is co-educational. It is not at all unusual for girls to show a different profile of mathematical ability from boys. Moreover, it is sometimes claimed that teachers make unwarrantable assumptions about gender differences in mathematical ability. Even if the sex ratio in this school is identical for Asians and whites, to understand Troyna's data we need to know whether the ability profile for girls and boys in the junior school ratings is similar, and whether the ability profile for Asian girls/boys is similar to the ability profile for white girls/boys. If, for example, Asian girls had a mathematical ability profile superior to white girls, but sex discrimination was implicated in setting decisions, this might show in the aggregate Troyna presents, but as ethnic discrimination rather than the sexual discrimination it might be more accurately labelled as.

ETHNIC INEQUALITY–ETHNIC EQUITY

As we have seen, there are various possibilities for modelling ethnic equity, and the figures for ethnic inequity fall out differently for each: although they are all very small. I think each of my models of ethnic equity has merits, but I can find no principled way of deciding between them. What certainly has no merit is Troyna's model, which is derived simply from comparing ethnic proportions in sets with the ethnic proportions in the cohort as a whole, without reference to differential ability, as in statements such as:

White pupils comprised over 74% of those in the six GCSE sets . . .
Asian pupils figured largely in the non-GCSE sets, comprising 54% of the

pupil population. Again, this compared unfavourably with the ratio of white and Asian pupils in the fifth year: that is 69% and 31% respectively.

If Troyna's model of ethnic equity is proportional distribution of ethnic groups through sets without reference to ability then it might seem puzzling that he should have bothered to provide any information representing ability at all. What he is actually doing is to use the data on ability, misleadingly, when it suits his argument, and to ignore it when it does not.

In addition, it is worth noting how Troyna presents this discrepancy between a crude ethnic proportional distribution and the actual situation. Look at the quotation above again. It refers to setting in years four and five. I challenge the reader to say whether this is a large or a small discrepancy. I suggest that few readers will be able to tell at a glance. This is because Troyna uses percentages and does not tell the reader how many pupils are in the top and bottom sets. It is possible to estimate this using simultaneous equations, [. . .] and the result is that the number of Asian pupils required to make up 54% of the bottom sets is about 17. The target figure of 31% for crude proportionality is about 11. The difference between actuality and crude proportionality is probably six. Thus the scandal which Troyna announces can only be a little one, and anyway we correctly expect schools to place pupils in sets according to ability, and not according to ethnicity.

WITHIN–GROUP DIFFERENCES

Not only do different models of ethnic equity generate different figures for ethnic inequity, they locate the disadvantages as being suffered by different pupils (sometimes by decimal points of pupils) or rather they locate the disadvantage nowhere in particular.

This may seem puzzling at first, so let me illustrate it with reference to the fate of the pupils rated average by the junior schools. Extrapolating from Table 2 gives the figures in Table 6 (note that the figures for Asians do not make 100% because of original rounding in Table 2).

What this shows is that 42 'average' pupils gained B or better placements while 24 did not. Nine of the losers were Asian, but then so were ten of the gainers. It would be perverse to say that the disadvantages of the eight Asian pupils were entirely due to the favourable treatment of the 32 white winners, without reference to what is going on within the Asian group. Twelve of the white winners were actually placed in sets A/AA, and only four of the Asian winners: a disadvantage equivalent to fractionally over one Asian pupil, by comparison with a proportional distribution. One more Asian pupil might have been placed in set A, but which of the 'average' Asian pupils should this have been: there are after all 14 contenders? And why should competition for an additional A/AA place be confined to Asians only?

Table 6 Allocation of 'average pupils' to maths sets

	Whites	*Asian*
Placement A/AA	25% (12)	22% (4)
Placement B/BB or better	67% (32)	56% (10)
Worse than B/BB	33% (16)	44% (8)

If we had started somewhere else in Table 2 then the distribution of advantage and disadvantage would have looked different. Although scrutinising the whole table will always show a marginal disadvantage for Asians, when compared to whites, there is no way of pinning this disadvantage on any particular Asian pupils. The situation is the same as in electoral studies where all voters and non-voters make a contribution to the outcome, but no one in particular can be held responsible for the majority of the winning candidate.

This has a very important implication. Ethnic inequality calculated in this way is a statistical product. This does not mean that it is not worth calculating, but it does mean that it cannot be tied to the careers of particular pupils. Using these procedures we can never choose, for example, which among a number of Asian pupils are in a lower set because places in the upper set were taken by whites, and which are in the lower set because places in the upper set were taken by other Asian pupils. There is no easy movement between, on the one hand, statistical calculations of ethnic inequity – whether these are of the crude proportional kind used by Troyna or the more sophisticated kinds suggested here – and on the other hand ethnographic case study approaches of the careers of known pupils of known measured ability. Each can be indicative for the other, but in the last resort they do not marry.

This is not just a methodological problem, it is also a practical one. If we told this school that their set placement practices disadvantaged the equivalent of three or four Asian pupils (or six if Troyna's wilder claims were used), the school would ask quite reasonably 'which ones?' And we could not tell them. If they chose to promote any three Asian pupils with a claim to having been under-placed, they would leave a much larger number of Asian pupils (and white pupils) able to say that an equally valid claim had been ignored. In an attempt to remedy the situation the school might take the tack of 'going back to basics'. To do this – to reach a result satisfactory to Troyna – they would first have to convince themselves that junior school teachers had a superior means for judging pupils' mathematical ability. Secondly they would have to disassemble their setting system. And, lastly, they would have to let junior school ratings constitute the sets, rather than the exigencies of the setting system moderate junior school ratings. I cannot image circumstances under which they would be prepared to do this or under which it would be sensible to do it. Crucial evidence to convince them is missing. This concerns the superiority of the junior school ratings and the workability of another system of ability setting. The resulting distribution of pupils would be likely to be administratively impossible in a system where sets have to rotate around sets. And if it is part of Troyna's thesis that setting should be abandoned in favour of mixed ability teaching, then it has to be said that the evidence with regard to the superior equitability of mixed-ability teaching in terms of outcomes is parlous (Reid, 1981; Ball, 1981, 1986).

All in all, then, on the evidence that Troyna provides, and no further, this school looks as if it is in line for congratulations rather than vilification. Given the logistical problems of its setting system, and in the face of the uncertainties of any kind of evidence about pupil ability, the distribution of pupils through sets is not inconsistent with a distribution strictly made on the basis of ability. It might also be consistent with a grievous degree of discrimination against girls or Asian or both. But Troyna provides no convincing evidence in this regard.

MOVEMENT BETWEEN SETS

The next stage of Troyna's argument refers to the small degree of movement of pupils between sets in the first three years. If pupils were wrongly setted then it is indeed inequitable that this should not be sorted out by moving pupils around when their true ability becomes apparent. There is already a problem here, however. Unless we assume, and we cannot, that junior school ratings were accurate and should be allowed 100% predictive validity for later achievement, then there are two reasons for moving pupils between sets: that they were wrongly setted on entry or that they were correctly setted on entry but have subsequently improved or declined in mathematical ability relative to their peers. However, without having some objective measures of pupils' mathematical ability, and tying these measures to the mobility of known pupils in the set system, we have no means of evaluating whether either the stability or the mobility of pupils was warranted.

One kind of evidence about pupil ability is not available: that of the crucial tests on which the school based its setting decisions. Troyna handles this evidence in one sentence. Writing of the results of the common year three examination he says:

> What we did find in the analysis of these results is that pupils in set D/DD in year 3 who obtained the same scores as pupils in higher year 3 mathematics sets did not move up to higher sets in transition from year 3 to year 4.

It is not at all clear what this means. Firstly how many pupils are being referred to? The numbers could be very small. It seems sensible to read this as referring to Asian *and* white pupils. If so, which ethnic category had the greater claim to being disadvantaged? It is not clear whether those D/DD pupils who scored more than some C/CC pupils were in fact promoted, and it is not stated whether C/CC or other higher set pupils who scored less than the best D/DD pupils were demoted. And in addition it has to be noted that schools rarely make setting decisions entirely on the basis of one examination, they usually take the year's overall performance into consideration, and can make a good case for this practice.

Troyna provides us with no data on the mobility of pupils of known ability through the set system, not even of pupils whose ability is 'known' from junior school ratings. Thus we have no way of judging whether mobility in the set system was equitable or not with regard to ability. He does quantify the amount of mobility in years 1–3, saying that 79% of pupils were in the same set in mathematics in year 1 as in year 3. This raises the question of how stable the system of placements should have been. If you take junior school assessments as the base line, and note that the school seemed to achieve a 79% match between ratings and sets, then a case could be made for saying that only 21% of pupils needed to be moved anyway. However, given the built-in inequality of the system, moving 21% of pupils would have redistributed the inequity by ability as much as remedying it. And, of course, we have no way of knowing whether the actual movements brought the pattern more into conformity with junior school ratings, or departed more from them. The secondary school test results would seem a more appropriate base-line for judging ability and mobility: it is a good bet that setting decisions were more consistent with these test results than with junior school ratings, and that teachers believed, rightly or wrongly, that few moves were warranted on an ability basis.

SHIFTY BASE FIGURES

Troyna also tells us that:

> the proportion of Asian pupils in the bottom sets for mathematics increased from 26% to 29% in these first three years whilst the proportion of white pupils in these sets fell from 18% to 13% in the same period.

However, we cannot make sense of this without knowing what 100% is. Troyna in fact uses three (and possibly four) sets of base figures for white and Asian pupils. But he does not always tell us which set he is using, while he almost exclusively cites data in percentages. Where each Asian pupil can amount to 2.27%, and white on Asian differences are small, quite small changes in base figures can have dramatic effects.

Troyna's Table 2 (our Table 1) gives one set of base figures: 120 whites and 44 Asians. If the paragraph above refers to this then two Asian pupils have been demoted, and six white pupils have been promoted. We do not know anything about these pupils but if we took junior school teachers' ratings as a measure of ability, the first year sets contained 11 white pupils who arguably should not have been in sets D/DD and six Asian pupils who arguably should have been in sets D/DD but were actually in sets C/CC. In other words, the actual movements could have been achieved as a partial attempt to match junior school ratings with ability setting, had anyone wanted to do this, which is doubtful.

In addition, we do not know whether these percentages refer to the pupils shown in Troyna's Table 2 or to the 'sample' of pupils which contained 138 whites (rather than 120) and 61 Asians (rather than 44), or to the whole school population including non-whites and non-SE Asians. So not only do we not know what these movements mean, we also do not know what their magnitude is in terms of numbers of pupils. Nor do we know whether they are boys or girls.

In terms of statistical methods and school processes the possibility that the base figures for Troyna's percentages are changing is a serious matter. His strongest claim for ethnic inequity is based on 120 whites and 44 Asians. The sample is 138 whites and 61 Asians. The cohort population is 153 whites, 67 South Asians and two others. If we want to judge the distribution of ethnic groups through sets (in the third year or later) against the ability profiles of ethnic groups, then we need to have some measure of the ability of 18 whites and 17 Asians (or 33 whites, 23 Asians and 2 others) for whom no ability data is given. For non-whites we can rightly be suspicious also that a percentage of those who do not appear in the primary school rating data were late arrivals to the UK with all the problems that late arrival constitutes for a pupil.

FOURTH AND FIFTH YEAR MATHS

Troyna also says that 82% of pupils did not move sets in the transition from the third year to the fourth year. This is a very odd thing to say, because in the third year there were eight mathematics sets, and in the fourth and fifth there were 10. Technically all pupils changed sets. The truth of the matter seems to be that there was a close correspondence between the populations of the eight sets and the ten sets, such that a majority of pupils in the top six sets of ten had been in sets A/AA and B/BB. Further than this, however, we are given no explicit details of the sizes of the new sets, the relationship between their populations and those of the old sets, or any direct information about ethnic composition. We are told that:

> White pupils comprised over 74% of those in the six GCSE sets . . . Asian pupils, by contrast, figured largely in the non-GCSE sets, comprising 54% of the pupil population.

But this does not mean anything unless we can establish some model of how many whites ought to have been in the top sets, and how many Asians ought to have been in the bottom sets, on the assumption that ethnicity was not implicated in the decision-making. Since we have no measure of the mathematical ability of these pupils *qua* set members, the data is entirely without meaning. It is, on the one hand, quite consistent with a distribution based entirely on ability – given that 100% of Asians and 100% of whites probably includes 18 whites and 17 Asians for whom no junior school ratings were available and pupils for whom first form school test results are missing, and that a 100% of all pupils may now contain two pupils from other ethnic groups. The data is also of course entirely consistent with a discriminatory policy towards Asian pupils. But we have no way of judging whether discrimination took place.

One thing we can work out from the scattered percentages is that Troyna is being misleading in referring to the top six sets as 'the GCSE sets'. If 74% of those in the top six sets were white, and if 83% of white pupils took GCSE, then some white pupils in the bottom four sets must have taken GCSE. Likewise with Asian pupils. Crossing our fingers and assuming the percentages refer to 199 pupils as given in the 'sample', and crossing the fingers of the other hand and assuming that all pupils in the top six sets took GCSE maths, then 13 Asians and 13 whites in the bottom four sets took GCSE: 38% of all bottom set pupils, 40% of Asian bottom set pupils, and 36% of white pupils. Fingers can be uncrossed because all other calculations give higher figures for GCSE takers from lower sets. These are evidently not 'non-GCSE sets'.

The implication that Troyna gives that placement in one of the lowest four sets eliminates one's chances of taking GCSE now have to be mitigated. Placement in such sets reduces the chance of taking GCSE but does not eliminate it. It reduces chances rather less for Asians and rather more for whites. It can be argued with equal plausibility that this shows that the lower sets obtained more Asian pupils who had the ability to take maths GCSE and should therefore have been in higher sets, or that the school took a more indulgent line with lower-setted Asian pupils who wanted to take maths. Nor would it help to know which of these lower-setted pupils actually passed, because for those who were not entered it could still be claimed that they might have passed had their true ability been recognised and entry been allowed. Troyna gives no data on scores in the common third year exam, and hence no data in relation to who did and who did not enter examinations. This might have been taken as indicative, but unless the assumption was made that ability in maths is frozen at the end of the third year it could not decide the matter with any finality.

INPUTS AND OUTPUTS

Troyna places more weight on junior school assessments as ability markers than I would do. But it is interesting to check the outputs in terms of GCSE maths entries with the inputs in terms of junior school ratings. Let us say that we would expect all pupils rated by junior schools as 'average' and above to be entered five years later for GCSE maths. Table 2 shows us that there are 86 white pupils and 31 Asian pupils in this category. On this basis we can say that there should be no fewer than 86 white and 31 Asian entrants for GCSE maths. The actual figures are 111 white entries and 41 Asian entries. Junior school ratings underpredict the numbers entering for GCSE. This is unsurprising since the actual entries include 18 whites and 17 Asians for whom there was no junior school data, and there has probably been some turnover in the cohort membership anyway. Two things can be said about this however. Firstly this data shows no inconsistency with the claim that all those pupils who were rated by their junior school as 'average' and above, were in fact finally entered for GCSE, whether white or Asian. Secondly and much more tentatively, junior school ratings under-predict GCSE maths entries for whites and Asians to much the same degree (14% for whites and 16% for Asians). The under-prediction implicates pupils for whom no junior school maths ratings were available, but as the evidence stands there is certainly none to show that white pupils were entered for the examination disproportionately more than would be predicted by junior school maths ratings, by comparison with Asian pupils.

MATHEMATICS: SUMMARY

In summary, so far as mathematics is concerned the data in this article do not:

provide clear cut evidence of the way Asian pupils, at the time of the study, were denied equality of opportunity in the school.

The most Troyna could claim for the evidence is that it suggests that three or four or 4.4 or three Asian pupils in this year – depending on how ethnic equity is defined – were setted lower than their junior school ratings would predict, by comparison with their white peers. Whether they should have been setted differently is entirely another matter. Since we do not have the school test results on which setting decisions were actually based, the third year examination results, nor any other ability data, we are not in a position even to consider whether school setting practices were better or worse, more or less accurate than what could have been based on junior school ratings. If there is any ethnic inequity here – and we cannot be sure there is – there is nothing to tell us whether it is determined by ethnic discrimination directly rather than by contingent factors (such as the decanting problem or the operation of setting systems) which happen to give a small minority of Asian pupils a raw deal in this particular year, or by sex differences and sexual discrimination, or indeed by differences in social class. The description of what happens in years four and five provides no evidence at all about the relationships between ethnicity, setting and examination entry which is inconsistent with examination entry allocated strictly on the basis of ability. Nor is the final pattern of examination entry inconsistent with the ability profile shown by junior school ratings. [. . .]

IMPUTING RACISM

Troyna's paper implies racial discrimination by the teachers at Jayleigh, and by other teachers elsewhere. This is a serious matter, and if such claims are merited they should be backed with good evidence. The imputations of racism made by Troyna are not warranted by the evidence he provides. [. . .]

If teachers engage in discriminatory practices these should be detected and corrected. But if they are accused of so doing when they are innocent, then they are put in a position where they can 'never do a thing right'. If they feel themselves to be in this position, they will give up bothering, even when the effort is warranted. It is especially worrying that the school staff at Jayleigh who afforded a research locale, and had every right to expect that their activities would be treated fairly, have been represented as racists when the evidence will not bear this interpretation.

There are also large constituencies who are either hostile to or complacent about the importance of ensuring ethnic equity in schools. In their hands an article like Troyna's would be a powerful weapon. A research report wherein data about ethnic inequity is so obviously massaged into place can be used as an excuse for dismissing all the other evidence past, present and future.

ACKNOWLEDGEMENTS

I would like to thank Peter Foster, Martyn Hammersley, and two anonymous reviewers for their comments on an earlier draft of this paper.

REFERENCES

Ball, S. (1981) *Beachside Comprehensive* (Cambridge, Cambridge University Press).
Ball, S. (1986) The Sociology of the school: streaming, mixed ability and social class, in: R. Rogers (Ed) *Education and Social Class* (Lewes, Falmer Press).
Reid, L. (1981) *Mixed Ability Teaching: Problems and Possibilities* (Windsor, NFER/ Nelson).
Troyna, B. (1984) Fact or Artefact? The 'Educational underachievement' of black pupils. *British Journal of Sociology of Education*, 5, pp. 153–66.
Troyna, B. (1991) Underachievers or underrated? The experience of pupils of South Asian origin in a secondary school. *British Educational Research Journal*, 17, pp. 361–76.

13

BEWARE OF WISE MEN BEARING GIFTS: A CASE STUDY IN THE MISUSE OF EDUCATIONAL RESEARCH

M. Hammersley and J. Scarth

The proper function of educational research is widely regarded as being to inform policy-makers and practitioners, and thereby to improve education. However, at the same time, there has long been concern about the lack of impact of research on policy and practice. Sometimes policy-makers and practitioners are blamed for taking insufficient account of research findings. Alternatively, research is criticized for being insufficiently relevant to the work of those whom it is intended to inform. Behind this conception of the role of research, and the complaints about its failure to fulfil this role effectively, there often seems to be an assumption that the influence of research on practice will necessarily be beneficial, so that it is in everyone's interests to maximize that influence. Few perhaps would go as far as MacDonald in rejecting the concept of information misuse completely (MacDonald, 1974, p. 18), but relatively little attention has been paid to the ways in which research findings can be misused and can have undesirable consequences. In this paper we examine a recent example of a government-sponsored discussion document that, in our view, misuses educational research findings in some highly significant ways.

In February 1992, the DES published what, even before it appeared, was widely dubbed the report of the 'Three Wise Men' (DES, 1992). The men involved were Robin Alexander, a professor of education, Jim Rose, the Chief Primary Inspector, and Chris Woodhead, Chief Executive of the National Curriculum Council. They had been appointed by Kenneth Clarke, the then Secretary of State for Education, to review evidence about the current state of primary education, and to make recommendations about school organization and teaching necessary for the successful implementation of the National Curriculum.

There has been relatively little sustained critical assessment of this report, in public at least. The only substantial assessments known to us are those by

Dadds (1992) and by David, Curtis and Siraj-Blatchford (1992), known collo-
quially as the 'Three Wise Women' report.[1] The first looks at the report in the
context of the current political climate, suggesting that the problem to which
the report offers itself as a solution is one that has been largely manufactured
by the government. It considers the prospects for a fruitful debate about the
educational issues raised, emphasizing both the value of educational theory
and research *and* the skilfulness of teachers, in the face of attacks on both.
David, Curtis and Siraj-Blatchford, on the other hand, show quite comprehen-
sively that research evidence can be marshalled to come to very different
conclusions to those of Alexander and his colleagues. While both of these
contributions are very useful, neither focuses in a very specific way on the
argument of the report itself. This is the focus we have adopted here. Above all,
we are interested in what sort of intervention in the long-running debate about
primary methods the report makes, how it draws on evidence, and how it
speaks to teachers.

It is important to understand the context in which this report was produced.
It is common to see the early 1970s as a watershed in the recent history of
British educational policy. At that point we see clear signs of a change of
direction in policy, most significantly in Prime Minister Callaghan's speech at
Ruskin College in 1976. However, this change was prefigured by the publication of a series of 'Black Papers' in the late 1960s and early 1970s. One of the
main targets of the Black Paper writers was what they took to be the widespread influence of progressivism on primary school practice. They saw the
Plowden Report of 1967 as representing an official endorsement of progressivism in primary schools, one that had to be challenged if further decline in
educational standards, and in society generally, was to be avoided (Cox and
Dyson, 1971; Wright, 1977).

A key event at this time was the publication of Neville Bennett's study
Teaching Styles and Pupil Progress, in which he claimed to have shown that:
'. . . formal teaching fulfils its aims in the academic area without detriment to
the social and emotional development of pupils, whereas informal teaching
only partially fulfils its aims in the latter area as well as engendering com-
paratively poorer outcomes in academic development' (Bennett, 1976, p. 162).
Bennett (1978, p. 26) notes that:

> These findings challenged one of the educational orthodoxies – that in-
> formal methods are more appropriate for primary school children. At the
> time of publication the orthodoxy was already under fire, fuelled mainly
> by the notorious William Tyndale affair, the closure of a so-called pro-
> gressive primary school in London at the instigation of parents and man-
> agers. Levels of public anxiety had also been raised by the question of
> falling standards, a question being answered by rhetoric rather than
> evidence, and capitalized on by yet another Black Paper. The publication
> of our report unwittingly gave the educational Right the research findings
> they had been waiting for. From the day of publication we found our-
> selves fighting a rearguard action against the excesses of the educational

Right. Despite protestations and disclaimers, members of the Conservative Party constantly misrepresented, over stated or sloganized our findings. The day after publication Rhodes Boyson exhorted parents to 'Go out to your schools and check on whether permissive rubbish is being used and if so demand a change'.

Wright (1977, p. 40) also provides a useful commentary on the events surrounding the publication of Bennett's book. He notes that in 1976 two studies were published:

> One was by John Gray, a researcher from Edinburgh University . . . Gray reported: 'My research suggests that there is no reason to suppose that formal teaching is significantly associated with greater reading progress.' He went on to warn that his findings cannot be generalised to other teachers, other localities, or other age groups. Gray's research received very little publicity. . . . The other study reported in 1976 was done by Neville Bennett of Lancaster University. It was received with enormous publicity in all newspapers, on the radio and television. . . . The *Daily Telegraph* summed up what it was all about: '*Old fashioned teaching is best, say Dons.* Children taught by traditional classroom methods do far better at school than those taught in a modern, "progressive" way, a research report by a team of dons at Lancaster says today'.

In the decade or so that followed there was recurrent public controversy about the effects of progressivism on primary schools, but the next major outburst was in 1990 and 1991, this time taking place against the background of the educational reforms of the late 1980s. In 1990 there was a debate about reading standards stimulated by a leaked report by nine educational psychologists claiming that standards in their LEAs had declined, and blaming teachers' use of 'progressive' methods that rely on 'real books' (see Stierer, 1991). In mid-1991 an evaluation of primary schooling in a sample of Leeds schools was published which was critical of some aspects of teaching in those schools, aspects which the author saw as stemming from teachers' commitment to progressive rhetoric. Both these reports were publicized by much of the national press in the same manner as Bennett's work had been treated a decade or so earlier. In December 1991 the Secretary of State for Education wrote a letter to headteachers, in which he expressed concern about the quality of teaching in primary schools and indicated that he had commissioned a report on primary education and the 'delivery' of the National Curriculum (Clarke, 1991). The report of the 'three wise men', so called partly because it was due to appear soon after Christmas, was subsequently published as a discussion paper, and responses to it monitored by HMI (Ofsted, 1993, see also NCC 1993).

AN ANALYSIS OF THE REPORT AND ITS USE OF EVIDENCE

The report covers many aspects of primary schooling, the conclusions being listed in the summary under the following headings: standards of educational achievement; the quality of teaching; subject expertise, teaching roles and staff deployment; initial training, induction and INSET; and the National Curriculum. We shall concentrate largely on the parts of the report dealing with educational standards and the quality of teaching, since these are the sections which have been given the most attention by the media and which were at the heart of the build-up to the commissioning of the report. Our particular concern will be the evidence needed to establish the claims that the authors make.

The main argument of the report in relation to these issues is as follows. First, it is claimed that the current level of pupil progress in primary schools is unsatisfactory. Thus in their summary the authors declare that there is 'some evidence of downward trends in important aspects of literacy and numeracy' among primary school children (para. 2); and this is repeated in the main body of the report (para. 50). Second, the diagnosis is made that this arises from poor quality teaching, produced by the persistence of elements of progressive doctrine among primary teachers. The authors write: 'over the last few decades the progress of primary pupils has been hampered by the influence of highly questionable dogmas which have led to excessively complex classroom practices and devalued the place of subjects in the curriculum' (para. 3.2). Finally, recommendations are made proposing the increased use of whole-class teaching, subject specialization, etc.; many, though not all, of these recommendations running counter to what the authors take to be progressivism.

Outlining the problem

The starting point for the report, then, is a claim that there has been a decline in standards of literacy and numeracy among primary-age children. However, the authors express caution. In the summary they comment that the data on primary pupils' achievement 'are in many ways inadequate' (para. 2). And in their discussion of the evidence they write that 'there are insufficient statistical data on primary performance over time' (para. 25). Of course, if these judgements about the adequacy of the evidence are correct, then strictly speaking these data cannot provide a reasonable basis for conclusions about trends in numeracy and literacy. The words 'inadequate' and 'insufficient' are not synonyms for 'less than ideal', 'poor', etc. They imply that the data are simply not good enough to provide a foundation for conclusions about trends in achievement, one way or the other. Furthermore, in our view the authors' judgement about the inadequacy of the data is sound. There are serious and largely unresolved problems involved in assessing accurately children's performance at school, even in such apparently straightforward matters as literacy and numeracy. The sources which the authors refer to in the body of their report exemplify the problems, and even at face value they provide very mixed evidence. Yet, despite all this, the authors feel able to claim that standards of literacy and numeracy have declined and to imply that this represents a serious problem that must be addressed as a priority. It seems as if the authors started from the conviction that there is a problem of declining standards, looked at the evidence and found that it did not support this conviction, but remained convinced. Of course, this conviction could be correct: the data do not count *against* it. However, the authors have no grounds for claiming that the various sources they discuss provide evidence for it. Some of their sources show a downward trend, others indicate an upward trend or no change; and all the sources are, as the authors admit, too weak to bear any conclusion one way or the other.

Identifying the cause

As we noted, the main cause that the authors identify as bringing about the claimed decline in standards is the commitment of some primary school teachers to 'highly questionable dogmas', by which they mean those ideas usually listed under the heading of 'progressivism'. They note that the 'commonly held belief that primary schools, after 1967, were swept by a tide of progressivism is untrue'. At the same time, though, they claim that (para. 20):

> the ideas and practices connoted by words like 'progressivism' and 'informal' had a profound impact in certain schools and LEAs. Elsewhere they were either ignored, or – most damagingly in our view – adopted as so much rhetoric to sustain practice which in visual terms might look attractive and busy but which lacked any serious educational rationale. Here they lost their early intellectual excitement and became little more than a passport to professional approval and advancement. The real problem was not so much radical transformation as mediocrity.

A first requirement for this explanation of the claimed decline in standards to be established is, of course, that the authors show that the views they list under the heading of dogmas are indeed widespread among primary school teachers. If this is not the case, these 'dogmas' can hardly serve as the cause of a general decline.

There are some conceptual problems here. The authors are referring to a collection of beliefs which are quite diverse in character and that do not necessarily go together. For example, at one point they list hostility to the idea that young children be exposed to subjects, the belief that subject divisions are inconsistent with the child's view of the world, the idea that children must be allowed to construct their own meanings, the view that subject teaching involves the imposition of a received version of knowledge, and the belief that the wholeness of the curriculum is more important than the distinct identities of individual subjects (para. 63). Now these ideas do not imply one another in a strict logical sense, nor is there evidence offered showing that they tend to go together empirically. For instance, one can believe that children must be allowed to construct their own meanings *and* that they should be introduced to subject knowledge, without contradiction. Furthermore, it would not be unreasonable to believe, and some teachers undoubtedly do believe this, that subject knowledge should be introduced to primary schoolchildren but not by teaching separate subjects.

These problems make the task of documenting the orientations of primary school teachers and their relationship to progressive doctrine much more difficult than the discussion in the report implies. Even putting such problems on one side, however, as the authors acknowledge, what evidence there is in this area suggests that the influence of progressivism has been much less than is commonly supposed by its critics: very few primary school teachers seem ever to have held progressive ideas in an unqualified way.[2]

Of course, even if it could be shown that progressive beliefs were widespread among primary school teachers and were acted on by them, and even if it had been shown that a decline in children's achievement had taken place, we still could not conclude without further evidence that the first had caused the second. It is quite possible for teachers to be doing all they reasonably can do, indeed to be organizing their work more effectively than before, and yet for the literacy and numeracy of succeeding cohorts of children to go down. Other factors, such as changes in the home circumstances of substantial numbers of children, could bring this about. Furthermore, there have been recent government-induced changes in the conditions of work of teachers that seem very likely to have had a negative effect on the quality of pupil learning. Tellingly, the latter are ruled out of consideration by the authors of the report. They express the hope that their readers 'can suspend their concern about overall levels of resourcing' (para. 41). But why should consideration of this factor be ruled out? The Secretary of State may not be prepared to consider it, but that is far from a sound basis on which to decide what is and is not relevant.

There are a number of studies that have investigated the relationship between teaching style and pupil progress. However, the results of those studies do not offer strong evidence for the idea that progressive teaching hampers pupil progress. The most famous study, still sometimes quoted as establishing such a relationship, is the book by Neville Bennett mentioned earlier (Bennett, 1976). However, scrutiny of his research has revealed that its conclusions are not well supported.[3] This is shown most strikingly by a reanalysis of the data carried out by Bennett himself and others, in which rather different results were produced (Aitken, Bennett and Hesketh, 1981).[4] In fact, most educational researchers, including Bennett, have come to the conclusion that the very aspiration of finding relationships between teaching styles and levels of pupil progress is misguided (Bennett *et al.*, 1984). In some places the authors of the report seem to recognize this and to claim relationships that are more specific, being concerned for example with the links between whole class or subject teaching and pupil progress. However, most of the severe methodological problems that arose with research on teaching styles, for example surrounding the operationalization of concepts and the establishment of causal effect, also apply to investigations of these more specific relationships, and they have not yet been satisfactorily resolved. This means that we should treat with great caution claims made about the effects of particular teaching strategies on pupils' progress. Obviously, teachers need to make decisions about how to organize pupils' learning, and research findings do provide some relevant information. But teachers themselves also have valuable practical experience of different modes of organization and their effects, and this experience should not simply be dismissed on the basis of research findings whose validity is very uncertain.

We must conclude on the basis of these arguments that the evidence for the authors' causal claim about the relationship between commitment to progressive dogmas on the part of primary school teachers and a decline in levels of literacy and numeracy is weak at all points. However, there is one other aspect of their argument to which we ought to give attention. We need to take account of the fact that when they claim that pupils' progress is being hampered, this is not just a causal claim but also an evaluative judgement. What is being implied is that the achievement levels of children are not what one could reasonably expect in the circumstances. This is an even more complex matter to investigate than the issue of causality. There is considerable scope for disagreement about what would be reasonable expectations in the varying conditions in which teachers work. And this relates closely to another claim of the authors: that many teachers' expectations of their pupils' achievement are too low and that this is itself responsible for hampering pupil progress (paras. 3.8 and 27). The evidence for this claim seems decidedly weak, and is probably based on over-generalization.[5] Certainly, there is *no* evidence of which we are aware which indicates that a large proportion of teachers in British primary schools have expectations that are too low. And the problems we have just mentioned indicate that such a conclusion would be very difficult to establish convincingly. Furthermore, while there has been a large amount of research on the *effects* of teachers' expectations on pupil achievement, even the results of this research are inconclusive (Rogers, 1982).

Ironically, a recurring counterpoint in the report is a recognition of some of the complexities we have just mentioned. The 'wise men' argue that good teaching requires the adoption by teachers of strategies and techniques according to fitness for purpose (para. 101). This seems very sensible. Yet it severely reduces the force of their criticism of primary practice and the value of the advice that they offer. To make a judgement about whether what a teacher is doing on a particular occasion is appropriate to his or her purposes and situation requires one to know quite a lot about those purposes and that situation. Certainly, aggregate data about the predominance of different teaching strategies in primary classrooms can tell us little or nothing about whether or not the teachers concerned are acting in ways that are appropriate.

Finally, some of the weight of the authors' argument rests on the suggestion that many teachers are at the mercy of dogmas. The implication is that they are unreflective practitioners, or at least that they are less reflective than they should be. For example, at one point the authors comment: 'If "Plowdenism" has become an ideology to which thousands of teachers have unthinkingly subscribed, then it is necessary to ask why the teachers concerned have stopped thinking for themselves and have apparently become so amenable to indoctrination' (para. 22).[6] But, again, we know of no evidence which establishes that this has occurred, and drawing this conclusion would rely on complex and uncertain judgements about how much reflection is desirable and of what kinds. Here as in some other areas the authors seem to be passing off their own opinions as established facts, and doing so on the basis of a spurious appeal to the findings of educational research.

THE INTERVENTION

We shall not discuss the detailed prescriptions that the report makes; some seem worth while, others not. For us, the manner in which the authors present their arguments is even more significant than the content of what they say. While it is labelled a discussion paper, in a crucial respect this document does not facilitate rational discussion about the issues with which it deals. Though the authors list the evidence to which they appeal in a bibliography, there are no specific links provided between their detailed claims and that evidence. The result is that unless one knows the literature very well it is not possible to make a reasonable judgement about whether particular claims that the authors make are supported by the evidence they cite. Thus, many readers, and this will include many teachers, are effectively forced into the position of either accepting what the authors say on the basis of their authority as 'wise men' who know the research literature, or of rejecting it and thereby leaving themselves open to the charge of holding on to their existing beliefs in a dogmatic fashion. And, as we have seen, the latter corresponds precisely with how the authors explicitly portray some potential members of their audience. It is implied that many primary school teachers continue to believe in 'the rhetoric of primary education' in the face of the 'demonstrable facts' (para. 63). Yet it should be clear from our discussion in this article that the authors' appeals to such facts are not well founded. They clearly believe that they know better than many teachers what facilitates pupil progress, and they seem to expect teachers who read this report who are not familiar with the educational research literature to accept what they say on the basis of their authority as experts. It seems to us that teachers would be well advised not to do so.

The authors' own argument that teachers must select teaching strategies on the basis of fitness for purpose suggests that a more collegial approach towards teachers would have been appropriate. Rather than accusing teachers of being dogmatists, the authors could have provided them with relevant evidence (along with guidance about its strengths and weaknesses), and suggested that they consider whether they make the best use of particular teaching strategies and whether their expectations about their pupils are sufficiently high. Teachers could then have been left to assess the arguments offered and to make adjustments, where necessary, on the basis of their local knowledge and professional judgement. In that form the report would have been appropriate as a communication between one set of professionals and another. By contrast, the approach adopted by the authors smacks of an attitude towards professionals in education and other fields, that seems to have become all too common over the past decade or so in government circles; and it is an attitude that itself exudes dogmatism. Indeed, we suspect that the effects of that attitude and the policies to which it has led have had as significant an effect on the quality of teaching and learning in schools as those matters with which the authors of the report are so preoccupied.

CONCLUSION

In our view, then, this report represents a misuse of the findings of educational research. We can summarize our criticisms under three headings. First, it employs selective interpretation of evidence, as in the case of its use of data about trends in literacy and numeracy. Second, it engages in over-interpretation of the evidence to support a particular view: claims are made which the evidence cited simply cannot support. The authors do not employ the judicious awareness of methodological problems that we have a right to expect from the 'wise'. The third ground for complaint concerns the relationship between the findings of research and educational practice that the report assumes, and the consequent relationship between educationists and teachers that it implies. In what they say, the authors clearly presume that the findings of research provide a strong basis not just for identifying problems but for recommending solutions. In our view, even were educational research to be much more highly developed than it currently is, having solved the serious methodological problems that currently bedevil it, there is little chance that it would be capable of playing the sort of directive role which the authors assume. This arises, in large part, from the character of educational practice. This does not consist of the implementation of policies, but rather of the employment of skills on the basis of judgements about situations that may be informed by research but will be shaped much more by the sedimented experience of the practitioner and his or her local knowledge (Schwab, 1969; Schon, 1978; Hirst, 1983; Carr, 1987). It is these characteristics of teaching that make it a profession. No doubt there are incompetent and wrong-headed teachers (just as there are incompetent and wrong-headed researchers), but their incompetence and wrong-headedness cannot be remedied by founding educational practice on research findings. Rather, what must be done, above all, is to create a context in which the development and exercise of the professional expertise of teachers is facilitated. Yet the interventions of which this report is a part are calculated to do quite the opposite, and this is reflected in the character of the report itself. These interventions seem to represent a concerted policy to establish and operate central control over education, and it is in the promotion of this goal that the findings of educational research have been misused in this report, whatever the intentions of the authors.

NOTES

1. For a shorter, and much more favourable, review, see Simon (1992).
2. Only a relatively small proportion of teachers in Bennett's sample were classified as progressive, and this finding was confirmed by the subsequent work of the ORACLE team (Galton, Simon and Croll, 1980).
3. See Gray and Satterly (1976, 1981), MacIntyre (1976); though see also Bennett (1978). There are also problems with other research in this field, such as that of Galton, Simon and Croll. See Scarth and Hammersley (1986), Croll and Galton (1986), and Scarth and Hammersley (1987).
4. Incidentally, while the authors of the report include Bennett's original study in their references, they do not cite this reanalysis or much of the critical assessment of Bennett's work. In this respect too they follow the Secretary of State (Clarke, 1991).
5. Alexander (1992) makes this claim in relation to the schools in Leeds that he studied, but his evidence is impressionistic: his research is much less systematic and explicit about its methodology than that of Bennett or Galton, Simon and Croll.
6. In the next sentence the authors equivocate, commenting that 'the word "if" is important'. Yet the bulk of their report is premissed on this claim being true. It is difficult to know how to interpret their equivocation, except perhaps as a compromise formulation to accommodate disagreement among the three authors.

REFERENCES

Aitken, M., Bennett, S. N. and Hesketh, J. (1981) Teaching styles and pupil progress: a re-analysis, *British Journal of Educational Psychology*, Vol. 51, pp. 170–86.

Alexander, R. (1992) *Policy and Practice in Primary Education*, Routledge, London.

Bennett, S. N. (1976) *Teaching Styles and Pupil Progress*, Open Books, London.

Bennett, N. (1978) Educational research and the media, *Westminster Studies in Education*, Vol. 1, pp. 23–30.

Bennett, S. N., Desforges, C., Cockburn, A. and Wilkinson, B. (1984) *The Quality of Pupil Learning Experiences*, Erlbaum, London.

Carr, W. (1987) What is an educational practice?, *Journal of Philosophy of Education*, Vol. 21, no. 2, pp. 163–75.

Clarke, K. (1991) *Primary Education, a Statement by the Secretary of State for Education and Science*, Department of Education and Science, London, 3 December.

Cox, C. B. and Dyson, A. E. (1971) *The Black Papers on Education*, Davis-Poynter, London.

Croll, P. and Galton, M. (1986) A comment on 'Questioning ORACLE' by John Scarth and Martyn Hammersley, *Educational Research*, Vol. 28, no. 3, pp. 185–9.

Dadds, M. (1992) Monty Python and the Three Wise Men, *Cambridge Journal of Education*, Vol. 22, no. 2, pp. 129–41.

David, T., Curtis, A. and Siraj-Blatchford, I. (1992) *Effective Teaching in the Early Years: Fostering Children's Learning in Nurseries and Infant Classrooms*, Organization Mondiale pour l'Education Prescolaire (UK), report, University of Warwick.

Department of Education and Science (1992) *Curriculum Organisation and Practice in Primary Schools: A Discussion Document*, HMSO, London.

Galton, M., Simon, B. and Croll, P. (1980) *Inside the Primary Classroom,* Routledge & Kegan Paul, London.

Gray, J. and Satterly, D. (1976) A chapter of errors: Teaching Styles and Pupil Progress in retrospect. *Educational Research,* Vol. 19, no. 1, pp. 45–56.

Gray, J. and Satterly, D. (1981) Formal or informal? A re-assessment of the British evidence, *British Journal of Educational Psychology,* Vol. 51, pp. 187–96.

Hirst, P. H. (1983) Educational theory, in P. H. Hirst (ed.) *Educational Theory and its Foundation Disciplines,* Routledge & Kegan Paul, London.

MacDonald, B. (1974) Evaluation and the control of education, in B. MacDonald and R. Walker (eds.) *SAFARI Innovation, Evaluation, Research and the Problem of Control,* Centre for Applied Research in Education, University of East Anglia.

MacIntyre, D. (1976) Review N. Bennett *Teaching Styles and Pupil Progress, British Journal of Teacher Education,* Vol. 2, pp. 291–7.

National Curriculum Council (NCC) (1993) *The National Curriculum at Key Stages 1 and 2,* York, National Curriculum Council.

Office for Standards in Education (Ofsted) (1993) *Curricular Organisation and Classroom Practice: A Follow-up Report,* HMSO, London.

Rogers, C. (1982) *The Social Psychology of Schooling,* Routledge & Kegan Paul, London.

Scarth, J. and Hammersley, M. (1986) Questioning ORACLE: an assessment of ORACLE's analysis of teachers' questions, *Educational Research,* Vol. 28, no. 3, pp. 174–84.

Scarth, J. and Hammersley, M. (1987) More questioning of ORACLE: a reply to Croll and Galton, *Educational Research,* Vol. 29, no. 1, pp. 37–46.

Schon, D. (1978) *Educating the Reflective Practitioner,* Jossey-Bass, San Francisco, Calif.

Schwab, J. (1969) The practical: a language for curriculum, *School Review,* Vol. 78, pp. 1–24.

Simon, B. (1992) Review of *Curriculum Organisation and Practice in Primary Schools: A Discussion Document, The Curriculum Journal,* Vol. 3, no. 1, pp. 91–7.

Stierer, B. (1991) Assessing reading standards: a continuing debate, *Cambridge Journal of Education,* Vol. 21, no. 2, pp. 119–27.

Wright, N. (1977) *Progress in Education: A Review of Schooling in England and Wales,* Croom Helm, London.

INDEX OF NAMES

INDEX OF SUBJECTS